MORE STREET FRENCH

Slang, Idioms,
and Popular Expletives

MORE STREET FRENCH

*Slang, Idioms,
and Popular Expletives*

David Burke

John Wiley & Sons, Inc.

New York • Chichester • Brisbane • Toronto • Singapore

Editor: Katherine Schowalter
Managing Editor: Ruth Greif
Editing, Design, and Production: Optima PrePress
Illustrator: Dave Jeno

Library of Congress Cataloging-in-Publication Data
Burke, David, 1956-
  More street French : slang, idioms, and popular
expletives / David Burke.
    p. cm.
Bibliography: p.
ISBN 0-471-50771-7
    1. French language – Slang.   2. French language – Idioms.
3. French language – Jargon.   4. French language – Textbooks
for foreign speakers – English.   I. Title.
PC3739.B86   1989
447'.09 – dc20   89-16418
                                                      CIP

Printed in the United States of America
90 91 10 9 8 7 6 5 4 3 2 1

THIS BOOK IS DEDICATED TO MY MOTHER

PREFACE

More Street French not only adds to the slang and idioms that make up its predecessor, *Street French*, but also goes one step further by exploring current slang inspired by specific groups such as mechanics, students, waiters, the entertainment industry, and even animals! These terms and expressions constantly infiltrate daily speech.

In addition, this book examines a living part of the French language that is certainly not covered in high school and college textbooks – popular obscenities. As censorship regulations in France are extremely lax, this wide range of slang terms and expressions appears frequently in the media, as well as in everyday conversations between family, friends and business people. For this reason, it is included here.

More Street French will lead you through the extensive world of slang in fifteen lessons. Each lesson is divided into five parts:

1. **DIALOGUE**: Here you will encounter about twenty to thirty new French slang words and expressions, indicated in boldface, that are used in context to demonstrate correct usage. An English translation of the dialogue is always given on the opposite page.

2. **VOCABULARY**: This section gives a detailed explanation of each term used in the dialogue, along with its synonym and/or antonym. In addition, a literal translation will be offered whenever possible. However, some words are actually a creation of slang and therefore have no literal translations.

3. **PRACTICE THE VOCABULARY**: These drills will allow you to test yourself on the slang from the dialogue. Feel free to write directly on the page as this is also your workbook. (The pages providing the answers to all the drills are indicated at the beginning of this section.)

4. **INSIDE INFO**: This section is designed to give you an inside look at some unspoken "rules" that are essential when using slang, as well as provide special lists of words that are rarely, if ever, taught in traditional French language books.

5. **PRACTICE**: This section presents a new set of drills devised to help test you on the **INSIDE INFO** section.

Following each sequence of five chapters is a review exam encompassing all of the words and expressions learned up to that point.

Also, unique to this book is a list of popular abbreviations that are *consistently* used in spoken French.

The secret to learning *More Street French* is to follow this simple checklist:

- Make sure that you have a good grasp of each section before proceeding to the drills. If you've made more than two errors in a particular drill, simply go back and review— then try again. Remember: This is a self-paced book, so take your time. You're not fighting the clock!

- It's very important that you feel comfortable with each chapter before proceeding to the next since words learned along the way *will* crop up in the following lessons. So feel comfortable before moving on!

- Read the dialogues and drills aloud. This is an excellent way to help you speak colloquially and think like a native!

WARNING

Slang must be used with discretion because it is a casual "language" that certainly should not be practiced with formal dignitaries or employers who you are trying to impress! This is why you need to pay close attention to the English equivalents and literal translations given in the vocabulary section. Their connotations are the same in the English definitions as in the French. Therefore, a general rule: *Use your own judgment.*

If you enjoyed reading *Street French*, or if you are encountering the secret world of slang for the first time, you will surely embrace *More Street French* as you discover the wealth of popular slang terms, expressions and expletives that, until now, were reserved exclusively for natives and inhabitants of France!

LEGEND

adj.	adjective	**m.**	masculine
adv.	adverb	**n.**	noun
exclam.	exclamation	**pl.**	plural
exp.	expression	**Prn.**	proper name
expl.	expletive	**qqch.**	quelque chose (something)
f.	feminine	**qqn.**	quelqu'un (someone)
interj.	interjection	**s.o.**	someone
(lit);	literal translation	**v.**	verb

IMPORTANT

The dialogues and exercises in *More Street French* have been entirely written using contractions. Their use is perhaps the single most critical element when speaking in slang.

The following is an abridged list of the shortcuts and contractions that you will find throughout this book (for a more detailed explanation, refer to *Street French*):

A. Commonly heard contractions

ce, cette = **c'te**	**Elle est jolie, c'te voiture!;** That car's pretty!
celui-là = **c'ui-là**	(Pronounced "sui-là") Only used with -**ce** or -**là**.
c'est un(e) = **c't'un(e)**	Past tense: c'était un(e) = **c't'ait un(e)**.
elle / elles = **è**	Only when followed by a consonant. **E parle trop vite;** She speaks too fast.
il faut = **faut**	**Il** may be dropped in all tenses of the verb *falloir*.
il y a = **y'a**	(Pronounced as one syllable, "ya") **Il** may be dropped in all tenses of the verb *avoir*.
il / ils = **y**	Il a = **y a** which is pronounced as two separate syllables.
ils = **z**	Only when followed by a vowel. **Z'ont de la chance;** They're lucky. Also common: **y z'ont**.
lui = **'ui**	**Lui** does *not* take on the form of **'ui** at the end of a sentence: **C'est pour lui;** *not* **pour 'ui**.
parce que = **pasque**	**Je porte un pullover pasque j'ai froid;** I'm wearing a sweater because I'm cold.
peut-être = **p't'êt'**	**P't'êt' qu'elle est malade;** Maybe she's sick.
plus = **pu**	**Je n'ai pu faim;** I'm full.
puis = **pis**	**J'ai rendez-vous à midi et pis à 1h;** I have a meeting at noon and then at 1:00.

puisque = **pisque**   **Y ne peut pas venir pisqu'y n'a pas d'argent;**
                              He can't come 'cuz he doesn't have any money.

quelques = **quèques**   **Tu peux me donner quèques francs?;**
                              Can you give me a few francs?

s'il te plaît = **s'te plaît** **Tu peux me passer le sel, s'te plaît?;**
                              Can you pass me the salt, please?

B. The omission of *ne*

In spoken French, **ne** is omitted entirely:

$$Je\ ne\ l'aime\ pas\ =\ \textit{\textbf{Je l'aime pas}}$$
$$Il\ n'est\ pas\ beau\ =\ \textit{\textbf{Il est pas beau}}$$
$$Ne\ partez\ pas!\ =\ \textit{\textbf{Partez pas!}}$$

C. The omission of *u* in *tu*

The letter **u** in **tu** may frequently be muted when followed by a vowel:

$$tu\ es\ =\ \textit{\textbf{t'es}}$$
$$tu\ ouvres\ =\ \textit{\textbf{t'ouvres}}$$
$$tu\ as\ =\ \textit{\textbf{t'as}}$$

D. The omission of *re*

When the **re** ending is followed by a consonant, it is not easy to articulate quickly even for the native speaker of French. For this reason, the **re** sound is often omitted:

$$le\ pauvre\ chat\ =\ le\ \textit{\textbf{pauv'}}chat$$
$$notre\ maison\ =\ \textit{\textbf{not'}}maison$$
$$votre\ voiture\ =\ \textit{\textbf{vot'}}voiture$$

The same rule applies to **re** verbs:

Il va mettre son cahier sur la table = *Y va **mett'**son cahier sur la table.*

E. The omission of *e*

$$je = \textit{\textbf{j'}}$$
Je veux prendre du dessert;
J'veux prend'du dessert.

$$te = \textit{\textbf{t'}}$$
Tu vas te coucher maintenant?;
Tu vas t'coucher maintenant?

$$me = \textit{\textbf{m'}}$$
Je me demande où elle est;
Je m'demande où elle est.

$$se = \textit{\textbf{s'}}$$
Il se met en colère facilement;
Y s'met en colère facilement.

ce = c'
Tu comprends ce qu'il dit?;
Tu comprends c'qu'y dit?

de = d'
Elle a décidé de partir;
Elle a décidé d'partir.

le = l'
Elles vont le faire plus tard;
E vont l'faire plus tard.

que = qu'
Il faut que je parte;
Faut qu'j'parte.

All -*er* verbs in the future
tense as well as *être*

je serai = je **s'rai**
tu seras = tu **s'ras**
il/elle sera = il/elle **s'ra**
nous serons = nous **s'rons**
vous serez = vous **s'rez**
ils/elles seront = ils/elles **s'ront**

Words containing a mute "e"

besoin = **b'soin**
venir = **v'nir**
demain = **d'main**
devant = **d'vant, etc.**

F.   Structure of a question when using interrogative pronouns

In colloquial French, a question is almost *always* constructed as a statement with
a question mark at the end. This structure replaces the traditional **est-ce que** and
inversion forms:

combien:
(how much)

Combien pèses-tu?
Combien tu pèses?

combien de:
(how many, how much)

Combien d'enfants a-t-elle?
Combien elle en a, des enfants?

comment:

Comment vas-tu?
Comment tu vas?

où:

Où vas-tu maintenant?
Où tu vas maintenant?

pourquoi:

Pourquoi as-tu acheté ça?
Pourquoi t'as acheté ça?

quand:

Quand est-ce qu'ils veulent venir chez nous?
Quand ils veulent venir chez nous?

quel(le):

Quelle heure est-il?
Quelle heure il est?

qui:
(as an object)

Qui rencontres-tu à l'aéroport?
Qui tu rencontres à l'aéroport?

quoi: Qu'est-ce qu'il prend avec lui?
                              Y prend quoi avec lui?
                              NOTE: **quoi** *is a little different from the other*
                              interrogative pronouns because it never begins a
                              statement but rather follows the verb.

à quoi: A quoi penses-tu?
                              A quoi tu penses?

de quoi: De quoi parles-tu?
                              De quoi tu parles?

ACKNOWLEDGMENTS

I owe a great deal of thanks to my family and friends for encouraging me to turn my slang notes, written on napkins and pastry wrappers, into a book that has now expanded into a second volume. It has always been their support and faith in me that has given me the strength and enthusiasm to persevere.

I am very grateful to Nancy Burke, Miguel Alvarez, and Christina Bauman for making the copyediting phase of the book such a pleasure. Their commitment, precision and diligence was greatly appreciated.

My very special thanks and fondness go to Katherine Schowalter and Ruth Greif of John Wiley & Sons for making the entire process so exciting.

CONTENTS

UNIT TWO
Popular Obscenities

MORE STREET FRENCH

Slang, Idioms,
and Popular Expletives

UNIT ONE - *French Slang & Idioms*

– 1 –

Au Cinéma

(At the Movies)

AU CINÉMA...

DIALOGUE

Sylvie raconte son aventure à Martine.

Martine:　J'espère qu'c't'un bon film.

Sylvie:　**Bof... Y'a à boire et à manger là-d'dans**. Hier, j'suis v'nue l'voir.

Martine:　Mais, pourquoi tu m'as pas dit ça avant?

Sylvie:　A vrai dire, j'l'ai pas vraiment vu à cause d'ce drôle d'**oiseau** qui m'a accompagnée. Y m'**assommait**, c'ui-là. Tu parles des **mains baladeuses**! T'aurais dû m'voir. J'étais tout **en nage**, moi. Ça m'**démangeait** d'le **tabasser**. J'te **fais cadeau du reste**!

Martine:　Mais, non! C't'une **histoire croustillante**! Vas-y... **affranchis**-moi.

Sylvie:　Faut qu'j'te fasse un dessin?

Martine:　Mais ouais! J'suis **tout oreilles**.

Sylvie:　Eh ben, y est v'nu m'**cueillir** à 8h et fallait être au **ciné** pour 8h15! Alors, on a **bombé** pour **arriver sur l'clou** mais y s'est fait coller un **biscuit** par un **cogne** pasqu'y **tapait du 95**.

Martine:　Oh, là là! Comment y **gagne son bifteck**, lui?

Sylvie:　C't'un **toubib**, alors y est pas **désargenté**, remarque! Mais, y est **près d'ses sous**! J'l'ai **catalogué** en un rien de temps. Que j'**me barbais**, moi! Pis pendant l'film, y voulait qu'on **s'lèche la pomme** mais j'avais pas vraiment envie d'**m'en jeter un vite fait** d'vant toute la **poulaille**!

Martine:　J'ai l'impression qu't'as pas vraiment **cordé** avec lui. Faut dire qu'**vous vous chauffez pas du même bois**.

AT THE MOVIES...

DIALOGUE

Sylvie tells Martine about her adventure.

Martine:	I hope this is a good film.
Sylvie:	Well… it's got good and bad stuff in it. Yesterday, I went to see it.
Martine:	Why didn't you tell me that before?
Sylvie:	To tell you the truth, I didn't actually see it because of this weirdo that came with me. He was bugging me to death. Talk about roving hands! You should have seen me. I was totally soaked in sweat. I was just itching to haul off and deck him. I'll spare you the rest of the details.
Martine:	No! This is a juicy one! Keep going… give me the lowdown.
Sylvie:	Do I have to draw you a picture?
Martine:	I'll say! I'm all ears.
Sylvie:	Well, he came over to pick me up at 8:00 and we had to be at the movie by 8:15! So, we hauled butt to get there on time but he got pulled over by a cop because he was doing 95.
Martine:	Wow wee! How does he make a living?
Sylvie:	He's a doctor so he's not exactly broke, right? But, is he ever a tight wad! I had that guy's number in no time flat. Was I ever bored out of my skull! Then during the movie, he wanted to make out but I didn't exactly feel like having a quickie in front of the whole audience!
Martine:	Something tells me you didn't really hit it off with him. I'd say you two don't exactly have a lot in common.

VOCABULARY

affranchir qqn. *v.* to bring s.o. up to date, to give s.o. the lowdown • (lit); to stamp s.o. (with the information) • *T' as été affranchi?;* Have you heard?
SYNONYM: **mettre qqn. à la coule** *exp.* (lit); to put s.o. in the flow (of news).

arriver sur le clou *exp.* to arrive on the dot • (lit); to arrive on the nail.
NOTE: Other synonyms of the verb *arriver* may certainly be used in this expression, e.g., *s'abouler, s'amener, débarquer, radiner, rappliquer, se pointer,* etc.

assommer *v.* to annoy greatly • (lit); to knock unconscious • *Oh, tu m'assommes avec tes questions!;* Oh, you're driving me crazy with your questions!
NOTE: **assommeur, euse** *n.* a crashing bore, "pain in the neck."
SYNONYM: **casser les pieds à qqn.** *exp.* • (lit); to break one's feet.

barber (se) *exp.* to be terribly bored. *J'me barbais pendant toute la classe;* I was bored to death during the entire class.
NOTE: **barber** *v.* to annoy. *Oh! Tu m'barbes!;* Oh! You're bugging me to death!
SYNONYM: **se barbifier** *v.*

bof *interj.* Used to denote indifference. *-Comment t'as trouvé l'film? -Bof!* -What did you think of the film?; -It was okay.

bomber *v.* to drive quickly, to move fast (like a bomb). *On a dû bomber pour n'pas être en r'tard;* We had to haul butt in order not to be late.

cataloguer *v.* to size up (s.o.) • (lit); to catalogue, to list • *Ma mère, è l'a catalogué tout d'suite;* my mother sized that guy up right away.
SYNONYM: **situer qqn.** *v.* • (lit); to situate (s.o.).

chauffer du même bois (ne pas se) *exp.* not to have anything in common • (lit); not to heat oneself with the same wood.

ciné *m.* Abbreviation of: *cinéma.*
SEE: *Unit Three - Popular Abbreviations,* p. 217.
SYNONYM: **cinoche** *m.*

cogne *m.* policeman, cop.
NOTE: This comes from the verb *cogner* meaning "to bump, to hit."
SYNONYM: **flic** *m.*

coller un biscuit (se faire) *exp.* to get a citation • (lit); to get oneself stuck with a biscuit • *Mon vieux, y va m'tuer quand y apprendra qu'je m'suis fait coller un biscuit!;* My old man's gonna kill me when he finds out I got a ticket!
NOTE: **biscuit** *m.* citation.
SYNONYM: **se faire coller une prune** *exp.* • (lit); to get oneself stuck with a plum.

corder *v.* to hit it off (with s.o.) • (lit); to string (together) • *J'ai cordé avec mon prof;* I hit it off with my teacher.
SYNONYM: **copiner** *v.* This comes from the noun *copin(e)* meaning "pal."
ANTONYM: **semer** *v.* to ditch (s.o.), to leave behind • (lit); to sow (seed).

cueillir *v.* to pick up (s.o.) • (lit); to pick (flowers, etc.) • *J' passe t' cueillir après l' dîner;* I'll come by to pick you up after dinner.
ANTONYM: **cracher** *v.* to drop off (s.o.) • (lit); to spit.

démanger *v.* to itch to do something • (lit); to itch • *Ça m' démange d' lui dire ses quat' vérités;* I'm itching to tell him what I think of him.
NOTE: **démangeaison** *f.* an itching to do something. *J' ai une démangeaison de dev' nir chanteur;* I have an itching to become a singer.

désargenté(e) (être) *adj.* to be broke • (lit); to be desilvered • *Tu peux m' prêter un franc? J' suis complètement désargenté;* Can you lend me a franc? I'm flat broke.
NOTE: This comes from the masculine noun *argent* meaning "money" or literally "silver."
ANTONYM: **argenté(e)** *adj.* • (lit); silvered.

en nage (être) *adj.* to be dripping in sweat. *Quand l' prof, y m' a fait plancher d' vant toute la classe, j' étais (tout) en nage;* When the teacher had me go up to the blackboard in front of the whole class, I was soaking wet.
NOTE: **nage** *f.* swimming, rowing.

faire cadeau du reste *exp.* to spare s.o. the details, to cut to the chase • (lit); to make a gift of the rest • *C' t' une longue histoire mais j' te fais cadeau du reste;* It's a long story but I'll spare you the details.

gagner son bifteck *exp.* to earn a living • (lit); to earn one's beefsteak • *Comment è gagne son bifteck?;* How does she make her living?
SYNONYM: **blot** *m.* job, line of work. *C' est quoi son blot?;* What kind of work does he do?
ALSO: **la lutte au bifteck** *exp.* rat race.

histoire croustillante *exp.* a good juicy story • (lit); crispy, crunchy story.
ANTONYM: **une histoire à dormir debout** *exp.* a long and boring story • (lit); a story that causes one to sleep standing up.

il y a à boire et à manger là-dedans *exp.* there are good points and bad points in it, "there are parts that are easy to swallow and others that are not" • (lit); there are things to drink as well as things to eat in it.

lécher la pomme (se) *exp.* to make out, to neck, to suck face • (lit); to lick each other's face • *Y z' ont passé toute une heure à s' lécher la pomme;* They spent an entire hour sucking face.
NOTE: **pomme** *f.* face • (lit); apple.
SYNONYM: **se sucer le citron** *exp.* • (lit); to suck each other's face • NOTE: **citron** *m.* face • (lit); lemon.

mains baladeuses (avoir les) *exp.* • (lit); to have wandering hands. *J' peux pas m' asseoir à côté d' lui... y a les mains baladeuses, c' ui-là!;* I can't sit next to him... that guy's got roving hands!

oiseau *m.* • (lit); bird • *un drôle d' oiseau;* a strange guy, "a strange bird."
SYNONYM: **un drôle de moineau** *m.* • (lit); a strange sparrow.

poulaille *f.* audience, public.
  NOTE: This comes from the masculine noun *poulailler* meaning "the top gallery of a theater or movie house" or literally, "the hen house."
  SYNONYM: **galerie** *f.*

près de ses sous (être) *adj.* to be stingy, tight fisted • (lit); to be close to one's money.
  NOTE: **sous** *m.pl.* money, coins.
  SYNONYM: **les lâcher avec un élastique** *exp.* • (lit); to release them (coins) with a rubberband.

tabasser *v.* to beat up (s.o.). *Les voisins, y z' ont tabassé l' cambrioleur;* The neighbors beat up the burglar.
  NOTE: **passer qqn. à tabac** *exp.* to beat s.o. to a pulp.

taper *v.* **1.** to reach a speed • (lit); to strike, hit •*Y a tapé du 95!;* He hit 95 (kilometers/miles)! • **2. taper** *v.* to stink. *Oh, ça tape!;* Oh, that stinks!

toubib *m.* doctor (Arabic).
  SEE: *Inside Info (2) - Professions in Slang*, p. 10.

tout oreilles (être) *exp.* • (lit); to be all ears.
  NOTE: Any other slang synonym for *oreilles* may certainly be used in this expression, e.g., *cliquettes, écoutilles, esgourdes, portugaises, etc.*

vite fait (s'en jeter un) *exp.* to have a quickie (with s.o.) • (lit); to throw oneself a "quickly done one."

PRACTICE THE VOCABULARY

[Answers to Lesson 1, p. 65]

A. Underline the appropriate word.

1. Y'a à boire et à (**parler, manger, chanter**) dans c'film.

2. Y a une voiture super rapide! E peut (**courir, prendre, taper**) du 150 comme ça!

3. Quel idiot! Faut dire qu'j'ai pas (**collé, coulé, cordé**) avec lui!

4. Hier, j'ai vu un bon film au (**ciné, cogne, magasin**).

5. On avait rien du tout en commun. J'suppose qu'on s'chauffe pas du même (**bâteau, bois, style**).

6. On a dû (**bomber, assommer, cueillir**) pour n'pas être en r'tard.

7. Le premier jour dans sa nouvelle voiture, è s'est fait (**jeter dedans, ramasser une pelle, coller un biscuit**).

8. Mais, raconte-moi c'qui s'est passé! J'suis tout (**pieds, oreilles, bras**)!

9. Ça m'(**démange, mange, manque**) d'apprendre à jouer du piano.

10. (**Garantis, Mentis, Affranchis**)-moi... elle a vraiment quitté son mari?

11. Tu sais, y s'parle tout l'temps! Quel drôle d'(**oiseau, éléphant, ours**)!

12. Attention de n'pas t'asseoir à côté d'lui... y a les mains (**marrantes, baladeuses, bleues**)!

B. Replace the word(s) in parentheses with the slang synonym from the right column.

1. J'*(m'ennuie)* _____ à c'te soirée!   A. **près d'ses sous**

2. Y font qu'*(s'embrasser)* _____ .   B. **tabassé**

3. J'ai fait tout mon possible pour arriver *(à l'heure)* _____ .   C. **me barbe**

4. Y est v'nu m'*(chercher)* _____ après l'dîner.   D. **désargenté**

5. Son père, y rent'toujours tard pasque c't'un *(agent de police)* _____ .   E. **croustillante**

6. Elle est très *(avare)* _____ , celle-là.   F. **s'lécher la pomme**

7. Quelle histoire *(intéressante)* _____ !   G. **assomme**

8. Les voisins, y z'ont *(battu)* _____ l'voleur.   H. **sur l'clou**

9. J't'ai pas *(tenu au courant)* _____ ?   I. **collé un biscuit**

10. Quel malheur! Le flic, y m'a *(donné une contravention)* _____ .   J. **cogne**

11. C'te prof, y m'*(ennuie)* _____ .   K. **toubib**

12. Son père, c't'un *(médecin)* _____ .   L. **tout en nage**

13. J'étais tellement nerveux qu'j'étais *(plein de sueur)* _____ .   M. **cueillir**

14. J'suis complètement *(pauvre)* _____ .   N. **affranchi**

C. Match the French with the English translations by writing the appropriate letter in the box.

☐ 1. On the way home, I got a ticket.

☐ 2. What happened? I haven't gotten the lowdown.

☐ 3. -How's it going? -Oh, I dunno... things are okay.

A. -Ça va? -Bof... ça va bien.

B. **Après sa première leçon d'conduite, elle était tout en nage.**

C. **C'te prof, y m'assomme.**

☐	4.	His father is a doctor.	D. **E s'en est jetée un vite fait avec le patron.**
☐	5.	After her first driving lesson, she was dripping wet!	
			E. **Comment è gagne son bifteck?**
☐	6.	She had a quickie with the boss.	F. **J'aimerais bien t'y accompagner mais j'suis désargenté.**
☐	7.	I quit my job. I'll spare you the details.	G. **Y est toubib, son père.**
☐	8.	How does she make a living?	H. **J'ai donné ma démission. J'te fais cadeau du reste.**
☐	9.	This darned teacher bores the living daylights out of me.	I. **En rentrant, je m'suis fait coller un biscuit.**
☐	10.	I'd really like to go there with you but I'm flat broke.	J. **Qu'est-c'qui s'est passé? On m'a pas affranchi.**

INSIDE INFO (1): *COLLOQUIAL USE OF PRESENT TENSE TO INDICATE FUTURE*

In colloquial French, the present tense is commonly used to indicate an event that will take place in the future. It is important to note that this construction is used by all social levels. For example:

> **On en parle plus tard.**
> We'll talk about it later.

> **Je reviens dans une heure.**
> I'll be back in an hour.

This also holds true when using "if" and "then" clauses. Ordinarily, when the "if" clause is in the present tense, the "then" clause is in the future tense.

> **Si tu m'rends ce service, j'te *donn'rai* mon nouveau disque.**
> If you do me this favor, I *will* give you my new record.

> **Si tu viens chez moi, j'te *f'rai* un bon dîner.**
> If you come to my house, I *will* make you a good dinner.

However, using the colloquial construction, the "then" clause remains in the present tense even though a reference to an event taking place in the future is being made.

> **Si tu m'rends ce service, j'te *donne* mon nouveau disque.**
> If you do me this favor, I *will* give you my new record.

> **Si tu viens chez moi, j'te *fais* un bon dîner.**
> If you come to my house, I *will* make you a good dinner.

PRACTICE USING THE PRESENT TENSE TO INDICATE FUTURE

A. Rewrite the following phrases by implementing the colloquial use of the present tense to indicate future.

1. On s'verra d'main, alors?
   (We'll see each other tomorrow then?)

   _____

2. J'te l'donn'rai après l'déjeuner.
   (I'll give it to you after lunch.)

   _____

3. On l'f'ra plus tard.
   (We'll do it later.)

   _____

4. On en discut'ra d'main.
   (We'll discuss it tomorrow.)

   _____

5. J'te la présent'rai à la soirée.
   (I'll introduce you to her at the party.)

   _____

6. Y'te l'rendra ce soir.
   (He'll give it back to you tonight.)

   _____

7. J'arriv'rai t'chercher à 8h.
   (I'll come by to pick you up at 8:00.)

   _____

8. Ce soir, è lui f'ra une grande surprise!
   (Tonight, she's going to give him a big surprise.)

   _____

9. C't'après-midi, on fêt'ra ton anniversaire.
   (This afternoon, we're going to celebrate your birthday.)

   _____

10. J'te pass'rai un coup d'fil d'main.
    (I'll give you a telephone call tomorrow.)

    _____

INSIDE INFO (2): *PROFESSIONS IN SLANG*

As learned in the opening dialogue at the beginning of this lesson, *toubib* is a slang term for "doctor." However, the following list demonstrates how slang has left virtually no vocation unmarked by its presence.

Artist

barbouilleur, euse *n.* bad artist
• (lit); one who makes a mess.
NOTE: **barbouiller** *v.* to make a mess, to dirty.

croûtier *v.* bad artist.
NOTE: This comes from the feminine noun *croûte* meaning "crust" which is also used to refer to a bad painting.

Butcher

louchébem *m.*
NOTE: This is a largonji transformation (SEE: **Street French**, p. 138) of the masculine noun *boucher*.

Butler

larbin *m.*

Dentist

quenottier *m.*
NOTE: This comes from the feminine noun *quenotte* meaning "tooth."

Dermatologist

peaussier *m.*
NOTE: This comes from the feminine noun *peau* meaning "skin."

Detective

bourrin *m.* • (lit); horse, donkey.

Doctor

toubib *m.* (Arabic).

Door-to-door salesman

posticheur *m.*
NOTE: **postiche** *f.* sales talk, sales spiel.

Female lavatory attendant

dame-pipi *f.*

Fireman

pomplard *m.*
NOTE: This comes from the verb *pomper* meaning "to pump (water, etc.)."

Hairdresser; Barber

coupe-tiffes *m.* • (lit); cut(ter of) hair.
NOTE: **tiffes** *m.pl.* hair.

figaro *m. (humorous)*
NOTE: This is from the Barber of Seville.

gratte-couenne *m.*
• (lit); scratch(er of) skin.
NOTE: **couenne** *f.* skin.

merlan *m.* • (lit); whiting.

perruquemar *m.*
NOTE: This comes from the feminine noun *perruque* meaning "wig."

pommadin *m.*
NOTE: This comes from the feminine noun *pommade* meaning "skin ointment."

tiffier *m.*
NOTE: This comes from the masculine noun *tiffe* meaning "hair."

Interpreter

inter *m*.
> NOTE: This is an abbreviation of *interprète* meaning "interpreter."

Laundress

briqueuse *f*.
> NOTE: **briquer** *v*. to clean well.

Lawyer

babillard *m*. • (lit); chatterbox, babbler.
> NOTE: This comes from the verb *babiller* meaning "to babble (of brook, person, etc.)"

blanchisseur *m*.
> NOTE: **blanchir** *v*. to clean (s.o.'s police record).

débarbe or **débarbot** *m*.
> NOTE: **débarboter** *v*. to clean (s.o.'s police record).

débarbotteur *m*. • (lit); cleaner (of s.o.'s police record).

parrain *m*. • (lit); godfather.

tabellion *m*. • (lit); scrivener.

Mechanic

mécano *m*.

Nurse

artilleur de la pièce humide *m*. male nurse • (lit); artilleryman of the wet gun.
> NOTE: **pièce humide** *f*. syringe • (lit); wet gun.

pique-fesse *f*. • (lit); prick-buttock.

tisanier *m*. • (lit); one who infuses (drugs into s.o.).
> NOTE: This comes from the feminine noun *tisane* meaning "infusion (of herbs, etc.)."

Obstetrician; Midwife

vise-au-trou *m*. • (lit); one who "looks at the hole."
> NOTE: **viser** *v*. to look, to see.

Orderly

canulard *m*.
> NOTE: This comes from the feminine noun *canule* meaning "the nozzle of a syringe."

Paper pusher

gratte-papier *m*.
• (lit); paper-scratcher.

Plumber

plombard *m*.
> NOTE: This comes from the masculine noun *plomb* meaning "lead."

Policeman

cognard *m*. • (lit); hitter.
> NOTE: This comes from the verb *cogner* meaning "to hit."

cogne *m*. Abbreviation of: *cognard*.

flic *m*.

flicard *m*.

fliquette *f*. police woman.

fliqueuse *f*. police woman.

hirondelle *f*. cycle cop
• (lit); swallow (bird).

pingouin *m*. • (lit); penguin.

Priest

coincoin *m*. • (lit); quacking of ducks.

Private investigator

fouille-merde *m*. (lit); one who rummages through shit, "shit rummager."

privé *m.* • (lit); private.

Professeur

prof *m. & f.*
NOTE: *professeur* is always masculine. However, in its abbreviated form *(prof)*, it is both masculine and feminine.

Psychiatrist

psi *m.* "shrink"
1. pschiatrist • 2. psycho.

Sailor; Blue-collar worker

col bleu *m.* • (lit); blue collar.

Taxi driver

loche *m. & f.*

Top surgeon

couteau *m.* • (lit); knife.
ALSO: **couteau** *m.* lead actor.

Veterinarian

véto *m.*
NOTE: This is an abbreviation of the masculine noun *vétérinaire* meaning "veterinarian."

Waiter

louf(f)iat *m.*

larbin *m.*
ALSO: **larbin** *m.* servant, butler.

White-collar worker

col blanc *m.* • (lit); white collar.

Writer

buveur *m.* writer, journalist • (lit); drinker (of ink).

scribouillard(e) *n.*
NOTE: This comes from the verb *scribouiller* meaning "to scribble, to write."

scribouilleur, euse *n.*
SEE: *scribouillard(e).*

PRACTICE USING PROFESSIONS IN SLANG

A. Match the columns by writing the correct letter in the box.

☐	1. private investigator	A. **prof**
☐	2. dentist	B. **scribouillard(e)**
☐	3. policeman	C. **toubib**
☐	4. butler	D. **mécano**
☐	5. psychiatrist	E. **merlan**
☐	6. professor	F. **blanchisseur**
☐	7. doctor	G. **flicard**
☐	8. lawyer	H. **couteau**
☐	9. surgeon	I. **psi**
☐	10. hairdresser	J. **fouille-merde**
☐	11. writer	K. **larbin**
☐	12. mechanic	L. **quenottier**

B. Underline the slang synonyms that match the vocation to the left.
Note: **There may be more than one answer in each case.**

1. **coiffeur**:
   a. pommadin   b. tiffier   c. plombard
   d. coupe-tiffes   e. blanchisseur   f. larbin

2. **agent de police**:
   a. merlan   b. flicard   c. prof
   d. pingouin   e. cognard   f. toubib

3. **écrivain**:
   a. psi   b. scribouilleur   c. loche
   d. scribouillard   e. flic   f. col bleu

4. **avocat**:
   a. blanchisseur   b. hirondelle   c. parrain
   d. débarbotteur   e. babillard   f. quenottier

5. **infirmière**:
   a. mécano   b. posticheur   c. tisanier
   d. pomplard   e. pique-fesse   f. inter

6. **investigateur**:
   a. col blanc   b. privé   c. buveur
   d. fouille-merde   e. couteau   f. cogne

7. **artiste**:
   a. barbouilleur   b. babillard   c. tisanier
   d. croûtier   e. bourrin   f. figaro

– 2 –

Vive l'Amour

(Hooray for Love)

VIVE L'AMOUR...

DIALOGUE

Margot et Jean discutent le mariage d'Yvette.

Margot: Après avoir **vécu à la colle** pendant deux **berges**, Yvette et Marc, y z'ont décidé de **s'marida**! C'était **couru**, ça. Au fait, y vont **prononcer l'conjugo** au mois d'mai!

Jean: Ouais, j'sais. **Mardoche**, Marc, y a **enterré sa vie d'garçon.** Y va vraiment **épouser l'gros sac,** c'ui-là.

Margot: Comme tu dis!

Jean: On dit qu'y vont s'installer dans un p'tit **bocal** à la **cambrousse.** Y vont **pend'la crémaillère** dès qu'y z'auront **des bouts d'bois.** Même maintenant, y sont obligés d'**coucher sur la dure.**

Margot: Mais, attends! Ça fait une bonne **trotte** d'ici. Pourquoi y veulent **nicher** à **Trifouillis-les-Oies**?

Jean: Pasque la **rem** de Marc, è **s'éternise** chez eux et Yvette, è veut pas s'faire **embellemerder.** S'y **s'décampaient** pas, j'suis sûr qu'elles finiraient à **s'peigner.**

Margot: Bravo pour Yvette, alors! J'parie qu'elle aura les **grelots** l'jour du mariage. Elle a toujours voulu **accrocher un mari** et après tout, è commence à **s'décatir.** En plus, y paraît qu'Marc, c't'un bon **chopin.** Y sais même **faire la popote.**

Jean: T'es pas **à la page**? Marc, y a toujours **mené une vie d'paillasson** et j'ai entendu dire qu'y a déjà **pris un p'tit à-côté**!

Margot: Ah, **l'affaire, è s'corse.**

HOORAY FOR LOVE...

DIALOGUE

Margot and Jean are discussing Yvette's wedding.

Margot: After shacking up for two years, Yvette and Marc have decided to get married! It was bound to happen. As a matter of fact, they're gonna tie the knot in May!

Jean: Yeah, I know. Tuesday, Marc had a bachelor party. That guy's really going to marry into money.

Margot: You know it!

Jean: I was told that they're going to get a little place somewhere out in the sticks. They're going to have a housewarming as soon as they get some furniture. Even now, they have to sleep on the floor.

Margot: But, wait! That's a real trek from here. Why do they want to live out in the boonies?

Jean: Because Marc's mom hangs out at their house all the time and Yvette doesn't want to be hounded all the time by her mother-in-law. If they didn't get outta there, I'm sure they'd end up tearing each other's hair out.

Margot: Then, good for Yvette! I bet she's gonna be shaking in her boots the day of the wedding. She always did want to land a husband and after all, she is starting to get up there. Besides, it seems like Marc is a good catch. He even knows how to cook.

Jean: You don't know the real story? Marc has always lived in the fast lane and I heard that he's already had a little on the side!

Margot: Ah, the plot thickens!

VOCABULARY

à la page (être) *exp.* to be in the know, caught up • (lit); to be (caught up) to the page
• *T' es pas à la page?;* You haven't heard the latest?
NOTE: **mettre qqn. à la page** *exp.* to bring s.o. up-to-date.
SYNONYM: **être à la coule** *exp.* • (lit); to be in the flow.

accrocher un mari *exp.* • (lit); to hook a husband.
NOTE: **avoir l'accroche de qqn.** or **être accroché(e) de qqn.** *exp.* to be hooked on s.o.
ANTONYM: **avoir qqn. dans le nez** *exp.* to dislike s.o. • (lit); to have s.o. in the nose.

berge *f.* year. *Elle a deux berges;* She's two years old.
SYNONYM: **pigette** *f.*

bocal *m.* house, premises, place • (lit); jar • *J' l' ai eu à son bocal;* I caught up with him
at his house.
SYNONYM: **baraque** *f.* house • (lit); barracks.

bouts de bois *m.pl.* • (lit); ends of wood • sticks of furniture.

cambrousse *f.* country, sticks, "Hicksville."
NOTE: **cambroussard(e)** *n.* one who lives in the country, hick.

chopin *m.* a catch (love). *Elle a fait un bon chopin;* She made a good catch.
NOTE: This comes from the slang verb *choper* meaning "to catch."

corser (se) *v. L'affaire se corse!;* The plot thickens • (lit); to make stronger (sauce,
drink, etc.), to intensify.
ANTONYM: **se tasser** *v.* to calm down • (lit); to settle, to set (of foundations) • *Mes
parents, y s'engueulaient pendant tout l'après-midi... maintenant tout s'est tassé;*
My parents have been screaming at each other all afternoon... now everything's
getting back to normal.

coucher sur la dure *exp.* to sleep on the floor • (lit); to sleep on the hard.
NOTE: **dure** *f.* floor.
SYNONYM: **coucher à barbette** *exp.* to sleep (on a matress) on the floor.

couru (être) *adj.* to be bound to happen • (lit); to be run • *Y s'est fait arrêter par les
flics. C'était couru!;* He got arrested by the cops. It was bound to happen!

décamper (se) *v.* to leave quickly • (lit); to decamp, clear out • *Les flics! On décampe!;*
The cops! Scram!
SYNONYM: **prendre la tangente** *exp.* to scram • (lit); to take the tangent.
ANTONYM: **radiner** *v.* to show up.

décatir (se) *exp.* to lose one's beauty, to age • (lit); to take off the gloss (of furniture,
etc.) • *Y commence à s'décatir;* He's starting to show his age.

embellemerder *v.* to be hounded by one's mother-in-law.
NOTE: This is a humorous transformation of the verb *emmerder*, which means "to
bug the shit out of s.o." Notice that within the verb *embellemerder* is the word
belle-mère meaning "mother-in-law" and *merde* meaning "shit."

enterrer sa vie de garçon *exp.* to have a bachelor party • (lit); to bury one's life as a boy.

épouser le gros sac *exp.* to marry into money (said of a man who marries a rich woman) • (lit); to marry the big sack (of money).

éterniser (s') *v.* to overstay and wear out one's welcome • (lit); to last forever, to drag on and on.

grelots (avoir les) *m.pl.* to be afraid, to have the jitters • (lit); to have bells, sleigh bells • *Cette maison, è m'donne les grelots;* This house gives me the jitters.
NOTE (1): This expression might be translated as "to have bells that are jingling (because the possessor is shaking from fear)."
NOTE (2): **grelotter** *v.* to shake with fear • (lit); to jingle.

mardoche *m.* slang transformation of mardi meaning "Tuesday."
SEE: *Inside Info - Slang Suffixes,* p. 22.

marida (se) *v.* slang transformation of *se marier* meaning "to get married." *Je m'suis marida la semaine dernière;* I got married last week.
NOTE: The verb *marida* is both an infinitive and past participle.
SYNONYM: **se caser** *v.* • (lit); to place, file (something) • *E va s'caser;* She's going to get married • *J'ai trois filles à caser;* I have three daughters to marry off.

mener une vie de paillasson *exp.* to lead a fast life • (lit); to lead a life of a doormat.
NOTE: This expression conjures up an image of a person who welcomes many different "houseguests" on a regular basis as does a doormat.

nicher *v.* to live • (lit); to build a nest, to nest • *J'niche à Paris;* I live in Paris.
SYNONYM: **crécher** *v.* *Y crèche à Paris;* He lives in Paris.

peigner (se) *v.* to fight, "to tear out each other's hair" (especially of women) • (lit); to comb one's hair.
SYNONYM: **se crêper le chignon** *exp.* • (lit); to frizz each other's bun (of hair).

pendre la crémaillère *exp.* to have a housewarming • (lit); to hang the pot hook.
NOTE: Years ago, when a family moved into a new home, a large pot containing food was hung from a hook above the fireplace as guests were invited to share in the meal.

popote (faire la) *exp.* kitchen, cooking • (lit); mess, canteen (military) • *C'est elle qui fait l'ménage et moi qui fait la popote;* She does the cleaning and I do the cooking.
SYNONYM: **faire la tambouille** *exp.*
NOTE: **cuistot(e)** *n.* chef.

prendre un petit à-côté *exp.* to have extramarital sex • (lit); to take a little something on the side.

prononcer le conjugo *exp.* to tie the knot • (lit); to announce the taking of one's conjugal vows.

rem *f.* verlan for *mère;* mother.
    SEE: *Street French*, Le Verlan, p. 130.
    NOTE: **rep** *m.* verlan for *père;* father.

Trifouillis-les-Oies *Prn.* boonies, boondocks, tules, "sticks," any imaginary faraway
    place. *Y z' ont décidé d' aller habiter à Trifouillis-les-Oies;* They've decided to go
    live out in the sticks.
    ALSO: **Tripatouille-les-Oies** *Prn.*

trotte *f.* a long distance • (lit); a trot • *Paris à Los Angeles, ça fait une bonne trotte;*
    Paris to Los Angeles, that's quite a trek.
    NOTE: **se trotter** *v.* to leave, to take off. *Y est déjà 7h? J' dois m' trotter;* It's already
    7:00? I've gotta be going.

vivre à la colle *exp.* to be unmarried and living together • (lit); to live like glue • *Mais,*
    ça fait des années qu' y vivent à la colle; They've been shacking up together for
    several years, now.

PRACTICE THE VOCABULARY

[Answers to Lesson 2, p. 66]

A. Underline the synonym.

1. **rem:**   a. déjeuner   b. mère   c. cuisine

2. **berge:**   a. enfant   b. année   c. dame

3. **cambrousse:**   a. campagne   b. père   c. voiture

4. **se peigner:**   a. se laver   b. s'en aller   c. se battre

5. **se décamper:**   a. partir   b. arriver   c. rester

6. **nicher:**   a. habiter   b. trouver   c. perdre

7. **à la page:**   a. stupide   b. au courant   c. fatigué

8. **bocal:**   a. maison   b. voiture   c. tête

9. **se décatir:**   a. s'ennuyer   b. s'amuser   c. âger

10. **la popote:**   a. les parents   b. la cuisine   c. le père

11. **bouts de bois:**   a. meubles   b. jambes   c. maisons

12. **dure:**   a. tête   b. meuble   c. plancher

B. **Rewrite the following phrases replacing the italicized word(s) with the appropriate slang synonym(s) from the right column. Make any other necessary changes.**

1. Encore 150 kilomètres?! Ça fait une *longue distance*.   **A. dure**

   _____

2. Mes deux frangines, è n'font qu'se *battre*.   **B. marida**

   _____

3. Y s'fait toujours *embêter par sa belle-mère*.   **C. trotte**

   _____   **D. rem**

4. On s'couche sur l'*plancher* pasqu'on a pas d'*meubles*.

   _____   **E. se décamper**

5. J'dois *partir* pour aller chercher ma *mère*.   **F. berge**

   _____

6. J'aime pas faire la *cuisine*, moi.   **G. peigner**

   _____

7. Sa fille, elle a trois *ans*.   **H. bouts de bois**

   _____   **I. popote**

8. Y vont bientôt s'*marier*.

   _____   **J. embellemerder**

C. **Complete the phrases by choosing the appropriate word(s) from the list below. Make any necessary changes.**

le gros sac	**crémaillère**	**se corser**
à la colle	**conjugo**	**chopin**
enterrer	**grelots**	**accrocher**
Trifouillis-les-Oies	**à-côté**	**nicher**

1. J'ai d'bonnes nouvelles! Ma frangine, è vient d'prononcer l' _____ .

2. Nancy, è s'est mariée à Dominique. Elle a d'la chance pasque c't'un très bon _____ .

3. Sa maison, è s'trouve à 100 kilomèt'de Paris. J'vois pas comment ça lui plaît d'habiter à _____ .

4. Y viennent d'acheter une nouvelle maison et la semaine prochaine, y vont pend'la _____ .

5. Félicitations! J'ai entendu dire qu't'as _____ un mari!

6. J'ai toujours voulu _____ à Paris.

7. J'veux pas entrer dans cette maison hantée; j'ai les _____ , moi!

8. Christophe, y est riche pasqu'y a épousé _____ .

9. Pisqu'y va bientôt s'marier, ce soir, y va _____ sa vie d'garçon.

10. Catherine, elle est furieuse pasqu'elle a appris qu'son mari, y a pris un p'tit _____ .

11. L'affaire, è _____ ! Quel scandale!

12. Irène, elle est pas contente qu'sa fille, è préfère vivre _____ avant de s'marier.

INSIDE INFO: *SLANG SUFFIXES*

In book one, **Street French**, we explored how conventional words can be easily transformed into slang and how slang words can be intensified by applying one of three formulae: *verlan*, *largonji*, and *javanais*.

There is yet another very popular formula which uses slang suffixes to create slang words. These suffixes include: *-aille, -ard, -arès, -asse (ace), -oche, -os, -osse, -ouille, -ouse (ouze)*, and *-uche*. By learning these slang suffixes, you will quickly be able to recognize them as well as create some interesting slang words of your own.

-aille(r)   **crevaille** *f.* huge meal.
        ORIGIN: **crever** *v.* to die, to explode.

discutailler *v.* to discuss.
        ORIGIN: **discuter** *v.*

duraille *adj.* hard.
        ORIGIN: **dur(e)** *adj.*

Franchecaille *f.* France.

gambergeailler *v.* to daydream.
        ORIGIN: **gamberger** *v.*

godaille *f.* food.

godailler *v.* to eat.

joncaille *f.* money.
        ORIGIN: **jonc** *m.*

lichailler *v.* to drink.
        ORIGIN: **licher** *v.*

mangeaille *f.* grub.
        ORIGIN: **manger** *v.* to eat.

pinailler *v.* to quibble, nit-pick.

poiscaille *m.* fish.
        ORIGIN: **poisson** *m.*

-ard   **cottard(e)** *adj.* difficult.

craspouillard(e) *adj.* dirty.

faiblard(e) *adj.* weak,
feeble.
ORIGIN: **faible** *adj.*

prétentiard(e) *n. & adj.*
pretentious; pretentious
person.
ORIGIN: **prétentieux,
-euse** *n. & adj.*

richard(e) *n. & adj.* rich.
ORIGIN: **riche** *adj.*

rigolard(e) *adj.* funny.
ORIGIN: **rigoler** *v.* to
laugh.

tartouillard *adj.* ugly.
ORIGIN: **tarte** *adj.*

-arès   **bouclarès** *adj.* closed.
ORIGIN: **boucler** *v.* to
close.

couparès *adj.* penniless
ORIGIN: **coupé** *adj.* cut
off (from funds).

emballarès *adj.* arrested.
ORIGIN: **se faire
emballer** *exp.* to get
arrested.

-asse   **blondasse** *f.* blonde.

fadasse *adj.* dull.
ORIGIN: **fade** *adj.*

follasse *adj. & n.* crazy
(of woman).
ORIGIN: **folle** *adj.*

-oche(r)   **cinetoche** *m.* movie
theater.
ORIGIN: **cinéma** *m.*

cinoche *m.* movie theater.
ORIGIN: **cinéma** *m.*

espadoches *f.pl.* espadrilles.

fantoche *f.* fantasy.
ORIGIN: **fantaisie** *f.*

filocher *v.* to shadow (s.o.).
ORIGIN: **filer** *v.*

glandocher *v.* to stroll and
hang out.
ORIGIN: **glander** *v.*

Invaloches *m.pl.* les
Invalides.

lapinoche *m.* rabbit.
ORIGIN: **lapin(e)** *n.*

mardoche *m.* Tuesday.
ORIGIN: **mardi** *m.*

médoche *f.* medal.
ORIGIN: **médaille** *f.*

patoche *f.* hand.
ORIGIN: **patte** *f.* hand
• (lit); paw.

peloche *f.* film
ORIGIN: **pellicule** *f.*

pétoche *f.* fart; fear.
ORIGIN: **pet** *m.*

téloche *f.* television.
ORIGIN: **télévision** *f.*

-os   **coolos** *adj.* cool (attitude).

-ose   **chouettose** *exclam.* fantastic.
ORIGIN: **chouette** *exclam.*

-ouille(r)   **charmouille** *adj.* charming.
ORIGIN: **charmant(e)** *adj.*

crachouiller *v.* to spit.
ORIGIN: **cracher** *v.*

crassouille *f.* filth, dirt.
ORIGIN: **crasse** *f.* dirt.

gidouille *m.* **1.** stomach
• **2.** belly button.

glandouiller *v.* to stroll;
hang out.
ORIGIN: **glander** *v.*

gratouiller *v.* to itch.
ORIGIN: **gratter** *v.*

mâchouiller *v.* to eat
without appetite.
ORIGIN: **mâcher** *v.*

merdouille *f.* shit.
ORIGIN: **merde** *f.*

papouille *f. faire des
papouilles à qqn.;* to
paw someone, to caress.

papouiller *v.* to paw and
caress.

patouille *f. faire des
patouilles à qqn.;* to paw
someone, to caress.
NOTE: **patte** *f.* paw.

péquenouille *m.* country
hick.
ORIGIN: **péquenot** *m.*

pétouille *f.* fart, fear.
ORIGIN: **pet** *m.*

-ouse(r) **cartouse** *f.* card.
ORIGIN: **carte** *f.*

cavouse *f.* wine cellar.
ORIGIN: **cave** *f.*

cravtouse *f.* tie
ORIGIN: **cravate** *f.*

filetouse *m.* string bag.
ORIGIN: **filet** *m.*

langouse *f.* tongue.
ORIGIN: **langue** *f.*

limouse *f.* shirt.
ORIGIN: **lime** *f.*

palpouser *v.* to earn money.
ORIGIN: **palper** *v.*

paradouse *m.* paradise,
heaven.
ORIGIN: **paradis** *m.*

perlouse *f.* pearl, fart.
ORIGIN: **perle** *f.*

pétouse *f.* fart, fear. *avoir
la pétouse;* to be scared
to death.
ORIGIN: **pet** *m.*

piquouser *v.* to shoot up
(with drugs).
ORIGIN: **piquer** *v.*

plaquouser *v.* to jilt, to
drop (responsibilities).
ORIGIN: **plaquer** *v.*

sacouse *m.* purse.
ORIGIN: **sac** *m.*

tantouse *f.* gay man,
"queen."
ORIGIN: **tante** *f.* aunt.

tartouse *adj.* ugly.
ORIGIN: **tarte** *adj.*

-uche **dabuche** *m.* father.
ORIGIN: **dab** *m.*

dolluche *m.* dollar.
ORIGIN: **dollar** *m.*

méduche *f.* medal.
ORIGIN: **médaille** *f.*

PRACTICE SLANG SUFFIXES

A. Rewrite the following terms using slang suffixes.

1. télévision:

6. folle:

2. dur(e):

7. cinéma:

3. licher:

8. prétentieux:

4. poisson:

9. riche:

5. fade:

10. glander:

– 3 –

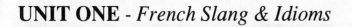

Au Travail

(At Work)

Leçon Trois

AU TRAVAIL...

DIALOGUE

Eric et David **parlent boulot**.

Eric:	Mais, **quelle mouche le pique?**
David:	Oh, Georges, y a toujours des **emmerdements** avec le **chapeau**. J'me **frott'rais** pas à lui si j'étais à sa place. En plus, j'ai entendu dire que l'patron, y va bientôt **dégraisser** et Georges, y est déjà **à deux doigts d'se faire envoyer sur les roses**.
Eric:	Avec le patron, **on sait jamais sur quel pied danser.**
David:	C'est vrai qu'c't'un **pompe-la-sueur**, mais y est **du bois dont on fait les flutes**! Tu l'laisses **tirer les ficelles** et y'a pas d'problème. Faut **faire dans la dentelle**, c'est tout!
Eric:	Bof... à mon avis, **c'est pain bénit** pour Georges. Y s'rend même pas compte qu'y a une vraie **assiette au beurre** avec d'bons **à-côtés**. D'accord, de temps en temps c't'un vrai **bagne**, mais faut s'y faire. En plus, y pense qu'y doit **s'coltiner** tout seul son boulot mais y r'fuse de **flécher**, c'est ça l'problème.
David:	Normalement, j'fais onze **battants bien tassés** d'**marne** et parfois les **jours chrômés**. Moi, j'**fais jamais l'pont** non plus et lui, y **s'casse** jamais! J'suis sûr que quelqu'un l'a **pistonné, c'est moi qui t'le dis.**
Eric:	Sans blague. Tiens! On est l'**combientième**, aujourd'hui?
David:	On est l'dix-huit. Pourquoi?
Eric:	Ah, encore deux jours, c'est **la Sainte-Touche**!
David:	Le patron! On **rembraye**!

28

AT WORK...

DIALOGUE

Eric and David talk shop.

Eric:	What's buggin' him?
David:	Oh, George is always having problems with the big cheese. I wouldn't tangle with him if I were in his shoes. Besides, I heard that the boss is going to be trimming the fat soon and George is already on the verge of getting canned.
Eric:	With the boss, you sure never know where you stand.
David:	True he's a slave driver but you can wrap him around your little finger! Just let him run the show and you won't have any problems. You just have to wear kid gloves, that's all!
Eric:	Oh, I dunno... in my opinion, it serves George right. He doesn't even realize that he's got a cushy job with good perks. Sure, sometimes it's a real grind but you just have to deal with it. Besides, he thinks he has to tackle his work all by himself and he refuses to be a team player, that's the problem.
David:	Normally, I do eleven solid hours of work and sometimes on Sundays and holidays. I never take Mondays off either and that guy never puts himself out! I'm sure someone pulled some strings to get him hired, I'll bet you anything.
Eric:	No joke. Hey! What's the date today?
David:	It's the eighteenth. Why?
Eric:	Ah, another two days till payday!
David:	The boss! Let's get crackin'!

VOCABULARY

à deux doigts (être) *exp.* to be on the verge, on the brink • (lit); to be two fingers away (from doing something) • *Elle est à deux doigts d' la mort;* She's at death's door.

à-côtés *m.pl.* perks • (lit); that which is on the side • *Ton boulot, ça comprend des à-côtés?;* Does your job come with any perks?

assiette au beurre *f.* cushy job • (lit); plate of butter • British equivalent: "Bum in butter."
NOTE: **c'est du beurre** *exp.* it's a cinch, a snap • (lit); it's butter.
SYNONYM: **fromage** *m.* • (lit); cheese • *Quel fromage!;* What a cush job!

bagne *m.* unpleasant job, grind • (lit); penal servitude • *Quel bagne!;* What a hellhole!

battants *m.pl.* hours • (lit); clappers (of a bell) • *Ça fait des battants qu'j'attends!;* I've been waiting for hours!
NOTE: **battante** *f.* watch.
SYNONYM: **plombes** *f.pl.*

bien tassé(e)s *adj.* solid (said of hours) • (lit); well compressed, packed • *Ça fait deux heures bien tassées qu'j'attends!;* I've been waiting for two solid hours.

c'est moi qui te le dis *exp.* • (lit); I'm telling you • *Y est pas réglo, c'ui-là... c'est moi qui t'le dis!;* That's guy's not on the up and up... I'm telling you!

c'est pain bénit *exp.* It serves him/her right • (lit); it's blessed bread • *Y s'est fait recalé à l'examen. C'est pain bénit... y a triché!;* He flunked his test. It serves him right... he cheated!
SYNONYM: **c'est bien fait pour sa gueule** *exp.* (lit); it's well done for his/her face.

casser (ne pas se) *v.* not to put oneself out • (lit); not to break oneself • *E s'casse pour personne;* She doesn't put herself out for anyone.
ANTONYM: **se plier en deux** *exp.* to bend over backwards (to do something) • (lit); to fold oneself in two.

chapeau *m.* big boss, he who wears the big hat • (lit); hat • *Attention! Voilà l'chapeau qui arrive!;* Look out! The boss man's coming!
SYNONYM: **singe** *m.* • (lit); monkey.

coltiner qqch. (se) *v.* to do, to get stuck doing something • (lit); **coltiner** *v.* to carry a heavy load on one's back • *Pourquoi c'est toujours moi qui dois m'coltiner tout c'boulot?;* Why do I always have to be the one to get stuck with all the work?

combientième *adv. On est l'combientième, aujourd'hui?;* What's the date today?
NOTE: This is a humorous way of asking for the correct date since *combientième* is actually a word that was created by adding the ordinal suffix *-ième* (as in *trois-ième, quatr-ième, cinqu-ième,* etc.) to the adverb *combien* meaning "how many/much."

dégraisser *v.* to make cutbacks • (lit); to skim the fat off (soup, etc.) • *Maintenant, nous avons qu' dix employés pasque l' chapeau, y vient de dégraisser;* Now, we only have ten employees because the boss just cut back the staff.
SYNONYM: **balayer** *v.* • (lit); to sweep • *Y a balayé tout l'personnel;* He made a clean sweep of the entire staff.

du bois dont on fait les flutes (être) *exp.* said of s.o. who can be wrapped around one's finger • (lit); to be the wood of which flutes are made (i.e., soft and pliable).

emmerdement *m.* annoyance, complication, problem, etc. • (lit); that which bugs the shit out of s.o. • *J'ai toujours des emmerdements avec lui;* I always have problems with him.
NOTE: **emmerder** *v.* to bug the shit out of s.o. (note that the root word is *merde* meaning "shit").

envoyer sur les roses (se faire) *exp.* to get oneself fired (from work) • (lit); to get oneself sent on the roses • *Y s'est fait envoyer sur les roses;* He got himself canned.
SYNONYM: **se faire saquer** *exp.* • (lit); to get oneself sacked.

faire dans la dentelle *exp.* to put on kid gloves, to handle carefully • (lit); to do (it) in lace • *Fais dans la dentelle... Ta mère, elle est d'mauvais poil!;* Go at it easy... Your mother's in a bad mood!

faire le pont *exp.* to take Monday off • (lit); to make the bridge (from Saturday to Monday) • *Le patron, y m'a dit qu' j'peux faire l'pont;* The boss said I can have Monday off.
SYNONYM: **faire le Saint-Lundi** *exp.* • (lit); to make Saint Monday (hence, a religious holiday).

flécher *v.* to stick together, to team up. *Si tu veux partir de bonne heure, faut flécher ensemble!;* If you want to leave early, we have to work together!
NOTE: This is from the feminine noun *flèche* meaning "arrow." Therefore, *flécher* might be loosely translated as "to point (and work) in the same direction as an arrow."

frotter à qqn. (se) *v.* to tangle with s.o • (lit); to rub up against s.o. • *Je m'suis frotté au patron, aujourd'hui;* I tangled with the boss today.

jour chrômé *m.* any Sunday or holiday • (lit); chromed day • *Y est interdit de s'garer ici les jours chrômés;* It's illegal to park here on Sundays and holidays.
NOTE: This is a humorous slang transformation of *jour férié* meaning "any non-working day." Since the first syllable of the word *férié* sounds like the masculine noun *fer* meaning "iron," the adjective *chrômé* meaning "chromed" has simply been used in its place.

marne *m.* work.
NOTE: **marner** *v.* to work hard.
SYNONYM: **boulot** *m.*

on sait jamais sur quel pied danser *exp.* you never know where you stand • (lit); you never know which foot to dance with.

parler boulot *exp.* to talk shop • (lit); to talk work • *Y n'fait qu'parler boulot;* All he ever does is talk shop.
NOTE: **boulot** *m.* work.

pistonner *v.* to recommend s.o. for a job, to pull strings (for s.o.). *Son père, y l'a pistonné;* His father pulled some strings for him.
SYNONYM: **chapeauter** *v.* to recommend s.o. for a job, to help s.o. become a boss *(un chapeau).*

pompe-la-sueur *m.* slave driver • (lit); sweat pumper.

quelle mouche le pique *exp.* what's bugging him? • (lit); what fly bit him.
SEE: *Inside Info - Fish, Insects, and Animals That Have Infiltrated French Slang,* p. 34.

rembrayer *v.* to get back to work, to get cracking • (lit); to put the clutch back in.
NOTE: **embrayer** *v.* to get to work • (lit); to put in the clutch.

Sainte-Touche (la) *f.* • (lit); the blessed payday.
NOTE: **toucher** *v.* to receive one's salary. *Combien tu touches par mois?;* How much do you make each month?

tirer les ficelles *exp.* to run the show • (lit); to pull the strings (of a theater curtain).
NOTE: Not to be confused with **pistonner** *v.* to pull strings (for s.o.).

PRACTICE THE VOCABULARY

[Answers to Lesson 3, p. 67]

A. Complete the phrase by choosing the appropriate word(s) from the list. Make any necessary changes.

pied	tassées	ficelles
pompe-la-sueur	emmerdements	se coltiner
battants	bagne	se casser

1. J'suis d'mauvaise humeur pasque j'ai toutes sortes d'_____ .

2. J'peux pas _____ tout seul c'boulot!

3. Y m'aide jamais. Faut dire qu'y _____ pas.

4. Y est difficile, lui. On sait jamais sur quel _____ danser.

5. J'en ai marre de c'boulot! Quel _____ !

6. Ça fait trois heures bien _____ qu'j'attends!

7. Ça fait trois _____ qu'j'attends!

8. C'est pas toi l'patron! Tu dois le laisser tirer les _____ !

9. Ce patron, y nous fait travailler sans arrêt. C't'un vrai _____ .

B. Match the French with the English translation by writing the appropriate letter in the box.

☐ 1. She's on the verge of cracking up.

☐ 2. He's bizarre... I'm telling you.

☐ 3. You have to handle her gently.

☐ 4. It serves him/her right.

☐ 5. What's the date today?

☐ 6. The boss gave me a raise.

☐ 7. I found a good job because my dad pulled some strings.

☐ 8. He got himself canned.

☐ 9. There are some perks with this job.

☐ 10. Tomorrow is payday.

☐ 11. What's eating you?

☐ 12. I refuse to work on Sundays and holidays.

A. **Le chapeau, y m'a augmenté.**

B. **Y s'est fait envoyer sur les roses.**

C. **C'est pain bénit.**

D. **Elle est à deux doigts d'craquer.**

E. **Y'a des à-côtés avec c'boulot.**

F. **Je r'fuse de travailler les jours chrômés.**

G. **Quelle mouche te pique?**

H. **Demain, c'est la Saint-Touche.**

I. **On est l'combientième aujourd'hui?**

J. **Y est bizarre... c'est moi qui t'le dis.**

K. **J'ai trouvé un bon boulot pasque mon père, y m'a pistonné.**

L. **Faut faire dans la dentelle avec elle.**

C. Underline the appropriate word(s) that best complete(s) the phrase.

1. Y a trouvé un bon boulot. C't'une vraie assiette au (**fromage, beurre, vin**).

2. J'crois qu'y va bientôt (**déménager, décatir, dégraisser**), l'patron. Le chômage, c'est pas marrant!

3. Oh, t'en fais pas. Elle est du bois dont on fait les (**arbres, violons, flûtes**).

4. J'te reverrai au boulot mardi. C'week-end, j'fais l'(**pont, bateau, voyage**).

5. Y faut (**flécher, dégraisser, s'marida**) ensemble pour faire un bon boulot.

6. Faut qu'j'aille au (**lit, marché, marne**). Le patron, y m'attend.

7. Y est pas gentil, c'ui-là. Faut pas t'(**carapater, frotter, barrer**) à lui!

8. Bon... (**voyons, regardons, parlons**) boulot. J'ai une bonne affaire qui va t'intéresser.

9. Après un bon déjeuner, y est toujours difficile de (**flécher, parler, rembrayer**).

10. J'peux pas t'accompagner maintenant. Y'a des (**marnes, bagnes, emmerdements**) chez moi.

11. J'peux pas m'(**marida, coltiner, flécher**) tout seul, c'boulot.

12. Je m'demande qui l'a (**rembrayé, pistonné, coltiné**) pour avoir c'boulot.

INSIDE INFO: *FISH, INSECTS, AND ANIMALS THAT HAVE INFILTRATED FRENCH SLANG*

We certainly owe a great deal of thanks to fish, insects, and animals that have graciously allowed themselves to be the subject of many American slang expressions such as: *to pig out, to be dog tired, to have a frog in one's throat, to worm something out of someone, to get one's goat, to smell fishy, to be a real fox, that's a lot of bull, "What are ya? Chicken?..." etc.*

Undeniably, the French hold their own in creating slang expressions out of anything that crawls, slithers, or flies, as demonstrated in the opening dialogue with the expression: *Quelle mouche le pique?*

The following are several words and expressions that have been inspired by the animal kingdom and are now part of the imaginative world of French slang:

Bears

avoir ses ours *exp.* to have one's period • (lit); to have one's bears.

ours *m.* manuscript that has been rejected repeatedly by publishers • (lit); bear.

Birds

à bientôt, mon oiseau! *exp.* see ya later, "alligator!"
• (lit); see you later, "sweetheart."

becquant *m.* • slang for "bird"
• (lit); "beaker."
NOTE: This comes from the masculine noun *bec* meaning "beak."

piaf *m.* slang for "bird"
• (lit); sparrow.

pinçant *m.* slang for "bird"
• (lit); "pincher."

rossignols *m.pl.* old merchandise.
• (lit); nightingales.

Cats

avoir un chat dans la gorge *exp.* to have a "frog" in one's throat
• (lit); to have a cat in the throat.

donner sa langue au chat *exp.* to give up (to a guess) • (lit); to give one's tongue to the cat.

écriture de chat *exp.* illegible writing, chicken scratch
• (lit); cat's writing.

greffier *m.* slang for "cat"
• (lit); scratcher.
NOTE: This comes from the verb *griffer* meaning "to scratch."

griffard *m.* slang for "cat"
• (lit); scratcher.
NOTE: This comes from
the verb *griffer* meaning
"to scratch."

grippart *m.* slang for "cat"
• (lit); pouncer.
NOTE: This comes from thea
verb *gripper* meaning
"to pounce."

lapin de gouttière *m.* slang for
"cat" • (lit); (roof-)gutter rabbit.

miron *m.* slang for "cat"
• (lit); looker.
NOTE: This comes from the
slang verb *mirer* meaning
"to look."

mistigri *m.* slang for "cat."

Chickens

des mollets de coq *exp.* thin legs,
bird legs • (lit); (leg-)calves of
a rooster.

faire la bouche en cul de poule
exp. to purse one's lips
• (lit); to make an expression
with one's mouth like the ass
of a hen.

pique-en-terre *m.* slang for
"chicken" • (lit); earth peckers.
NOTE: This comes from the
verb *piquer* meaning "to pick,
to peck, to bite."

Cows

cornante *f.* slang for "cow"
• (lit); that which has horns.

pleuvoir comme vache qui pisse
exp. to rain heavily • (lit); to
rain like a pissing cow.

tête de veau *m.* idiot, fool
• (lit); calf's head.

travailler comme un bœuf *exp.*
to work like a "horse"
• (lit); to work like an ox.

vache *f. & adj.* **1.** mean, nasty,
rotten. *Elle est vache avec lui;*
She's really nasty with him •
2. bastard. *Bande de vaches;*
Bunch of bastards •
3. policeman • **4.** *Oh, la
vache!;* Wow!• (lit); cow.

vaches à roulettes *f.pl.* cycle cops
• (lit); cows on wheels.

Crickets

cricri *m.* cricket.

Dogs

avoir du chien *exp.* to have
charm and sex appeal
• (lit); to have dog.

avoir un caractère de chien *exp.*
to have a nasty disposition
• (lit); to have a dog's
disposition.

avoir un chien pour quelqu'un
exp. to have a crush on s.o.
• (lit); to have a dog for s.o.

avoir un mal de chien *exp.* to be
in great pain • (lit); to have
pain like a dog.

cabot *m.* slang for "dog."

chienchien *m.* affectionate term
for dog, doggy.

chien coiffé *m.* very ugly person,
a "real dog" • (lit); dog with a
hairdo.

chien(ne) (être) *adj.* to be mean
• (lit); to be dog(-like).

clébard *m.* slang for "dog."

clebs *m.* (pronounced: *kleps*)
slang for "dog."

mon chien *exp.* my darling
• (lit); my dog.

ouah-ouah *m.* (pronounced *wawa*) doggy.

piquer un chien *exp.* to take a "cat" nap • (lit); to take a dog (nap).

quel chien t'a mordu? *exp.* what's gotten into you?
• (lit); what dog bit you?

se donner un mal de chien pour faire qqch. *exp.* to bend over backwards to do something
• (lit); to cause oneself the pain of a dog (great pain) to do something.

temps de chien *exp.* horrible weather • (lit); dog's weather.

vie de chien *exp.* • (lit); dog's life.

Donkeys

monté comme un âne (être) *exp.* to be hung like a "horse"
• (lit); to be mounted like a donkey.

oreillard *m.* slang for "donkey"
• (lit); that which has ears.

peau d'âne *f.* diploma
• (lit); donkey skin.

plein(e) comme une bourrique (être) *exp.* to be drunk as a "skunk" • (lit); to be full (drunk) like a donkey.

Ducks

barbot *m.* slang for "duck"
• (lit); that which likes to paddle.
NOTE: This comes from the verb *barbotter* meaning "to paddle."

barboteux *m.* slang for "duck"
• (lit); that which likes to paddle.
NOTE: This comes from the verb *barbotter* meaning "to paddle."

sirop de canard *m.* water
• (lit); duck syrup.

Elephants

comme un éléphant dans un magasin de porcelaine *exp.* like a "bull" in a china shop
• (lit); like an elephant in a porcelain shop.

Fish

faire des yeux de merlan frit *exp.* to make goo-goo eyes at s.o. • (lit); to make fried marlin eyes at s.o.

finir en queue de poisson *exp.* to fizzle out • (lit); to end up like a fish's tail.

pescal(e) *m.* slang for "fish."

poiscaille *m.* slang for "fish."

Fleas

chercher des puces à qqn. *exp.* to nitpick • (lit); to look for fleas in s.o.

Flies

c'est une fine mouche *exp.* he/she's a crafty devil
• (lit); that's a fine fly.

quelle mouche te pique? *exp.* what's bugging you?
• (lit); what fly's biting you?

tuer les mouches à quinze pas *exp.* to have bad breath
• (lit); to kill flies fifteen steps away.

Foxes

aller au renard *exp.* to throw up • (lit); to go to the fox.

Frog

sirop de grenouille *m.* water • (lit); frog syrup.

Goats

bique *f.* slang for "nanny-goat."

chèvre coiffé *m.* very ugly person • (lit); goat with a hairdo.

Horses

bourdon *m.* slang for "horse, old nag."

bourrin *m.* slang for "horse" • (lit); donkey.

canasson *m.* slang for "horse, old nag."

carcan *m.* slang for "horse, old nag."

carne *f.* slang for "old horse" • (lit); meat (Spanish).

cocotte *f.* horse • used in *Hue, cocotte!;* Giddy up!

dada *m.* horsey (child's language).

fièvre de cheval *exp.* raging fever • (lit); fever of a horse.

gail *m.* slang for "horse."

canard *m.* slang for "horse, old nag." • (lit); duck.

manger avec les chevaux de bois *exp.* to go without food • (lit); to eat with the wooden horses.

mémoire de cheval *exp.* excellent memory, memory of an "elephant" • (lit); memory of a horse.

Kangaroos

voler au kangourou *exp.* to shoplift (and hide the stolen goods under one's clothing like a kangaroo would do in its pouch) • (lit); to steal kangaroo style.

Lice

orgueilleux comme un pou *exp.* proud as a "peacock" • (lit); to be proud as a louse.

sale comme un pou *exp.* filthy dirty • (lit); dirty as a louse.

Mice

c'est la montagne qui accouche d'une souris *exp.* what a lot of fuss about nothing • (lit); it's like the mountain giving birth to a mouse.

trottante *f.* slang for "mouse" • (lit); that which trots around. NOTE: This comes from the verb *trotter* meaning "to trot."

Oysters

huître *f.* gob of snot, "loogie." • (lit); oyster

plein(e) comme une huître (être) *exp.* to be drunk as a "skunk" • (lit); to be full *(drunk)* as an oyster.

Pigs

amis comme cochons (être) *exp.* to be great friends • (lit); to be friends like pigs.

bacon *m.* slang for "pig" • (lit); a (piece of) bacon.

bouant *m.* slang for "pig." NOTE: This comes from the feminine noun *boue* meaning "mud."

cochonner *v.* to botch up • (lit); to make something look "pig-like."

cochonnerie *f.* smut, dirty trick.

soûl comme un cochon *exp.* drunk as a "skunk" • (lit); drunk as a pig.

travail de cochon *exp.* botched job, slap dash work • (lit); the work of a pig.

Pigeons

pigeon *m.* sucker • (lit); pigeon.

Rabbits

jeannot *m.* slang for "rabbit, bunny."

lapinoche *m.* slang for "rabbit." SEE: *Lesson Two: Inside Info - Slang Suffixes*, p. 22.

lever un lièvre *exp.* to bring up a touchy subject • (lit); to raise a hare.

mon petit lapin *exp.* my darling • (lit); my little rabbit.

poser un lapin à qqn. *exp.* to stand s.o. up • (lit); to raise a rabbit to s.o.

trottin *m.* slang for "rabbit." NOTE: This comes from the verb *trotter* meaning "to trot (around)."

un fameux lapin *exp.* a great guy • (lit); a terrific rabbit.

une mère lapine *f.* woman with many children • (lit); mother rabbit.

Rats

fabriqué(e) comme un rat (être) *exp.* to be done for, to have one's "goose" cooked • (lit); to be done (for) like a rat.

gaspard *m.* slang for "rat."

mon petit rat *exp.* my darling • (lit); my little rat.

mon petit raton *exp.* my darling • (lit); my little baby rat.

Sheep

bêlant *m.* slang for "sheep." NOTE: This comes from the verb *bêler* meaning "to bleat."

chercher le mouton à cinq pattes *exp.* to look for the impossible • (lit); to look for the sheep with five paws.

revenons à nos moutons *exp.* let's get back to the subject • (lit); let's get back to our sheep.

Squirrels

écureuil à roulettes *m.* cyclist • (lit); squirrel on wheels.

Whales

se marrer comme une baleine *exp.* to laugh like a "hyena" • (lit); to laugh like a whale.

Worms

nu(e) comme un ver (être) *exp.* to be naked as a "jaybird" • (lit); to be naked as a worm.

tirer les vers du nez à qqn. *exp.* to worm something out of s.o. • (lit); to pull worms from s.o.'s nose.

PRACTICE USING FISH, INSECTS, AND ANIMALS IN FRENCH SLANG

A. Match the English with the French translations by writing the appropriate letter in the box.

☐ 1. It's raining cats and dogs.

☐ 2. She's always nasty.

☐ 3. I'm in such pain.

☐ 4. What a lousy disposition.

☐ 5. What horrible weather.

☐ 6. He's drunk as a skunk.

☐ 7. He's a crafty devil.

☐ 8. The project fizzled out.

A. **Y est plein comme une bourrique.**

B. **Le projet, y a finit en queue d'poisson.**

C. **Y pleut comme vache qui pisse.**

D. **Quel temps d'chien.**

E. **Elle est toujours vache.**

F. **C't'une fine mouche, lui.**

G. **J'ai un mal d'chien.**

H. **Quel caractère d'chien.**

B. Underline the appropriate word that best completes the sentence.

1. J'suis fatigué. J'vais piquer un (**éléphant, chien, poisson**).

2. Quelle mauvaise haleine! Y tue les (**mouches, cochons, lapins**) à quinze pas!

3. Quel travail d'(**souris, renard, cochon**)!

4. E l'a volé au (**cheval, kangourou, mouton**).

5. Elle a perdu du poids pasqu'è mange avec les (**pigeons, poux, chevaux**) d'bois.

6. J'suis malade, moi. J'ai une fièvre d'(**cheval, cochon, lapin**).

7. Je m'suis marré comme une (**baleine, vache, mouche**).

8. Y a essayé de m'tirer les (**baleines, rats, vers**) du nez.

9. Revenons à nos (**moutons, rats, vers**).

10. Ça fait deux heures bien tassées qu'j'attends. J'crois qu'è m'a posé un (**oiseau, poisson, lapin**).

11. J'suis fabriqué comme un (**kangourou, mouton, rat**), moi.

12. Mais, pourquoi t'as demandé ça? Tu vois pas qu't'as levé un (**lièvre, cheval, cochon**)?

C. Choose the slang synonym of the word in italics by writing the letter of the correct response in the space provided.

1. _____ ; *chat*
   a. mistigri   b. bêlant   c. bourrin

2. _____ ; *chien*
   a. barbot   b. cabot   c. griffard

3. _____ ; *cheval*
   a. piaf   b. pescale   c. canasson

4. _____ ; *cochon*
   a. bouant   b. trottin   c. gaspard

5. _____ ; *vache*
   a. cornante   b. bourrin   c. bouant

6. _____ ; *mouton*
   a. clébard   b. greffier   c. bêlant

7. _____ ; *oiseau*
   a. trottin   b. cornante   c. piaf

8. _____ ; *canard*
   a. barbot   b. canasson   c. carcan

9. _____ ; *poulet*
   a. clebs   b. pique-en-terre c. piaf

— 4 —

Au Café

(At the Café)

AU CAFÉ...

DIALOGUE

Marc et Clint font la **bamboula** à un p'tit **bistrot**.

Marc:	J'ai **décroché l'contrat**!
Clint:	Bravo! **Ça s'arrose.**
Marc:	**C'est pas d'refus**, ça. J'crois qu'j'ai b'soin d'**basculer un godet** pour m'**ravigoter** après tout ça. J'étais tellement tendu qu'j'ai grillé tout un **paquet d'bleues**!
Clint:	Oh, t'**frappe pas l'biscuit**, mon vieux. Si on prenait une **roteuse** et un p'tit **cale dent**?
Marc:	Pour l'instant, juste un **chouïa** d'café... avec une **larme** de rhum dedans, ce s'rait parfait.
Clint:	Mais, pourquoi tu prends pas un **roméo**? J'pensais qu't'avais l'**gosier blindé**, toi!
Marc:	Si j'bois trop d'rhum, ça m'**réussit** pas. Et si j'bois avant d'me **caler l'bide**, **j'en ai vite dans l'casque** et j'peux même pas m'**dépieuter** le lendemain. La dernière fois, j'ai **fait l'tour du cadran**.
Clint:	Pour moi, ça m'donne une **cuite carabinée**. La dernière fois pour moi, j'avais la **tête en compote** et ça durait trois jours, remarque. T'aurais dû m'voir **festonner**! Heureusement qu'j'ai pris une **bâfrée** avant de v'nir cette fois-ci.
Marc:	Tu sais, y z'ont un bon **abrevoir** ici par rapport à celui du coin. C'est toujours plein d'mecs **rétamés** qui n'font qu'**écumer les bars**. D'ailleurs, j'crois que l'**proprio**, y **sale la note**.
Clint:	Mais, ce soir, on fait la bamboula! On **recharge les accus**!

AT THE CAFÉ...

DIALOGUE

Marc and Clint are partying it up at a little café.

Marc: I landed the contract!

Clint: Congratulations! That calls for a drink.

Marc: Don't mind if I do. I think I could use a drink to get myself going again after all that. I was so uptight that I polished off an entire pack of Gauloise cigarettes!

Clint: Don't get yourself so worked up, buddy. What do ya say we get a bottle of bubbly and something to munch on?

Marc: For right now, just a little coffee... with a drop of rum in it would be perfect.

Clint: Why don't you have a "rum and water?" I thought you could handle the strong stuff.

Marc: If I drink too much rum, it doesn't agree with me. And if I drink before putting something in my stomach, it goes right to my head and I can't even get up the next day. The last time, I slept the whole day away.

Clint: It gives me a monster hangover. When I did that last time, I had a killer headache that lasted three days, I'll have you know. You should have seen me stagger around! Luckily, I porked out before coming here this time.

Marc: You know, they have a good bar here compared to the one around the corner. It's always full of these guys who are totally bombed and do nothing but barhop. Besides, I think the owner pads the bill.

Clint: But tonight, we're going to live it up! Let's stack 'em up again!

VOCABULARY

abrevoir *m.* bar, pub • (lit); drinking trough • *Y' a toujours trop d' monde à c' t' abrevoir;* There are always too many people at this bar.

bâfrée *f.* a huge meal, a real blowout.
NOTE: **se bâfrer** *v.* to pig out.
SYNONYM: **gueuleton** *m.* This comes from the feminine noun *gueule* meaning "mouth."

bamboula (faire la) *exp.* to party it up, to go out on a bender. *Y z' ont fait la bamboula toute la sainte soirée;* They were partying the whole blessed night.

basculer un godet *exp.* to drink • (lit); to rock (back) a glass • *J' l' ai vu basculer un godet au déjeuner!;* I saw him drinking during lunch!
NOTE: **godet** *m.* glass.
SYNONYM: **s'en jeter un derrière le bouton de col** *exp.* • (lit); to throw one behind the collar button.

bistrot *m.* café-bar.
SYNONYM: **troquet** *m.*

c'est pas de refus *exp.* don't mind if I do • (lit); it's not refused.

ça s'arrose *exp.* that calls for a drink • (lit); that waters itself.
NOTE (1): **s'arroser la gorge** *exp.* to wet one's whistle.
NOTE (2): **arroser** *v.* to buy the drinks. *C' est moi qui arrose;* Drinks are on me.

cale dent *m.* snack • (lit); that which steadies "hunger" • *Y m' faut un p' tit cale dent avant l' dîner;* I need a little snack before dinner.
NOTE: **avoir la dent** *exp.* to be hungry.
SYNONYM: **casse-croûte** *m.* snack • (lit); crust breaker (as in "to break bread").

caler le bide (se) *exp.* to take the edge off one's hunger • (lit); to steady one's stomach • *Tiens... ça t' cal' ra l' bide avant l' dîner;* Here... that'll take the edge off before dinner.
SYNONYM: **se caler les amygdales** *exp.* to eat well • (lit); to steady one's tonsils.

carabiné(e) *adj.* extreme, violent. *Une fièvre carabinée, une tempête carabinée, un rhume carabiné;* A raging fever, a violent storm, a heavy cold.

casque (en avoir dans le) *m.* to feel tipsy • (lit); to get some in one's head • *Si j' bois du vin, j' en ai vite dans l' casque;* If I drink wine, it goes right to my head.
NOTE: **casque** *m.* head • (lit); helmet.
SYNONYM: **être ébréché(e)** *adj.* to be tipsy, buzzed • (lit); to be chipped.

chouïa *adv.* (Arabic) a small amount. *J' en prends un chouïa;* I'll have just a bit.

cuite *f.* state of drunkeness • (lit); a frying (of one's brain cells due to excessive drinking) • *Elle a pris une sacrée cuite;* She got totally wasted.
NOTE (1): **prendre une cuite** *exp.* to get drunk.
NOTE (2): **se cuiter** *v.* to get drunk.
SYNONYM: **poivrade** *f.* • (lit); peppering • NOTE: **se poivrer** *v.* to get drunk • (lit); to pepper oneself.

décrocher un contract *exp.* to land a contract • (lit); to unhook a contract.
SYNONYM: **accrocher une affaire** *exp.* to sew up a deal • (lit); to hook a deal.

dépieuter (se) *v.* to get out of bed • (lit); to unstake oneself • *J'ai du mal à m'dépieuter l'matin;* I have trouble getting up in the morning.
NOTE: **pieu** *m.* bed • (lit); stake • *Au pieu!;* Off to bed (to get staked down for the night)!
ANTONYM: **se pieuter** *v.* to go to bed.

écumer les bars *exp.* to barhop • (lit); to scour, rove bars • *Y passe tout son temps à écumer les bars;* He spends all his time barhopping.

festonner *v.* to stagger about drunkenly • (lit); to walk in the pattern of festoons.

frapper le biscuit (se) *exp.* to worry oneself sick • (lit); to hit oneself in the head • *Arrête de t'frapper l'biscuit!;* Stop driving yourself crazy!
NOTE: **biscuit** *m.* head • (lit); biscuit.
SYNONYM: **se faire du mauvais sang** *exp.* • (lit); to make oneself bad blood.
ANTONYM: **être peinard(e)** *adj.* to be calm and relaxed.

gosier blindé (avoir le) *exp.* to be able to handle strong liquor, to be able to pack it away • (lit); to have the armored throat.
NOTE: **gosier** *m.* throat • (lit); gullet.
ANTONYM: **avoir la cuite facile** *exp.* to get drunk easily.

larme *f.* a drop • (lit); tear • *J'ai mis une larme de whisky dans son café;* I put a drop of whisky in his coffee.
SYNONYM: **larmichette** *f.*

paquet de bleues *m.* a pack of Gauloise cigarettes • (lit); a packet of blues (since Gauloise cigarettes come in a blue packet).
SYNONYM: **paquet de goldu** *m.*

proprio *m.* (male) owner; landlord • (lit); Abbreviation of: *propriétaire.*
NOTE: **propriote** *f.* (female) owner.
SEE: *Unit Three - Popular Abbreviations*, p. 217.

ravigoter (se) *v.* to perk oneself (back) up, to revive oneself. *Si tu prends à boire, ça t'ravigot'ra;* If you get something to drink, it'll perk you back up.
SYNONYM: **se requinquer** *v.*
ANTONYM: **partir en brioche** *exp.* to go downhill.

recharger les accus *exp.* to set 'em up (the glasses for another round of drinks) • (lit); to recharge the batteries.
SYNONYM: **recharger les wagonnets** *exp.* to recharge the tipcarts.

rétamé(e) (être) *adj.* to be bombed • (lit); to be retinned (to be so drunk that one can barely move as if made of tin).
SYNONYM: **être bourré(e)** *adj.* • (lit); to be stuffed (with alcohol, food, etc.).

réussir *v.* to be good for one's health • (lit); to succeed (in digesting something) • *La cuisine piquante, ça m' réussit pas;* Spicy food doesn't agree with me.

roméo *m. (rhum et eau = roméo)* an alcoholic drink consisting of rum and water.

roteuse *f.* bottle of champagne • (lit); the burper, that which causes burping.
NOTE: **roter** *v.* • (lit); to burp.
SYNONYM: **champe** *m.*

saler la note *exp.* to pad the bill • (lit); to salt the bill (with extra charges).
NOTE: **être salé(e)** *adj.* to be expensive.

tête en compote (avoir la) *exp.* to have a terrible headache • (lit); to have a head that feels like compote.
SYNONYM: **avoir les pieds en compote** *exp.* to have aching feet.

tour du cadran (faire le) *exp.* to sleep round the clock • (lit); to take a tour of the face of the clock.
SYNONYM: **faire la grasse matinée** *exp.* to sleep in • (lit); to make the fat morning.

PRACTICE THE VOCABULARY

[Answers to Lesson 4, p. 68]

A. Underline the synonym.

1. **abrevoir:**   a. maison   b. bar   c. boisson

2. **cuite:**   a. ivresse   b. champagne   c. faim

3. **roteuse:**   a. bar   b. champagne   c. un peu

4. **rétamé:**   a. fatigué   b. ivre   c. heureux

5. **un chouïa:**   a. beaucoup   b. rien   c. un peu

6. **bâfrée:**   a. maison   b. grand repas   c. bébé

7. **ravigoter:**   a. revigorer   b. arriver   c. partir

8. **se dépieuter:**   a. aller au lit   b. sortir du lit   c. pleurer

9. **se caler le bide:** a. s'arrêter   b. réussir   c. manger

10. **carabiné:**   a. extrême   b. faible   c. amusant

B. Write the letter of the answer that best completes the sentence.

1. J'ai soif. J'ai envie d' _____ .
   a. **décrocher un contrat**   b. **saler la note**   c. **basculer un godet**

2. Félicitations pour ton nouveau boulot! Allons _____ !
   a. **faire le tour du cadran**   b. **faire la bamboula**   c. **nous dépieuter**

3. J'peux pas manger trop d'chocolat. Ça m' _____ pas.
   a. **réussit**   b. **festonne**   c. **parle**

4. Je m'sens pas bien aujourd'hui. J'ai _____ .
   a. **le tour du cadran**   b. **le gosier blindé**   c. **la tête en compote**

5. C'restaurant, y est trop cher! J'crois qu'on a _____ .
   a. **décroché un contrat**   b. **salé la note**   c. **festonné**

6. Tu veux prendre un peu d'dessert? _____ .
   a. **c'est pas d'refus**   b. **ça s'arrose**   c. **roméo**

7. Arrête de _____ ! Le patron, y va pas t'sacquer!
   a. **recharger les accus**   b. **t'frapper l'biscuit** c. **festonner**

8. J'ai envie d'fumer. J'vais acheter un _____ .
   a. **chouïa**   b. **cale dent**   c. **paquet d'bleues**

9. Y a bu trois verres de rhum! Faut dire qu'y a _____ .
   a. **l'gosier blindé**   b. **écumé les bars**   c. **réussit**

10. J'ai mis une _____ d'whisky dans mon café.
    a. **bâfrée**   b. **casque**   c. **larme**

C. Match the columns by writing the appropriate letter in the box.

☐ 1. After one glass of wine, I start to stagger.

☐ 2. This calls for a drink.

☐ 3. Get out of bed right now!

☐ 4. I'll have a rum and water.

☐ 5. Stack 'em up for another round!

☐ 6. I need a little snack.

☐ 7. If I drink too much whisky, it goes right to my head.

☐ 8. I don't like barhopping.

☐ 9. My landlord raised the rent.

☐ 10. You can really pack it away.

A. **Ça s'arrose.**

B. **J'prends un roméo, moi.**

C. **Recharge les accus!**

D. **Mon proprio, y a augmenté l'loyer.**

E. **Si j'bois trop d'whiskey, j'en ai vite dans l'casque.**

F. **Après un verre d'vin, j'commence à festonner.**

G. **J'aime pas écumer les bars, moi.**

H. **T'as l'gosier blindé, toi.**

I. **J'ai b'soin d'un p'tit cale dent.**

J. **Dépieute-toi tout d'suite!**

INSIDE INFO: *SLANG BAR TERMS AND EXPRESSIONS*

It's hard to think of France without conjuring up an image of elegant food, delicate pastries, and, of course, fine wines and liqueurs. It's certainly common to see the neighborhood watering hole crawling with local natives who have come together to "raise their spirits" after a long day.

Without a doubt, if you are interested in learning slang, this is the place to start… just sit back and listen. However, since drinking is truly a part of the French culture, here you are bound to encounter not only everyday slang, but slang that is specific to drinking as well.

Below are some common words and phrases that one can expect to hear in any bar in France:

Absinthe
douanier *m.* • (lit); customs officer.
NOTE: This may be due to the dark color of the uniform.
pure *f.* • (lit); "a pure thing."
purée *f.* • (lit); puree.
verte *f.* • (lit); "a green thing."

Adulterated drink, Mickey Finn
Mickey *m.*

After-dinner liqueur
pousse-café *m.* • (lit); a coffee pusher.
rincette *f.* • (lit); "a rinser."

Aperitif
apéro *m.*

Beaujolais
Beaujoli *m.*
Beaujolpif *m.*

Beer
bibine *f.* poor quality beer.
bock *m.* quarter liter of beer.
demi-pression *m.* half a liter of beer on tap.

distingué *m.* large glass of beer
• (lit); something distinguished.

galopin *m.* quarter liter of beer
• (lit); street urchin.

mariée *f.* half a liter of beer
• (lit); a bride.
NOTE: This is due to the white foam that slides down one side of the mug which resembles the train of a bride.

moussante *f.* • (lit); that which foams.
NOTE: This comes from the feminine noun *mousse* meaning "foam."

pisse d'âne *f.* poor quality beer
• (lit); donkey piss.

sérieux *m.* liter glass of beer
• (lit); the serious one.

un demi *m.* half a liter of beer.

Brandy
eau d'affe *f.* Abbreviation of: *eau-de vie.*

gniole *f.*

lampion *m.* • (lit); lantern.

riquiqui *m.* • (lit); **1.** the little finger, pinky • **2.** undersized person.

schnaps *m.* (from German)

tord-boyaux *m.* • (lit); gut twister, "rot gut."

Café owner

troquet *m.* **1.** café owner • **2.** café.

Café

bistro(t) *m.*

resco *m.* poor quality café or restaurant.

troquet *m.* **1.** café owner • **2.** café.

Champagne

champe *m.*

roteuse *f.* bottle of champagne • (lit); burper.

Coffee

bain de pieds *m.* coffee and milk served in a large glass • (lit); foot bath.

cafiot *m.*

caouah *m.*

caoudji *m.*

grand noir *m.* large cup of coffee • (lit); big black.

jus de chapeau *m.* poor quality coffee • (lit); hat juice.

noir *m.* • (lit); black.

petit noir *m.* small cup of coffee • (lit); little black.

roupies de café *f.pl.* coffee dregs • (lit); coffee snot.

tortillard *m.* expresso • (lit); that which has been twisted.

Cognac

cognebi *m.*

Drinks in general

gobette *f.*
NOTE: This comes from the verb *gober* meaning "to gulp down."

Early morning nip (of booze)

pousse-dehors *m.* • (lit); that which pushes one outside.

Glass of Calvados drunk between two courses of a meal

trou normand *m.* • (lit); Normandy hole.
NOTE: This is a strong drink that is taken to "burn a hole" right through to the stomach in order to make room for more food.

Grenadine

tomate *f.* • (lit); tomato.

Ice, "on the rocks"

cailloux *m.pl.* • (lit); pebbles.

Lemonade

diablo *m.*

Mint syrup

perroquet *m.* • (lit); parakeet.
NOTE: This refers to its green color.

On the house

aux frais de la princesse *exp.* • (lit); at the expense of the princess.

Orgeat syrup

mauresque *f.* • (lit); **1.** Moorish woman • **2.** Moresque pattern.

Red wine

brouille-ménage *m.* humorous for red wine • (lit); household jumbler.
NOTE: This literally translates as "that which stirs up the household" since husbands and wives may get into fights after having too much to drink.

brutal *m.* poor quality red wine • (lit); that which is brutal.

casse-pattes *m.* • (lit); foot ("paw") breaker.

casse-poitrine *f.* poor quality red wine • (lit); chest breaker.

chocolat de déménageur *m.* • (lit); chocolate furniture remover.

décapant *m.* • (lit); scouring solution.

gros qui tache *m.* poor quality red wine • (lit); fat one that stains.

gros rouge *m.* • (lit); fat red one.

jus de chique *m.* poor quality red wine • (lit); tobacco juice.

petit-velours *m.* • (lit); little velvet.

picrate *f.* • (lit); picrate (from picric acid which is very bitter).

picton *m.*

pif *m.*

pinard *m.*

pousse au crime *f.* poor quality red wine • (lit); that which pushes one to crime.

rouquemoute *m.* Variation of: *rouquin* meaning "red."

rouquin *m.* • (lit); "red."

rouquinos *m.* Variation of: *rouquin* meaning "red."

tutu *m.*

un coup de rouge *m.* • (lit); a hit of the red stuff.

Round of drinks

tournée *f.* • (lit); a round.

Rum and water

roméo *m. (rhum et eau)*

Rhum and orgeat syrup

romaine *f.* • (lit); Roman woman.

"The same thing again"

à refaire *exp.* • (lit); to do again.

Second after-dinner liqueur

surrincette *f.* • (lit); a rinser.

Seltzer water

eau à ressort *m.* • (lit); spring (coil) water.

"Set 'em up again!"

recharger les wagonnets *exp.* • (lit); recharge the tipcarts.

Slice of lemon added to tea

soleil *m.* • (lit); sun.

Tip

violette *f.*

Waiter, servant

larbin *m.*

Water

bouillon *m.* • (lit); broth.

bouillon de canard *m.* • (lit); duck broth.

Château-la-Pompe *m.* • (lit); Château Waterpump.

flotte *f.* • (lit); that which floats.
NOTE: **flotter** *v.* to rain.

fraîche *f.* carafe of ice water • (lit); a fresh one.

jus de grenouille *m.* • (lit); frog juice.

lance *f.* • (lit); urine.

lancequine *f.* • (lit); urine.
NOTE: **lancequiner** *v.* to rain • (lit); to urinate.

sirop de parapluie *m.*
• (lit); umbrella syrup.

White wine

blanco *m.* • (lit); Spanish for "white."

pivois savonné *m.* • (lit); washed (out) peony plant.
NOTE: The peony, part of the buttercup family, is known for its large colorful red, pink, and white flowers, which represent the colors of wine.

PRACTICE USING SLANG BAR TERMS AND EXPRESSIONS

A. Match the French word in the left column with its slang synonym from the right column by writing the appropriate letter in the box.

☐ 1. eau-de-vie

☐ 2. café-bar

☐ 3. champagne

☐ 4. Calvados

☐ 5. vin rouge

☐ 6. garçon de café

☐ 7. carafe d'eau froide

☐ 8. vin blanc

☐ 9. demi-litre de bière

☐ 10. apéritif

A. **un demi**

B. **du blanco**

C. **un apéro**

D. **un trou normand**

E. **de la gniole**

F. **une fraîche**

G. **un bistro(t)**

H. **du champe**

I. **du pinard**

J. **larbin**

B. Underline the words that are *not* synonyms of the word(s) in boldface. *Note:* There may be more than one answer in each case.

1. **Brandy:**
   a. gniole
   b. eau d'affe
   c. un demi
   d. un apéro
   e. schnaps
   f. tord-boyaux

2. **Coffee:**
   a. diablo
   b. grand noir
   c. petit noir
   d. trou normand
   e. caouah
   f. tortillard

3. **Water:**
   - a. larbin
   - b. pinard
   - c. flotte
   - d. jus de grenouille
   - e. bouillon de canard
   - f. sirop de parapluie

4. **Beer:**
   - a. bibine
   - b. demi-pression
   - c. un distingué
   - d. moussante
   - e. un sérieux
   - f. un galopin

5. **Absinthe:**
   - a. un demi
   - b. un sérieux
   - c. verte
   - d. purée
   - e. douanier
   - f. mariée

6. **Poor quality red wine:**
   - a. pousse au crime
   - b. picrate
   - c. flotte
   - d. décapant
   - e. violette
   - f. rincette

7. **White wine:**
   - a. sirop de parapluie
   - b. brutal
   - c. blanco
   - d. pivois savonné
   - e. roteuse
   - f. perroquet

– 5 –

Au Magasin

(At the Store)

AU MAGASIN...

DIALOGUE

Christine et Pascale sont en ville.

Christine: Ah, j'adore **faire du lèche-vitrine**. D'ailleurs, j'ai pas vraiment d'choix. J'suis **dans la dèche**, moi.

Pascale: Oh, **change de disque**! Tu m'as dit qu't'as un **bas d'laine** bien garni!

Christine: Ben ouais, mais c'est pas pour **fiche en l'air** sur les **frippes**, ça! Mais on verra. Peut-êt'que j'pourrai **dégauchir** quèque chose pour **pas cher**.

Pascale: Tiens! C'te robe, è coûte un **malheureux** trois cents francs et c'est **l'dernier cri**, c'te style-là. On y **jette un coup d'œil**?

Christine: Ce s'rait d'la **braise flambée**, ça. C'te truc, ça vaut cent francs **à tout casser**. D'ailleurs, elle est **d'la courtille**, c'te robe.

Pascale: Allez... on y **antiffe**!

(plus tard...)

Pascale: V'là la robe. Tiens! Comme tu dis, elle est plutôt courte. T'**as l'compas dans l'œil**, toi.

Christine: J'suis **brouillée** avec les dates et les chiffres, mais les mesures, **ça m'connaît**.

Pascale: Et ça coûte cinq cents francs! Quel **coup d'matraque**! J'vais pas **cracher** toute ma salaire sur une robe quand même! Tu parles de t'faire **étriller**!

Christine: Y'a pas grand' chose dans c'te **magase**. Y a vraiment été **dévalisé**. Tu sais, la semaine dernière, un **Jules** de dix-huit **pigettes**, y a essayé d'**chouraver** une **toquante** mais y s'est fait **cueillir** par **les en bourgeois**. Y l'ont **pipé sur l'tas**.

AT THE STORE...

DIALOGUE

Christine and Pascale are in the city.

Christine: Ah, I love going window-shopping. Besides, I don't really have a choice. I'm flat broke.

Pascale: Oh, get off it! You told me you have quite a nest egg!

Christine: Well yeah, but it's not to blow on clothes! But we'll see. Maybe I'll be able to come across something that's not expensive.

Pascale: Hey! That dress costs a measly 300 francs and it's the latest style. Want to go take a look?

Christine: That would be money down the drain. That thing is worth 100 francs at the outside. Besides, that dress is on the short side.

Pascale: Oh, come on... let's go in!

(later...)

Pascale: There's the dress. Hey! Just like you said, it's kind of short. You've really got a good eye.

Christine: I may be lousy at dates and numbers but when it comes to measurements, I'm great.

Pascale: And it costs 500 francs! What a rip-off! As if I'm really going to cough up my entire salary for a dress! Talk about getting totally fleeced!

Christine: There isn't a whole lot in this store. It's really been cleaned out. You know, last week, an eighteen-year-old guy tried to rip off a watch but got caught by plainclothesmen. They caught him red-handed.

VOCABULARY

à tout casser *exp.* **1.** at the outside • (lit); to break everything • *Cette chemise, ça vaut 50 francs à tout casser;* This shirt is worth 50 francs at the very most • **2.** fantastic, extraordinary. *C't'un film à tout casser;* It's one helluva film.

antiffer *v.* to enter. *J'veux pas y antiffer, moi;* I don't want to go in there.
SYNONYM: **encarrer** *v.* This verb comes from the feminine noun *carrée* meaning "room."
ANTONYM: **décarrer** *v.* to exit, to leave a room.

bas de laine *m.* savings, money put aside for a rainy day • (lit); woolen sock (into which money is hidden away) • *Elle a un bas d'laine bien garni;* She has a nice nest egg.
SYNONYM: **un magot** *m. Elle a un joli magot;* She has a nice nest egg • NOTE: **un gros magot**: *Y a épousé un gros magot;* He married into money.

braise *m.* money, "dough" • (lit); live charcoal • *Elle a payé 500 francs cette robe. A mon avis, c'est d'la braise flambée!;* She paid 500 francs for that dress. In my opinion, it's money down the drain!
SYNONYM: **fric** *m.*

brouillé(e) (être) *adj.* to be hopelessly bad at something • (lit); to be jumbled, mixed, confused • *J'suis brouillé avec les dates;* I'm bad at dates.
NOTE: **être brouillé(e) avec qqn.** *adj.* to be on bad terms with s.o. *Nous sommes brouillés!;* We're through!

ça me connaît *exp.* that's right up my alley • (lit); it knows me • *La danse, ça m'connaît;* I'm great when it comes to dancing.
SYNONYM: **être dans ses cordes** *exp.* to be right up one's alley • (lit); to be in one's cords • *Chanter, c'est pas dans mes cordes;* Singing isn't one of my strong points.

changer de disque *exp.* to change the subject, to give it a rest • (lit); to change the record • *Change de disque! J'en ai marre d'en parler!;* Give it a rest! I'm tired of talking about it!
SYNONYM: **Basta!** *interj.* enough • (lit); enough (Italian) • *Basta! J'en ai marre!;* That's enough! I've had it!

chouraver *v.* to steal, swipe. *Elle a chouravé mon cahier!;* She stole my notebook!
NOTE (1): **chouraveur** *m.* thief.
NOTE (2): The verb *chouraver* comes from the masculine noun *chourave* meaning "kohlrabi," which is a vegetable from the cabbage family known for its edible root. Therefore, *chouraver* might be loosely translated as "to steal something right from the root (therefore leaving no trace)."

compas dans l'œil (avoir le) *exp.* to have a good eye for measurements • (lit); to have the compass in one's eye.

coup de matraque *m.* overcharging, rip-off, fleecing • (lit); a blow or hit by a bludgeon • *Ça coûte combien, ça? Quel coup d'matraque, ça!;* How much is that? What a rip-off!
SYNONYM: **coup de massue** *m.* • (lit); a blow or hit by a club or bludgeon.

courtille (être de la) *adj.* to be on the short side. *Y est d'la courtille, c'te pantalon;* These pants are on the short side.
NOTE: This comes from the adjective *court(e)* meaning "short."

cracher *v.* **1.** to cough up (money) • (lit); to spit • *J'ai dû craché mille francs au mécano pour faire réparer ma bagnole;* I had to cough up 1,000 francs for the mechanic to fix my car • **2. cracher** *v.* to drop s.o. off. *Y m'a craché chez moi à minuit;* He dropped me off at my house at midnight.
SEE: *cueillir.*
SYNONYM: **abouler** *v.* to bring, to hand over. *Aboule-moi ça!;* Hand it over!
ANTONYM: **piquer** *v.* to take, to steal.

cueillir (se faire) *v.* to get arrested • (lit); to get oneself picked • *Y s'est fait cueillir par les flics;* He got nabbed by the cops.
NOTE: **cueillir** *v.* to pick s.o. up. *J'pass'rai t'cueillir à midi;* I'll come by to pick you up at noon.
SYNONYM: **se faire agrafer** *exp.* • (lit); to get oneself stapled.

dèche (être dans la) *exp.* • (lit); to be in poverty • *Ça fait deux mois qu'y est dans la dèche;* It's been two months that he's been on the skids.
NOTE: **déchard(e)** n. one who is always broke, hard up for cash.
SYNONYM: **être dans la débine** *exp. Y est tombé dans la débine;* He's fallen on hard times.

dégauchir *v.* to find, uncover • (lit); to "un-left" (something) • *J'peux pas dégauchir mon parapluie;* I can't find my umbrella.
NOTE: The verb *dégauchir* comes from the expression *mettre qqch. à gauche*, which means "to put something away, to store" or literally, "to put something to the left."
SYNONYM: **dégotter** *v.*

dernier cri (le) *m. & adj.* the latest fashion • (lit); the latest cry • **1.** *m. C'est l'dernier cri d'Paris;* It's the latest style from Paris • **2.** *adj. Ça, c't'une chemise dernier cri;* That shirt is the latest thing.

dévaliser *v.* to clean out (a store, a refrigerator) of its stock. *A minuit, j'ai dévalisé l'frigo;* At midnight, I raided the fridge • *Y a été dévalisé, c'magase;* This store's been cleaned out.

en bourgeois *m.* plainclothesmen • (lit); like a citizen, townsman • *Attention aux en bourgeois!;* Watch out for the plainclothesmen!

étriller *v.* to ripoff (s.o.), to fleece • (lit); to currycomb (s.o. of all his money) • *Je m'suis fait étriller à c't'hôtel;* I got taken for a ride at this hotel.
SYNONYM: **rouler** *v.* to ripoff, to cheat • (lit); to roll • *Y m'a roulé, c'ui-là!;* That guy cheated me!

fiche qqch. en l'air *exp.* to chuck something away • (lit); to throw something into the air • *Y a fichu toute sa fortune en l'air;* He blew his entire fortune.
NOTE: The verb *fiche* has replaced its old form *ficher.*
SYNONYM: **foutre en l'air** *exp.* The verb *foutre* has a much stronger meaning than its euphemism *fiche* since its literal translation is "to fuck." It is, however, extremely popular.
SEE: *Unit Two - Popular Obscenities.*

frippes *f.pl.* clothes, threads • (lit); wrinkles • *Tu vas pas sortir avec ces frippes-là, non?;* You're not going out dressed like that are you?
SYNONYM: **nippes** *f.pl.* clothes • NOTE: **nipper** *v.* to dress. *Où tu vas nippé comme ça?;* Where are you going dressed like that?

jeter un coup d'œil *exp.* to have a look • (lit); to throw a "quick" eye • *J'dois jeter un coup d'œil au bébé;* I have to take a peek at the baby.
SYNONYM: **jeter un œil** *exp.*

Jules, jules *m.* man in general, boyfriend, husband. • (lit); Julius • *J'te présente mon Jules;* I'd like you to meet my boyfriend (or husband) • *Regarde c'te drôle de Jules!;* Look at that weird dude!
ANTONYM: **Julie, julie** *f.* girlfriend, wife.

lèche-vitrine (faire du) *exp.* to go window-shopping • (lit); to go out licking store windows • *J'adore faire du lèche-vitrine;* I love going window-shopping.

magase *m.* Abbreviation of: *magasin* meaning "store."

malheureux *adj.* measly, mere • (lit); wretched, poor • *Ça coûte un malheureux dix francs;* It costs a mere ten francs.

pas cher *exp.* cheap • (lit); not expensive • *J'l'ai eu pour pas cher;* I got it cheap.
NOTE: French natives are the first to admit that they are basically pessimists and that "the glass is half empty" before it is "half full." This is an extremely popular style of communication in spoken French:

> *c'est pas cher*   not   *c'est un bon marché;*
> *c'est pas mauvais*   not   *c'est bon;*
> *elle est pas bête*   not   *elle est intelligente,* etc.

pigette *f.* year. *Ça fait une bonne pigette depuis ma dernière visite ici;* It's been a good year since my last visit here.
SYNONYM: **pige** *f.* / **berge** *f.*
NOTE: **plombe** *f.* hour / **broquille** *f.* minute / **journaille** *f.* day / **marcotin** *m.* month.

piper qqn. sur le tas *exp.* to catch s.o. red-handed • (lit); to lure s.o. on the stack • *On l'a pipée sur l'tas;* They caught her in the act.
SYNONYM: **prendre qqn. sur le tas** *exp.* • (lit); to take s.o. on the stack.

toquante *f.* watch • (lit); "ticker."
NOTE: This refers to that which goes "tic toc."
SYNONYM: **oignon** *m.* • (lit); onion.

PRACTICE THE VOCABULARY

[Answers to Lesson 5, p. 68]

A. Complete the sentence by filling in the blank with the appropriate word(s) from the list below. Make any necessary changes.

à tout casser	**chouraver**	**dévaliser**
toquante	**frippes**	**antiffer**
pigettes	**magase**	**braise**
bas d'laine	**Jules**	**étriller**

1. T'es beau dans tes nouvelles _____ .

2. L'addition, y était astronomique! Je m'suis fait _____ à c'restaurant!

3. Quelle heure il est? J'ai pas d' _____ .

4. Tu peux m'prêter d'la _____ .

5. Ce supermarché, y a été _____ .

6. On a _____ mon portefeuille.

7. J'veux pas _____ dans c'te maison. Ça m'fait peur.

8. J'dois aller au _____ pour faire des achats.

9. Carole, è va s'marida à son _____ .

10. Elle est pas aussi pauv'qu'elle en a l'air. Elle a un _____ bien garni.

11. Ça fait trois _____ que nous sommes mariés.

12. C'te truc, y vaut trois francs _____ .

B. Underline the word(s) that best complete(s) the phrase.

1. Les flics, y l'ont (**pipé, trouvé, vu**) sur l'tas.

2. Pour un (**heureux, contents, malheureux**) dix francs, pourquoi tu l'achètes pas?

3. On va aller en ville pour faire du (**mange, lèche, avale**)-vitrine.

4. J'adore c'te chapeau! C'est l'dernier (**des derniers, cri, sourire**)!

5. Y a (**fait, fichu, mis**) tout son fric en l'air.

6. J'peux pas (**dévaliser, cracher, dégauchir**) mes clés!

7. Tu peux pas porter c'pantalon. Y est d'la (**courtille, longueur, mode**).

8. Ça a coûté combien?! Quel coup d'(**barre, magase, matraque**), ça!

9. Oh, change de (**chemise, disque, balle**)! C'est ridicule c'que tu racontes.

10. Jouer du piano... ça m'(**connaît, reconnaît, regarde**)!

11. J'suis (**malheureux, en bourgeois, brouillé**) avec les dates.

12. Merci beaucoup pour la chemise. E m'va comme un gant! Mais tu dois avoir l'(**coup d'matraque, compas, dernier cri**) dans l'œil, toi!

C. Choose the appropriate slang synonym of the italicized word(s). Write the corresponding letter of the correct answer in the box.

1. Y s'est fait *arrêter* par la police.

2. J'vais y *regarder*.

3. J'suis dans la *misère*.

4. Ça fait deux *ans* qu'on s'est pas vus!

5. Y sont supers, tes *vêtements*.

6. J'l'ai eu *à bon prix*, ça!

7. Y a *volé* mon sac!

8. J'vais pas *payer* 100 francs ces chaussures!

9. Tu peux m'prêter un peu d'*argent*?

10. C't'une nouvelle *montre*, ça?

11. J'ai *jeté* tout mon fric en l'air.

12. Cette robe, c'est *très à la mode*.

A. **toquante**

B. **pour pas cher**

C. **cueillir**

D. **cracher**

E. **fichu**

F. **braise**

G. **jeter un coup d'œil**

H. **dèche**

I. **frippes**

J. **chouravé**

K. **le dernier cri**

L. **pigettes**

INSIDE INFO: *EXPRESSIONS THAT CONTAIN PROPER NAMES*

In the previous chapter, we saw how animals have crept their way into French slang providing us with an unlimited supply of colorful expressions. But wait! People are animals, too! Have we humans been unfairly neglected? There is only one answer to that question, "No way, José!"

In American slang, we have certainly heard proper names crop up in expressions like: *for Pete's sake, good-time Charlie, plain Jane, Joe Blow, jack-of-all-trades, to go to the john, etc.* The French certainly keep pace when it comes to creating expressions of this sort, as presented in the dialogue in which the proper name *Jules* was used to mean "man."

Proper names have given birth to many other imaginative expressions in French as demonstrated by the following list:

"Nom"

ça n'a pas de nom! *exp.* that's incredible! • (lit); it has no name.

Adam

pomme d'Adam *f.* • (lit); Adam's apple.

je ne le connais ni d'Eve ni d'Adam *exp.* I don't know him from Adam • (lit); I don't know him from Eve or Adam.

manger qqch. avec la fourchette du père Adam *exp.* to eat with one's fingers • (lit); to eat something with the fork of father Adam.

Alfred

le bonjour d'Alfred *exp.* tip, "pourboire" • (lit); the hello from Alfred.

Anatole

ça colle, Anatole? *exp.* Hey Joe, whadya know? • (lit); does it stick, Anatole?

Arthur

se faire appeler Arthur *exp.* to get reprimanded • (lit); to get oneself called Arthur.

Auguste

comme de juste, Auguste! *exp.* You said it, Charlie! • (lit); Exactly, Auguste!

Azor

appeler Azor *exp.* to boo and hiss • (lit); to call Azor.

Azor *Prn.* Fido, Rover.

Ben Hur

arrête ton chard, Ben Hur! *exp.* Stop exaggerating • (lit); stop your chariot, Ben Hur!

Bouffi

tu l'as dit, Bouffi! *exp.* You said it, Charlie!

Charles

Charles-le-Chauve *Prn. & m.* penis • (lit); Charles the Bald.

tu parles, Charles! *exp.* You said it, Charlie!

Charlot

Charlot *Prn. & m.* good-time Charlie.

cravate à Charlot *f.* sanitary napkin • (lit); Charlie's tie.

Diane

un prix de Diane *exp.* a very pretty girl • (lit); Diane's prize.

Etienne

à la tienne, Etienne! *exp.* Here's to you! • (lit); to yours, Steve!

Eve

je ne le connais ni d'Eve ni d'Adam *exp.* I don't know him from Adam • (lit); I don't know him from Eve or Adam.

François

faire le coup du père François à qqn. *exp.* to strangle s.o. • (lit); to do the Father François hit to s.o.

Gaston

cravate à Gaston *f.* sanitary napkin • (lit); Gaston's tie.

Georges

Georges *Prn. & m.* (aviation) automatic pilot.

Gustave

cravate à Gustave *f.* sanitary napkin • (lit); Gustave's tie.

Henriette

Henriette *Prn. & f.* heroin.

Jacques

Pierre, Paul et Jacques *exp.* Tom, Dick and Harry.

Jean

comme un petit Saint Jean *exp.* naked • (lit); like a little Saint John.

Joseph

faire son Joseph *exp.* to act self-righteous and smug • (lit); to do one's Joseph.

Joséphine

faire sa Joséphine *exp.* to play the prude, to be all goody-goody • (lit); to do one's Josephine.

Jules

Jules *Prn. & m.* **1.** husband, boyfriend • **2.** chamber pot.

se faire appeler Jules *exp.* to get reprimanded • (lit); to get oneself called Jules.

Julie

Julie *Prn. & f.* wife.

Jupiter

se croire sorti(e) de la cuisse de Jupiter *exp.* to think highly of oneself, to be conceited • (lit); to believe oneself to have come from Jupiter's thigh.

Léon

vas-y, Léon! *exp.* • (lit); Go for it (Leon)!

Lisette

pas de ça, Lisette! *exp.* • (lit); Let's have none of that (Lisette)!

Louis

avoir des jambes Louis XV *exp.* to be bowlegged • (lit); to have legs like Louis XV.

Louisette

Louisette (la) *Prn. & f.* guillotine.

Madeleine

    pleurer comme une Madeleine
    exp. to cry one's eyes out
    • (lit); to cry like a Madeleine.

Marcel

    chauffe, Marcel! *exp.* Go for it!
    • (lit); heat up, Marcel!

Marie

    Marie-couche-toi-là *Prn. & f.*
    woman of easy morals
    • (lit); Marie lay yourself
    there.

    Marie-salope *Prn. & f.* bloody
    Mary (drink)
    • (lit); Marie-bitch.

Marie-Chantal

    Marie-Chantal *Prn. & f.*
    C't'une Marie-Chantal;
    She's a rich airhead.

Marie-Jeanne

    Marie-Jeanne *Prn. & f.*
    marijuana.

Paul

    Pierre, Paul et Jacques *exp.*
    Tom, Dick, and Harry.

Pierre

    Pierre, Paul et Jacques *exp.*
    Tom, Dick, and Harry.

Robert

    roberts *m.pl.* big breasts.

Sophie

    faire sa Sophie *exp.* to behave
    prudishly • (lit); to do one's
    Sophie.

PRACTICE USING PROPER NAMES

A. Choose the letter of the appropriate name that goes with the expression.

1. Ma mère, elle était furieuse. Je m'suis fait appeler ____ en rentrant.
    a. **Etienne**   b. **Auguste**   c. **Arthur**

2. Tu parles, ____ !
    a. **Georges**   b. **Charles**   c. **Gaston**

3. Y s'croit sorti d'la cuisse de ____ .
    a. **Jupiter**   b. **Paul**   c. **Pierre**

4. Ça colle, ____?
    a. **Henriette**   b. **Anatole**   c. **Marie**

5. Regarde c'te fille! Quels ____ .
    a. **Georges**   b. **roberts**   c. **Jules**

6. L'acteur, y s'est fait appeler ____ .

   a. **Auguste**   b. **François**   c. **Azor**

7. Allez! Chauffe ____ !

   a. **Léon**   b. **Joseph**   c. **Marcel**

8. C't'un drogué, lui. Y prend d'l' ____ .

   a. **Henriette**   b. **Madeleine**   c. **Lisette**

9. Elle a pleuré comme une ____ , la pauvre.

   a. **Louisette**   b. **Henriette**   c. **Madeleine**

10. Y s'est fait décapoter par la ____ .

   a. **Diane**   b. **Sophie**   c. **Louisette**

ANSWERS TO LESSONS 1-5

LESSON ONE - *Au Cinéma*

Practice the Vocabulary

A.
1. manger
2. taper
3. cordé
4. ciné
5. bois
6. bomber
7. coller un biscuit
8. oreilles
9. démange
10. Affranchis
11. oiseau
12. baladeuses

B.
1. C
2. F
3. H
4. M
5. J
6. A
7. E
8. B
9. N
10. I
11. G
12. K
13. L
14. D

C.
1. I
2. J
3. A
4. G
5. B
6. D
7. H
8. E
9. C
10. F

INSIDE INFO(1):
Practice Using the Present Tense to Indicate Future

A.
1. On s'voit d'main, alors?
2. J'te l'donne après l'déjeuner.
3. On l'fait plus tard.
4. On en discute d'main.
5. J'te la présente à la soirée.
6. Y t'le rend ce soir.
7. J'arrive t'chercher à 8h.
8. Ce soir, è lui fait une grande surprise.
9. C't'après-midi, on fête ton anniversaire.
10. J'te passe un coup d'fil d'main.

INSIDE INFO(2) :
Practice Vocations in Slang

A.				B.			
1. J		7. C		1. a, b, d		5. c, e
2. L		8. F		2. b, d, e		6. b, d
3. G		9. H		3. b, d		7. a, d
4. K		10. E		4. a, c, d, e		
5. I		11. B				
6. A		12. D				

LESSON TWO - *Vive l'Amour*

Practice the Vocabulary

A.		
1. b		7. b
2. b		8. a
3. a		9. c
4. c		10. b
5. a		11. a
6. a		12. c

B. 1. Encore 150 kilomètres? Ça fait une longue trotte.
    2. Mes deux frangines, è n'font qu'se peigner/que s'peigner.
    3. Y s'fait toujours embellemerder.
    4. On s'couche sur la dure pasqu'on a pas d'bouts d'bois.
    5. J'dois m'décamper pour aller chercher ma rem.
    6. J'aime pas faire la popote, moi.
    7. Sa fille, elle a trois berges.
    8. Y vont bientôt s'marida.

C.		
1. conjugo		7. grelots
2. chopin		8. le gros sac
3. Trifouillis-les-Oies		9. enterrer
4. crémaillère		10. à-côté
5. accroché		11. se corse
6. nicher		12. à la colle

INSIDE INFO:
Practice Slang Suffixes

A. 1. téloche
    2. duraille
    3. lichailler
    4. poiscaille
    5. fadasse

    6. follasse
    7. cinoche, cinetoche
    8. prétentiard
    9. richard
    10. glandouiller

LESSON THREE - *Au Travail*

Practice the Vocabulary

A. 1. emmerdements
    2. m'coltiner
    3. s'casse
    4. pied
    5. bagne

    6. tassées
    7. battants
    8. ficelles
    9. pompe-la-sueur

B. 1. D
    2. J
    3. L
    4. C
    5. I
    6. A

    7. K
    8. B
    9. E
    10. H
    11. G
    12. F

C. 1. beurre
    2. dégraisser
    3. flûtes
    4. pont
    5. flécher
    6. marne

    7. frotter
    8. parlons
    9. rembrayer
    10. emmerdements
    11. coltiner
    12. pistonné

INSIDE INFO:
Practice Using Fish, Insects, and Animals in French Slang

A. 1. C
    2. E
    3. G
    4. H

    5. D
    6. A
    7. F
    8. B

B. 1. chien
    2. mouches
    3. cochon
    4. kangourou
    5. chevaux
    6. cheval

    7. baleine
    8. vers
    9. moutons
    10. lapin
    11. rat
    12. lièvre

C. 1. a
    2. b
    3. c
    4. a
    5. a

    6. c
    7. c
    8. a
    9. b

LESSON FOUR - *Au Café*

Practice the Vocabulary

A. 1. b   6. b   B. 1. c   6. a
   2. a.   7. a   2. b   7. b
   3. b   8. b   3. a   8. c
   4. b   9. c   4. c   9. a
   5. c   10. a   5. b   10. c

C. 1. F   6. I
   2. A   7. E
   3. J   8. G
   4. B   9. D
   5. C   10. H

INSIDE INFO:
Practice Using Slang Bar Terms and Expressions

A. 1. E   6. J   B. 1. c, d   5. a,b,f
   2. G   7. F   2. a, d   6. c, e, f
   3. H   8. B   3. a, b   7. a, b, e, f
   4. D   9. A   4. NONE
   5. I   10. C

LESSON FIVE - *Au Magasin*

Practice the Vocabulary

A. 1. frippes   7. antiffer   B. 1. pipé   7. courtille
   2. étriller   8. magase   2. malheureux   8. matraque
   3. toquante   9. Jules   3. lèche   9. disque
   4. braise   10. bas d'laine   4. cri   10. connaît
   5. dévalisé   11. pigettes   5. fichu   11. brouillé
   6. chouravé   12. à tout casser   6. dégauchir   12. compas

C. 1. C   7. J
  2. G   8. D
  3. H   9. F
  4. L   10. A
  5. I   11. E
  6. B   12. K

INSIDE INFO:
Practice Using Proper Names

A. 1. c   6. c
  2. b   7. c
  3. a   8. a
  4. b   9. c
  5. b   10. c

REVIEW EXAM
FOR LESSONS 1-5

[Answers to Review, p. 74]

A. Choose the words or expressions that are associated with the terms to the left. *Note:* **There may be more than one answer in each case.**

1. **to drink**:
   - a. abrevoir
   - b. chopin
   - c. cuite
   - d. ça s'arrose
   - e. braise
   - f. bistrot

2. **to bore**:
   - a. antiffer
   - b. chouraver
   - c. se barber
   - d. tabasser
   - e. cataloguer
   - f. assommer

3. **up-to-date**:
   - a. couru
   - b. à la page
   - c. dévalisé
   - d. affranchi
   - e. dégauchi
   - f. rétamé

4. **year**:
   - a. à-côté
   - b. marne
   - c. berge
   - d. pigette
   - e. larme
   - f. pas cher

5. **work**:
   - a. marne
   - b. bagne
   - c. cogne
   - d. assiette au beurre
   - c. bâfrée
   - d. bistrot

6. **to fight**:
   - a. se tabasser
   - b. étriller
   - c. se peigner
   - d. rembrayer
   - e. flécher
   - f. démanger

7. **policeman**:
   - a. berge
   - b. cogne
   - c. cale dent
   - d. en bourgeois
   - e. abrevoir
   - f. toquante

8. **to eat:**   a. bâfrée   b. pigette   c. cale dent
                  d. bistrot   e. se caler le bide   f. pistonner

9. **money:**   a. bas de laine   b. être dans la dèche   c. braise
                  d. s'éterniser   e. désargenté   f. marne

B. Complete the following sentences by choosing the appropriate word(s) from the list below. Make any necessary changes.

sur le clou	bamboula	nage
dégraisser	trotte	taper
nicher	décatir	cueillir
dépieuter	brouillé	biscuit

1. On va aller faire la _____ ce soir!

2. C'est déjà ton anniversaire? Tu commences à _____ .

3. J'ai _____ dans cette maison toute ma vie.

4. Je m'suis fait coller un _____ .

5. Y s'est fait _____ par la police.

6. Attention… le patron, y va bientôt _____ .

7. J'dois être au boulot dans une heure. J'dois m'_____ .

8. C't'une voiture super! Ça peut _____ du 150 en trois secondes!

9. Ça fait une bonne _____ , ça. J'peux pas y aller à pied.

10. J'étais tout en _____ tellement j'étais nerveux.

11. C'est quand ton anniversaire? J'suis _____ avec les dates, moi.

12. Tu vois… j'suis pas en r'tard. J'suis arrivé _____ .

C. Underline the word(s) that best complete(s) the sentence.

1. C'est l'patron! On (**sale la note, rembraye, niche**)!

2. Mais, t'frappe pas l'(**biscuit, roméo, cogne**). Tout va très bien.

3. J'ai trop bu. J'suis (**dévalisé, étrillé, rétamé**).

4. Comment tu arrives à boire c'la? Tu dois avoir l'(**gosier, emmerdement, chapeau**) blindé, toi.

5. C'lundi, j'fais l'(**ciné, casque, pont**).

6. Le dimanche, c't'un jour (**chouravé, chrômé, dépieuté**).

7. Quel boulot super! C't'une vraie (**toquante, berge, assiette au beurre**).

8. J'ai faim, moi. J'vais aller trouver un p'tit (**cale dent, en bourgeois, bagne**).

9. Y est bizarre, c'ui-là. J'l'ai (**catalogué, cordé, couru**) tout d'suite.

10. Cécile et Jim, y vont s'(**tabasser, marida, bomber**) au mois d'mai.

11. J'peux pas l'supporter. On s'chauffe pas du même (**chapeau, bois, casque**).

12. Ça m'(**démange, rembraye, niche**) d'aller habiter à Paris.

13. Ce patron, y nous fait travailler sans arrêt. C't'une vraie (**cambrousse, pompe-la-sueur, popote**).

14. Faut qu'j'm'achète de nouvelles (**frippes, berges, pigettes**) pour aller à la soirée.

15. J'veux pas l'faire. J'ai les (**frippes, compas dans l'œil, grelots**), moi.

D. Match the columns.

☐ 1. I advise you not to tangle with him.

☐ 2. It's payday.

☐ 3. I have to take off.

☐ 4. She lives in the sticks.

☐ 5. The plot thickens.

☐ 6. He's a good catch.

☐ 7. May I have a little cake?

☐ 8. I've got a splitting headache.

☐ 9. He sure never puts himself out.

☐ 10. I'm going to go window-shopping.

☐ 11. I really porked out.

☐ 12. I prefer sleeping on the floor.

☐ 13. What's today's date?

☐ 14. He's the one who runs the show.

A. **C'est la Sainte-Touche.**

B. **C't'un bon chopin.**

C. **J'ai la tête en compote.**

D. **J'vais faire du lèche-vitrine.**

E. **Elle habite à Trifouillis-les-Oies.**

F. **C'est lui qui tire les ficelles.**

G. **J'te conseil de n'pas t'frotter à lui.**

H. **J'préfère m'coucher sur la dure.**

I. **L'affaire, è s'corse.**

J. **Je m'suis bien calé l'bide.**

K. **On est l'combientième, aujourd'hui?**

L. **J'peux prendre un chouïa d'gâteau?**

M. **Y s'casse pas, lui.**

N. **J'dois m'décamper.**

E. Choose the word or expression that goes with the definition.

1. **se faire embêter par sa belle-mère:**
   a. épouser l'gros sac
   b. emmerdement
   c. embellemerder

2. **avare:**
   a. rétamé
   b. bien tassé
   c. près d'ses sous

3. **un travail dur et désagréable:**
   a. bagne
   b. berge
   c. bâfrée

4. **plein de sueur:**
   a. tout en l'air
   b. à tout casser
   c. tout en nage

5. **se sentir un peu ivre:**
   a. en avoir dans l'casque
   b. cataloguer
   c. bomber

6. **un lieu très distant:**
   a. Trifouillis-les-Oies
   b. Sainte-Touche
   c. Jules

7. **faire la cuisine:**
   a. faire la bamboula
   b. faire le pont
   c. faire la popote

8. **reprendre le travail:**
   a. tabasser
   b. rembrayer
   c. pistonner

9. **aider qqn. à se faire engager:**
   a. démanger qqn.
   b. pistonner qqn.
   c. tabasser qqn.

10. **une bouteille de champagne:**
    a. casque
    b. bocal
    c. roteuse

11. **dormir toute la journée:**
    a. faire l'tour du cadran
    b. faire d'la dentelle
    c. s'éterniser

12. **un tout petit peu:**
    a. un chapeau
    b. une larme
    c. un chopin

13. **voler:**
    a. chouraver
    b. cataloguer
    c. vivre à la colle

14. **manger beaucoup:**
    a. jeter un coup d'œil
    b. se caler l'bide
    c. saler la note

15. **conduire très vite:**
    a. bomber
    b. parler boulot
    c. décatir

ANSWERS TO REVIEW FOR LESSONS 1-5

A. 1. a, c, d, f
   2. c, f
   3. b, d
   4. c, d
   5. a, b, d

   6. a, c
   7. b, d
   8. a, c, d, e
   9. a, b, c, e

B. 1. bamboula
   2. décatir
   3. niché
   4. biscuit
   5. cueillir
   6. dégraisser

   7. dépieuter
   8. taper
   9. trotte
   10. nage
   11. brouillé
   12. sur le clou

C. 1. rembraye
   2. biscuit
   3. rétamé
   4. gosier
   5. pont
   6. chrômé
   7. assiette au beurre
   8. cale dent

   9. catalogué
   10. marida
   11. bois
   12. démange
   13. pompe-la-sueur
   14. frippes
   15. grelots

D. 1. G
   2. A
   3. N
   4. E
   5. I
   6. B
   7. L

   8. C
   9. M
   10. D
   11. J
   12. H
   13. K
   14. F

E. 1. c
   2. c
   3. a
   4. c
   5. a
   6. a
   7. c
   8. b

   9. b
   10. c
   11. a
   12. b
   13. a
   14. b
   15. a

– 6 –

Rien Que Des Racontars

(Nothing But Gossip)

RIEN QUE DES RACONTARS...

DIALOGUE

Cécile et Josette **s'tombent d'ssus** au supermarché.

Cécile:	**Sous l'sceau du secret**, Hélène était **laissée en carafe** pendant sa lune de miel à cause d'une aut'femme!
Josette:	Jean, y a toujours aimé **fréquenter les lits** mais à c'point-là! Bon ben, **on apprend pas à un vieux singe à faire la grimace**.
Cécile:	**Un d'ces quat'**, y va avoir **un réveil pénible**! C'est vraiment dommage… tout l'monde pensait qu'y **avait l'étoffe** d'un bon mari.
Josette:	C'est bizarre d'penser qu'j'étais là l'moment où y **a fait sa déclaration**. Alors dis-moi, quand è s'est **mise à la coule**, Hélène, elle a dû êt'**prise au dépourvu**, non?
Cécile:	**C'est l'moins qu'on puisse dire**! Maintenant, j'vais **t'en boucher un coin**. Après l'**tissu d'mensonges** qu'y lui a balancé, y a promis qu'y **f'rait peau neuve** si è l'laissait rentrer.
Josette:	E lui en a dit quoi, alors?
Cécile:	«**Rien à faire**!» Y sait très bien qu'y **s'la coule douce** depuis bien longtemps et maintenant **comme on fait son lit on s'couche**. Maintenant c'est elle qui **a l'dessus**.
Josette:	C'est **bien fait pour sa gueule**! Hélène, elle **est pas aussi bête qu'elle en a l'air**. Y pensait qu'y pourrait lui **jeter d'la poudre aux yeux** mais **rien lui échappe**.
Cécile:	Chez l'amour, ma dévice, c'est pas «**plus on est d'fous plus on rit**!»
Josette:	Ben, non! C'est plutôt «**à deux on s'distrait, à trois on s'ennuie**!»

Lesson Six

NOTHING BUT GOSSIP...

DIALOGUE

Cécile and Josette bump into each other in the supermarket.

Cécile: Just between us, Hélène was dumped during her honeymoon because of another woman!

Josette: Jean always did like to sleep around but come on! Well, you can't teach an old dog new tricks.

Cécile: One of these days he's going to have a rude awakening! It's really a shame... everyone thought he had the makings of a good husband.

Josette: It's weird to think that I was there the moment he popped the question. So tell me, when Hélène figured out what was going on, she sure must have been caught off guard, huh?

Cécile: You can say that again! Now I'm gonna really freak you out. After the pack of lies he gave her, he promised he'd turn over a new leaf if she let him come back.

Josette: So, what did she tell him?

Cécile: "No way!" He knows very well that he's slid by long enough and now he's made his bed, so he can just lie in it. Now she's the one with the upper hand.

Josette: Well, it serves him right! Hélène is not as stupid as she looks. He thought he could just pull the wool over her eyes but nothing gets by her.

Cécile: When it comes to love, my motto is not, "The more the merrier!"

Josette: No way! It's more like, "Two's company, three's a crowd!"

VOCABULARY

à deux on se distrait, à trois on s'ennuie *exp.* two's company, three's a crowd • (lit); with two it's fun, with three it's boring.

bien fait pour sa gueule *exp.* it serves him/her right • (lit); well done for his/her face. NOTE: **gueule** *f.* insulting term for "face" or "head" • (lit); mouth (of animal). SYNONYM: **c'est pain bénit** *exp.* • (lit); it's blessed bread.

c'est le moins qu'on puisse dire *exp.* • (lit); that's the least one can say • *-Y est bizarre, c'ui-là! -C'est l'moins qu'on puisse dire!;* -That guy is weird! -That's the least you can say! SYNONYM: **tu parles!** *exp.* you said it!

comme on fait son lit on se couche *exp.* you've made your bed, now lie in it • (lit); since one makes one's bed, one lies down (in it).

dessus (avoir le) *exp.* • (lit); to have the upper (hand) • *Maintenant, c'est moi qui ai l'dessus;* Now, I'm the one with the upper hand.

en boucher un coin *exp.* to surprise, to flabbergast • (lit); to stop up a corner of it (with a cork) • *Tu m'en bouches un coin!;* You really surprise me! or That's a corker! SYNONYM: **en boucher une surface à qqn.** *exp.*

étoffe (avoir l') *exp.* to have the makings (of something) • (lit); to have the fabric • *Elle a l'étoffe d'un bon médecin;* She has the makings of a good doctor.

faire peau neuve *exp.* to turn over a new leaf • (lit); to make new skin • *Après l'premier d'l'an, j'fais peau neuve;* After the first of the year, I'm turning over a new leaf.

faire sa déclaration *exp.* to pop the question • (lit); to make one's declaration (of love) • *Maman! Y vient d'faire sa déclaration!;* Mom! He just popped the question!

fréquenter les lits *exp.* to sleep around, to bed hop • (lit); to frequent beds • *J'aime pas les mecs qui fréquentent les lits;* I don't like guys who sleep around.

jeter de la poudre aux yeux *exp.* to pull the wool over one's eyes • (lit); to throw powder in one's eyes • *C'est la dernière fois qu'y m'jète d'la poudre aux yeux!;* It's the last time he's gonna pull that on me!

la couler douce (se) *exp.* to have it easy • (lit); to flow sweetly through it (life) • *Y habite dans une grande maison, possède une chouette bagnole. Y s'la coule douce, lui;* He lives in a big house, owns a great car. That guy really has it easy.

laisser qqn. en carafe *exp.* to jilt s.o., to leave s.o. high and dry • (lit); to leave s.o. like a carafe (after it's been all used up) • *C'est vrai qu'y l'a laissée en carafe?;* Is it true he dumped her? SYNONYM: **laisser qqn. en plan** *exp.* • (lit); to leave s.o. just standing there like a plant • NOTE: *plan* is an erroneous spelling of *plant* meaning, "a group of plants all of the same variety."

mettre à la coule *exp.* to bring (s.o.) up-to-date, to give (s.o.) the lowdown • (lit); to put (s.o.) in the flow • *Tu sais pas c' qui s' est passé? J' te mets à la coule;* You don't know what happened? Let me give you the lowdown.
SYNONYM: **mettre à la page** *exp.* • (lit); to bring (s.o.) up to the page (of events).

ne pas être aussi bête qu'on en a l'air *exp.* • (lit); not to be as dumb as one looks.
NOTE: Any slang synonym of *bête* could certainly be used in this expression such as: *cinglé, con, déplafonné, dingue, empaillé, empaqueté, emplâtré, enflé, fada, siphoné, etc.*

on apprend pas à un vieux singe à faire la grimace *exp.* you can't teach an old dog new tricks • (lit); you can't teach an old monkey to smile.

plus on est de fous plus on rit *exp.* the more the merrier • (lit); the more "crazies" there are, the more we'll laugh.

pris(e) au dépourvu (être) *exp.* to be taken off guard • (lit); to be taken short (as in destitute).

réveil pénible *m.* rude awakening • (lit); painful awakening • *Un d' ces jours, y va avoir un réveil pénible, c'ui-là;* One of these days, that guy's gonna have a rude awakening.

rien à faire *exp.* no way • (lit); nothing doing • *Tu veux qu' j' te prête du fric?! Rien à faire!;* You want me to lend you money?! No way!
SYNONYM: **rien à chiquer** *exp.* • (lit); nothing chewing (English equivalent: "I'm not swallowing that").

rien lui échappe *exp.* • (lit); nothing escapes him/her.

sous le sceau du secret *exp.* on the qt, just between you and me • (lit); under the seal of secrecy. *J' te raconte c' qui s' est passé mais seulement sous l' sceau du secret;* I'll tell you what happened but it can't go any further than us.
SYNONYM: **entre quat'z'yeux** *exp.* • (lit); between four eyes.

tissu de mensonges *exp.* pack of lies • (lit); a tissue of lies • *J' ui parle plus. E m' raconte toujours un tissu d' mensonges;* I don't speak to her anymore. She always hands me a pack of lies.

tomber sur qqn. *or* **tomber dessus** *exp.* to run into (s.o.) • (lit); to fall on (s.o.) • *J' ui suis tombé d' ssus au ciné;* I ran into him at the movies.

un de ces quat' *exp.* one of these days • (lit); one of these four • *Un d' ces quat', j' vais donner ma démission;* One of these days, I'm gonna up and quit!
NOTE: This is a shortened version of the expression *un de ces quatre matins* (pronounced: *un d' ces quat' matins*) meaning "one of these four mornings."

PRACTICE THE VOCABULARY

[Answers to Lesson 6, p. 133]

A. Complete the sentences by choosing the appropriate word(s) from the list below. Make any necessary changes.

réveil	tissu	dessus
gueule	boucher	peau neuve
fréquenter	poudre	carafe
à la coule	sceau	quat'

1. Un d'ces _____ , tu vas avoir un _____ pénible.

2. Elle a essayé d'me jeter d'la _____ aux yeux avec son _____ d'mensonges.

3. Comme j'suis ton patron, c'est moi qui ai l' _____ .

4. C'est bien fait pour sa _____ .

5. T'as l'air étonné. J't'en ai _____ un coin?

6. Tu vas pas croire c'qui s'est passé. J'te mets _____ .

7. Ça s'renouvell'ra jamais. J'te promets qu'je f'rai _____ .

8. Y m'a laissé en _____ .

9. Ça lui plaît d' _____ les lits.

10. J'vais t'raconter quèque chose sous l' _____ du secret.

B. Underline the word(s) in parentheses that best complete(s) the sentence.

1. A deux on s'distrait, (**se la coule douce, rien à faire, à trois on s'ennuie**).

2. J'suis (**arrivé, tombé, parti**) sur un bon copain au magase.

3. Elle est pas bête, celle-là. Rien lui (**attrape, échappe, agrafe**).

4. E pouvait pas l'croire. Faut dire qu'elle était prise au (**dépourvu, dénouement, dèche**).

5. Elle a l'(**écorse, étoffe, compas**) d'une bonne chanteuse.

6. Ma sœur, è va s'marida. Son jules, y vient d'faire sa (**carafe, grimace, déclaration**).

7. Y est bizarre, c'ui-là. C'est l'(**plus, moins, assez**) qu'on puisse dire.

8. Rejoignez-nous! Plus on est d'(**nombreux, fous, bizarres**) plus on rit!

9. Ah, la bonne vie. Je m'la (**cours vite, marche vite, coule douce**).

10. J'en ai assez d'son (**tissu, étoffe, casque**) d'mensonges!

11. On apprend pas à un vieux singe à (**faire la popote, faire peau neuve, faire la grimace**).

12. Elle est pas aussi bête qu'elle en a l'(**air, dessus, gueule**).

C. Match the columns.

☐   1. He has the upper hand.

☐   2. You really surprised me.

☐   3. He has it easy.

☐   4. You're gonna have a rude awakening.

☐   5. The more the merrier.

☐   6. Nothing gets by her.

☐   7. You've made your bed, now lie in it.

☐   8. He has the makings of a good father.

☐   9. She pulled the wool over my eyes.

☐ 10. She likes to bed hop.

☐ 11. No way.

☐ 12. He's turning over a new leaf.

A. **Rien à faire.**

B. **Tu m'en as bouché un coin.**

C. **E m'a jeté d'la poudre aux yeux.**

D. **Y fait peau neuve.**

E. **Rien lui échappe.**

F. **Tu vas avoir un réveil pénible.**

G. **Y a l'étoffe d'un bon papa.**

H. **Comme on fait son lit on s'couche.**

I. **Elle aime fréquenter les lits.**

J. **Y s'la coule douce, lui.**

K. **Y a l'dessus.**

L. **Plus on est d'fous, plus on rit.**

INSIDE INFO: *THE USE OF NUMBERS IN SLANG EXPRESSIONS*

From time to time, numbers creep into our own slang in expressions such as: *to be dressed to the 9's, to be in 7th heaven, catch 22, cloud 9, to 86 someone, to put 2 and 2 together, etc.*

The French seem to have beaten us hands down in the "numbers game" with an assortment of colorful phrases:

"Numéro"

tirer un bon numéro *exp.* to pick a winner • (lit); to pull a good number.

un drôle de numéro *m.* a weird person • (lit); a strange number.

0 (zéro)

à zéro *adv.* completely • (lit); to zero.

avoir le morale à zéro *exp.* to be very depressed • (lit); to have the morale down to zero.

double zéro *m.* a real loser • (lit); a double zero.

les avoir à zéro *exp.* to be frightened • (lit); to have them (one's testicles) down to zero.

1/3 (tiers)

s'en moquer du tiers comme du quart *exp.* not to give a damn • (lit); not to care a third or a fourth about it.

1/4 (quart)

les trois quarts du temps *exp.* most of the time • (lit); three-quarters of the time.

faire passer un mauvais quart d'heure *exp.* to worry (s.o.) greatly • (lit); to make (s.o.) go through a bad quarter of an hour.

s'en moquer du tiers comme du quart *exp.* not to give a damn • (lit); not to care a third or a fourth about it.

1 (un/une)

être sans un *exp.* to be broke • (lit); to be without one (a franc).

la une *f.* front page of a newspaper • (lit); the number one (page) • *C't'un événement qui fait la une;* It's an event that made the front page.

un(e) de ces *exp.* a real... • (lit); one of these • *C't'un d'ces menteurs!;* He's a real liar!

2 (deux)

à la six-quat'-deux *adv.* quickly, lickety-split • (lit); in six-four-two.

en deux temps, trois mouvements *adv.* quickly, lickety-split • (lit); in 2/4 time, three mouvements (said of music).

en moins de deux *adv.* quickly • (lit); in less than two (seconds).

nous sommes à deux de jeu *exp.* two can play at that game • (lit); we are two at that game.

se casser en deux *exp.* to double up with laughter • (lit); to break oneself in two.

se plier en deux *exp.* to bend over backwards in order to do something • (lit); to fold oneself in two.

3 (trois)

en deux temps, trois mouvements *adv.* quickly, lickety-split • (lit); in 2/4 time, three mouvements (said of music).

les trois quarts du temps *exp.* most of the time • (lit); three-quarters of the time.

4 (quatre)

à la six-quat'-deux *exp.* quickly, lickety-split • (lit); in six-four-two.

en quatrième vitesse *adv.* quickly • (lit); in fourth gear.

entre quat'z'yeux *exp.* just between you and me • (lit); between four eyes.

fichu comme quat'sous *exp.* to be dressed any old way • (lit); to be made like four francs.

la semaine des quat'jeudis *exp.* never • (lit); the week of the four Thursdays.

malle à quat'nœuds *f.* handkerchief containing one's savings • (lit); trunk with four knots.

quatre à quatre *adv.* very quickly • (lit); four by four • *Y a descendu l'escalier quatre à quatre;* He took the stairs four at a time.

tiré à quatre épingles (être) *exp.* to be dressed to the "nines" • (lit); pulled with four pins.

un de ces quat' *exp.* one of these days • (lit); one of these four (mornings).

un de ces quat'matins *exp.* one of these days • (lit); one of these four mornings.

5 (cinq)

en cinq secs *adv.* very quickly • (lit); in five seconds.

il était moins cinq *exp.* it was a narrow escape • (lit); it was less than five.

je t'en écrase cinq *exp.* gimme five! • (lit); I'll crash five of them (fingers) down on you.

je vous reçois cinq sur cinq *exp.* I read you loud and clear • (lit); I receive you five on five.

les cinq lettres *exp.* "four" letter word (like *merde* meaning "shit") • (lit); the five letters.

tape cinq *exp.* gimme five! • (lit); hit five (fingers).

un cinq à sept *m.* a quickie, a quick screw • (lit); a five-to-seven (a sexual act that lasts from five to seven minutes).

y aller de cinq *exp.* to shake hands • (lit); to go at it with five (fingers).

6 (six)

à la six-quat'-deux *adv.* quickly, lickety-split • (lit); in six-four-two.

7 (sept)

un cinq à sept *m.* a quickie, a quick screw • (lit); a five-to-seven (a sexual act that lasts from five to seven minutes).

11 (onze)

prendre le train d'onze heures *exp.* to go by foot • (lit); to take the 11:00 train.

12 (douze)

faire un douze *exp.* to make a mistake • (lit); to make a twelve.

13 (treize)

treizième mois *m.* Christmas bonus • (lit); the thirteenth month.

14 (quatorze)

chercher midi à quatorze heures *exp.* to look for problems where there are none • (lit); to look for noon at 2:00 (p.m.).

15 (quinze)

tuer les mouches à quinze pas *exp.* to have bad breath • (lit); to kill flies fifteen paces away.

22 (vingt-deux)

vingt-deux! *interj.* let's scram!

31 (trente et un)

se mettre sur son trente et un *exp.* to get all dressed up, to dress to the "nines" • (lit); to get on one's thirty-one.

33 (trente-trois)

trente-trois *interj.* (doctor to patient) *Dites trente-trois!;* Say "ah!"

36 (trente-six)

en voir trente-six chandelles *exp.* to see stars after getting hit in the head • (lit); to see thirty-six candles.

tous les trente-six du mois *exp.* once in a blue moon • (lit); each thirty-sixth of the month.

40 (quarante)

quarante-quatre *interj.* (doctor to patient) *Dites quarante-quatre!;* Say "ah!"

s'en foutre comme de l'an quarante *exp.* not to give a damn • (lit); to care about (something) as much as the year forty.

se mettre en quarante *exp.* to get angry • (lit); to put oneself in forty.

"50" (cinquante)

faire fifti *exp.* (Americanism) to go halves, "fifty-fifty."

100 (cent)

être aux cent coups *exp.* to be worried sick • (lit); to be at one hundred blows, to feel as though you've been hit in the head one hundred times due to so much worrying.

numéro cent *m.* restroom • (lit); the number one hundred.

1000 (mille)

c'est du mille feuilles *exp.* it's a piece of cake • (lit); it's a Napoléon pastry (also referred to as a *mille feuilles*).

faire du millimètre *exp.* to economize • (lit); to make millimeters.

je te le donne en mille *exp.* you will never guess • (lit); I will give it to you in one thousand.

taper dans le mille *exp.* to be successful • (lit); to be making in the thousands.

PRACTICE EXPRESSIONS THAT CONTAIN NUMBERS.

A. Circle the correct French translation of the word(s) in italics.

1. I was *totally* bombed.
   a. à la six-quat'-deux
   b. à zéro
   c. la une

2. I'll do it *right away.*
   a. double zéro
   b. cinq à sept
   c. à la six-quat'-deux

3. He *made a mistake* on his test.
   a. a fait un douze
   b. était sans un
   c. s'est plié en deux

4. She's *such a big* liar.
   a. un drôle de numéro
   b. une de ces
   c. treizième mois

5. *Let's beat it!*
   a. vingt-trois
   b. vingt-cinq
   c. vingt-deux

6. She couldn't sleep because she was *terribly worried.*
   a. aux cents coups
   b. un d'ces quat'
   c. j't'en écrase cinq

7. After he got hit in the head, he *saw stars.*
   a. en a vu 36 chandelles
   b. y est allé d'cinq
   c. était aux cent coups

8. He *got so angry* about it.
   a. s'est mis en quarante
   b. y est allé d'cinq
   c. a fait fifti

9. I have to go to the *bathroom.*
   a. quarante-quatre
   b. vingt-deux
   c. numéro cent

10. He sure is *a strange dude.*
   - a. un drôle d'numéro   b. un d'ces   c. à zéro

11. Boy, what a *loser!*
   - a. drôle de numéro   b. double zéro   c. trente-trois

12. Could you hand me the *front page*, please?
   - a. deux de jeu   b. treizième mois   c. la une

– 7 –

Les Nouveaux Voisins

(The New Neighbors)

LES NOUVEAUX VOISINS...

DIALOGUE

Irène et Jacques espionnent les nouveaux voisins.

Jacques: Tiens! Voilà les nouveaux voisins! Ta sœur, è m'a dit qu'è les a déjà rencontrés.

Irène: Ouais, j'sais. Mais elle était dans **ses p'tits souliers**! Au début, elle a **trouvé porte de bois**. Pis elle a entendu un **chahut pas croyable**... un vrai **badaboum**! Monsieur **Machin**, y était en train d'**coller** une **pâtée maison** à son fils. Elle **en restait comme deux ronds d'flan**.

Jacques: Si j'avais des **croulants** comme ça, j'**me caval'rais presto** pour m'**sauver les côtelettes**! Je m'demande s'y'a toujours du **tiraillement** comme ça entre ces deux-là.

Irène: Pas du tout. Selon ma sœur, y semblaient **réglos**. Enfin, elle a causé avec la femme qui lui a dit qu'y z'**en avaient vu d'toutes les couleurs** pasque des **faucheurs**, y z'ont essayé d'**déménager** leur **gourbi** l'premier jour. Heureusement qu'les **lardus**, y sont **tombés à pic**. C'est pour ça qu'son jules, y était **au bout d'sa corde**.

Jacques: Ah, d'accord. Alors, comment y sont... et la maison? Elle a pas **fouiné** un peu?

Irène: Bien sûr! Lui, y est **déboisé**, assez **balaise** et, selon sa femme, un **tire-au-flanc fini** et la dame, c't'une vraie **bouboule** mais sympa **comme tout**. La pauvre, elle avait l'**coup d'pompe** pasqu'è passe tout son temps à **briquer**.

Jacques: J'comprends. C'te maison-là, elle a toujours été **craspèque** à cause des **fumerons** qui y habitaient avant eux. Et qu'est-c'que ça **fouettait** là-d'dans!

THE NEW NEIGHBORS...

DIALOGUE

Irène and Jacques are spying on the new neighbors.

Jacques: Hey! There are the new neighbors! Your sister told me she already met them.

Irène: Yeah, I know. But she was never so embarrassed! At first, no one answered the door. Then she heard this unreal commotion... a real free-for-all! Mr. What's-his-name was giving his son a thrashing, big time. She just stood there with her mouth hanging open.

Jacques: If I had parents like that, I'd be outta there in no time flat just to save my butt! I wonder if there's always tension like that between those two.

Irène: Not at all. According to my sister, they seemed very normal. She finally chatted with the wife who told her that they've been through the mill because some burglars tried to ransack their house the first day. Fortunately, the cops showed up just in the nick of time. That's the reason her husband was at the end of his rope.

Jacques: Ah, okay. So, what do they look like... and the house? Didn't she snoop around a little?

Irène: Of course! The guy is bald, sort of muscular and, according to his wife, just one big lazy bum and the woman is a real fatso but very nice. The poor thing, she was wrecked because she spends all her time cleaning.

Jacques: I'm not surprised. That house has always been disgusting because of those smokers who used to live there before them. And did it ever stink in there!

VOCABULARY

au bout de sa corde (être) *exp.* • (lit); to be at the end of one's rope.
NOTE: **être au bout du rouleau** *exp.* to be at death's door • (lit); to be at the end of one's roller or spool.

badaboum *m.* free-for-all fight. *Y' avait un vrai badaboum au concert hier soir;* There was a real knock-down-drag-out at the concert last night.
SYNONYM: **torchée** *f.*

balaise (être) *adj.* to be big and strong. *Y est balaise, c' mec!;* That guy's built!
SYNONYM: **être baraqué** *adj.* to be well built • NOTE: This comes from the feminine noun *baraque* meaning "house."

bouboule *m. & f.* fatso.
SYNONYM: **patapouf** *m.* (used only for men) *Quel gros patapouf!;* What a fatso! •
ALSO: **boudin** *m.* (used only for women) *Quel boudin!;* What a blimp!

briquer *v.* to clean thoroughly, to scrub. *J' ai passé deux heures à briquer c' te maison;* I spent two hours cleaning this house.
NOTE: **se briquer** *v.* to clean oneself, to freshen up.
SYNONYM: **astiquer** *v.*

cavaler (se) *v.* to run away, to make a run for it. *Les flics! On s' cavale!;* The cops! Let's beat it!
NOTE (1): **être en cavale** *adj.* to be on the run (from the police), to be on the lamb.
NOTE (2): **cavaler qqn.** *v.* to annoy s.o. greatly. *Oh, tu m' cavales!;* Oh, you drive me crazy!
SYNONYM: **s'éclipser** *v.* • (lit); to eclipse oneself.

chahut *m.* loud noise, racket. *Arrêtez d' faire c' te chahut!;* Stop making that noise!
NOTE: **chahuter** *v.* **1.** to make a lot of noise • **2.** to boo a performer. *L' acteur, y s' est fait chahuter;* The actor got himself booed (off the stage).
SEE: *Inside Info - Slang Movie and Theater Terms,* p. 96.
SYNONYM: **chambard** *m.*

coller *v.* **1.** to put (with force) • (lit); to stick • *Colle ça sur la table;* Stick it on the table • **2.** to give. *Y lui a collé une pâtée maison;* He gave him/her a real thrashing.
SYNONYM: **fiche(r)** *v.*

comme tout *adj.* very, extremely • (lit); like everything • *Ce bébé, y est mignon comme tout;* This baby is just the cutest thing.

coup de pompe (avoir le/un) *m.* to be suddenly exhausted. *J' peux pu continuer. J' ai l' coup d' pompe, moi;* I can't go any further. I'm wiped out.
NOTE (1): This expression comes from the verb *pomper* meaning "to exhaust" or more literally, "to pump (s.o.) of all his energy."
NOTE (2): **être pompé(e)** *adj.* to be pooped.
SYNONYM: **avoir le coup de barre** *exp.* to be suddenly exhausted • (lit); to feel as if you were just hit over the head with a bar.

craspèque *adj.* filthy dirty. *Pourquoi tes frippes, è sont tellement craspèques?;* Why are your clothes so dirty?
SYNONYM: **cradeau** *adj.*
ANTONYM: **nickel** *adj.* spotlessly clean.

croulants *m.pl.* parents, "old folks." *Y z'habitent où, tes croulants;* Where do your parents live?
NOTE: This comes from the verb *crouler* meaning "to collapse, to crumble."
SYNONYM: **vieux** *m.pl.* • (lit); old folks.

déboisé(e) (être) *adj.* to be bald • (lit); to be "untimbered."
SYNONYM: **être chauve comme un genou** *exp.* • (lit); to be bald as a knee.

déménager *v.* **1.** to ransack a house • (lit); to move, to "unhome" • *Les cambrioleurs, y z'ont tout déménagé;* The burglars cleaned out everything • **2.** to talk absolute nonsense. *Tu déménages, toi!;* You're off your rocker!
SYNONYM: **nettoyer** *v.* • (lit); to clean (out a house during a burglary).

faucheur *m.* thief.
NOTE: This comes from the verb *faucher* meaning "to steal."
SYNONYM: **barboteur** *m.* This comes from the verb *barboter* meaning "to steal."

fini *adj.* through and through, complete • (lit); finished • *C't'un menteur fini;* He's a total liar.
SYNONYM: **sacré(e) / beau (bel / belle)** *adj.* • (lit); blessed / handsome (pretty) • *C't'un sacré menteur; He's a real liar / C't'une belle tricheuse;* She's a real cheater • NOTE: *sacré(e)* and *beau (bel / belle)* precede the noun they modify, whereas *fini* follows the noun.

fouetter *v.* to stink to high heaven • (lit); to whip • *Y fouette d'la bouche, lui;* That guy's got the worst breath.
SYNONYM: **taper** *v.* • (lit); to hit • *Oh, ça tape, ça!;* Boy, does that stink!

fouiner *v.* to snoop around • (lit); to do like a weasel *(une fouine)* • *Pourquoi tu fouines dans ma chambre?;* Why are you snooping around my room?
NOTE: **fouine** *f.* snoop • (lit); weasel.

fumeron *m.* heavy smoker, chain-smoker.
SYNONYM: **fumer comme un pompier** *exp.* • (lit); to smoke like a fireman.

gourbi *m.* house • (lit); shack, dirty house.
SYNONYM: **baraque** *f.* house • (lit); barracks.

lardu *m.* policeman • (lit); the "fat one" • *Attention! Les lardus!;* Watch out! The cops!
NOTE: This comes from the masculine noun *lard* meaning "fat" or "bacon."
SYNONYM: **flic** *m.* cop.

Machin(e) *n.* What's-his-name / What's-her-name. *Y est très gentil, Monsieur Machin;* Mr. What's-his-name is very nice.
NOTE: When in lowercase, the meaning of *machin* becomes "thing" or "thingamajig." *C'est quoi, c'machin?;* What is this thing?

pas croyable *adj.* unbelievable, terrific • (lit); not believable. *C'est pas croyable, ce synthétiseur;* This synthesizer is unreal.
NOTE: This is a popular replacement for *incroyable*.
SYNONYM: **génial(e)** *adj. Tu vas aller en Amérique pour les vacanaces? Génial!;* You're going to America on vacation? Fantastic!

pâtée maison *f.* a thrashing. *Son père, y lui a collé une pâtée maison;* His father gave him a beating.
NOTE: The word *pâtée* literally means "a mash used for poultry." However, it is also used to mean "a thrashing," because it conjures up an image of someone getting beaten to a pulp. Since *pâtée* is pronouned the same as the masculine noun *pâté*, meaning "ground meat or vegetables," the word *maison* has been added as a play on words. This is because the word *pâté* is commonly seen on restaurant menus followed by the word *maison* meaning "the pâté of the house."

petits souliers (être dans ses) *exp.* to be very embarrassed or ill at ease • (lit); to be in one's little shoes • *J'ai déchiré ma robe à la soirée. Que j'étais dans mes p'tits souliers!;* I ripped my dress at the party. Was I ever embarrassed!
NOTE: This expression conjures up an image of a person who is so ill at ease, that he/she cannot keep from fidgeting and moving around as if he/she were wearing shoes that were unbearably small and uncomfortable.

presto *adv.* immediately (from Italian). *Allez, presto!;* Hurry it up!
NOTE: **illico-presto** *adv.* variation of: *presto*.
SYNONYM: **dare-dare** *adv.* quickly. *On est en r'tard! Faut s'habiller dare-dare!;* We're late! We'd better get dressed fast!
ANTONYM: **mollo-mollo** *adv.* slowly, carefully.

réglo (être) *adj.* to be on the level, normal.
NOTE: This comes from the verb *régler* meaning "to regulate, to keep (something) in order."
SYNONYM: **être terre-à-terre** *adj.* to be down-to-earth. *Cette dame-là, elle est pas du tout prétentieuse. J'la trouve très terre-à-terre;* That woman's not at all pretentious. I find her very down-to-earth.

rester comme deux ronds de flan (en) *exp.* to be flabbergasted • (lit); to stay there like two slices of custard (hence "motionless").
SYNONYM: **en rester baba** *v.* to be speechless with astonishment (that only the sound "baba" can be uttered).

sauver les côtelettes (se) *exp.* to save one's hide • (lit); to save one's cutlets or chops • *Y était furibard! Alors, j'ai filé pour m'sauver les côtelettes;* He was furious! So, I darted out of there to save my skin.
NOTE: **se sauver** *v.* to leave in a hurry.

tiraillement *m.* tension, friction • (lit); pulling, yanking • *Y'a toujours du tiraillement entre ces deux-là;* There's always friction between those two.
NOTE: This comes from the verb *tirailler* meaning "to pull in different directions."

tire-au-flanc *m.* a lazy individual • (lit); a "pull-by-his-side," one who has to be pulled while on his side because he's always lying down.
NOTE: **tirer au flanc** *v.* to be lazy. *Tu fais qu'tirer au flanc, toi;* All you ever do is lie around.
SYNONYM: **cossard** *m.* lazy bum • NOTE: **avoir la cosse** *exp.* to be lazy.
ANTONYM: **péter du feu** *exp.* to have tons of energy • (lit); to fart fire.

tomber à pic *exp.* to arrive in the nick of time • (lit); to fall like a pickaxe.
SYNONYM: **tomber bien** *exp. Que t'es tombé bien, toi!;* Boy, did you ever get here just in the nick of time!

trouver porte de bois *exp.* to find no one at home • (lit); to find a wooden door.

voir de toutes les couleurs (en) *exp.* to be having a very hard time of it, to be going through the mill • (lit); to see it from every color • *La pauvre, elle en a vu de toutes les couleurs;* The poor thing, she's been through the wringer.

PRACTICE THE VOCABULARY

[Answers to Lesson 7, p. 134]

A. Replace the word(s) in italics with the slang synonym from the right column.

1. T'es *arrivé au bon moment* _____ .
2. C't'un vrai *paresseux* _____ , c'ui-là.
3. Pourquoi tes vêtements, y sont *sales* _____ ?
4. Y est *fort* _____ , c'garçon.
5. J'dois manger *vite* _____ pasque j'suis en r'tard.
6. Y habite toujours avec ses *parents* _____ .
7. J'dois *partir tout d'suite* _____ !
8. Y est tout à fait *chauve* _____ , mon frère.
9. Ça *pue* _____ dans c'te maison!
10. Quel *fumeur* _____ !
11. Y lui a *donné* _____ un coup d'poings.
12. J'ai passé deux heures à *nettoyer* _____ la maison.
13. C'est *fantastique* _____ , c'te voiture!
14. Attention! C't'un *voleur* _____ !

A. **m'cavaler**
B. **briquer**
C. **tombé à pic**
D. **pas croyable**
E. **tire-au-flanc**
F. **craspèques**
G. **faucheur**
H. **presto**
I. **fouette**
J. **croulants**
K. **balaise**
L. **déboisé**
M. **collé**
N. **fumeron**

B. Fill in the blank with the appropriate letter.

1. J'sais pu quoi faire. J'suis au bout ____ .
    a. **d'la rue**   b. **du fil**   c. **d'ma corde**

2. Quel ____ ! J'n'ai jamais entendu un bruit pareil!
    a. **bouboule**   b. **gourbi**   c. **badaboum**

3. J'en restais comme deux ____ .
    a. **ronds d'flan**   b. **secs**   c. **six-quat'-deux**

4. Y est très ____ , c'te mec.
    a. **réglo**   b. **chahut**   c. **lardu**

5. Arrête de ____ dans mes affaires!
    a. **fouetter** ·   b. **fouiner**   c. **faucher**

6. Y'avait un cambrioleur armé chez moi mais je m'suis sauvé les ____ .
    a. **côtelettes**   b. **bras**   c. **jambes**

7. J'vais aller m'coucher. J'ai l'coup d' ____ .
    a. **pouce**   b. **pompe**   c. **vieux**

8. Son père, y lui a donné une ____ .
    a. **tire-au-flanc**   b. **pâtée maison**   c. **bouboule**

9. E mange sans arrêt, celle-là. Quelle ____ .
    a. **bouboule**   b. **baraque**   c. **bagnole**

10. C't'un menteur ____ , c'ui-là.
    a. **enfin**   b. **à finir**   c. **fini**

11. Le pauvre… y en a vu d'toutes les ____ .
    a. **maisons**   b. **couleurs**   c. **chemises**

12. Le garçon de restaurant, y a cassé huit verres! Y a dû êt'dans ses ____ .
    a. **grandes chaussures**   b. **petites chaussettes** c. **petits souliers**

13. V'là M'sieur ____ .
    a. **Machin**   b. **Machine**   c. **Mauvais Poil**

14. Les cambrioleurs, y z'ont ____ leur maison.
    a. **briqué**   b. **déboisé**   c. **déménagé**

15. Y est mignon ____ , c'te bébé.
    a. **comme tous**   b. **comme tout**   c. **comme toute**

C. Underline the correct definition of the slang term(s) to the left.

1. **balaise:**   a. petit et faible   b. grand et fort

2. **chahut:**   a. grand bruit   b. grand silence

3. **se cavaler:**   a. partir   b. arriver

4. **coller:**   a. donner; mettre   b. prendre

5. **faucheur:**   a. fumeur   b. voleur

6. **gourbi:**   a. voiture   b. maison

7. **lardu:**   a. homme gros   b. agent de police

8. **presto:**   a. lentement   b. rapidement

9. **tire-au-flanc:**   a. enfant énergique   b. paresseux

10. **fouetter:**   a. puer   b. arriver

11. **fumeron:**   a. pompier   b. fumeur

12. **fini:**   a. joli   b. sacré

INSIDE INFO: *SLANG MOVIE AND THEATER TERMS*

Slang has infiltrated just about every profession from the distinguished medical community to the flamboyant world of the performing arts. Depending upon whether you're in a pastry shop, a bookstore, at the races, or in a casino at Monte Carlo, you will inevitably hear a different type of slang being spoken, since each group has created a "lingo" all its own.

The same certainly holds true in the English language. For instance, when speaking with a friend about a television show or movie, we might use expressions such as: *that show was a turkey, she brought the house down, he really bombed, what a flop, that actor's a real ham, he got panned by the critics, she can act circles around the others, she flubbed her lines, etc.*

In French slang, the movie and theater industries have inspired the creation of numerous words and expressions bound to be heard at any theatrical presentation. Once you've studied the following list, you'll know that if someone says that a movie is a real "turnip," you'd be better off not going!

acteuse *f.* actress devoid of talent. SEE: *cabotin / panne / ringard / théâtreux, euse.*

balayer les planches *exp.* to act as the show opener • (lit); to sweep the boards (of the stage).

bouler *v.* to fluff (one's lines) • (lit); to make a *boulette* meaning "blunder, mistake."

brûler les planches *exp.* to act with fire • (lit); to burn the boards (of the stage).

cabotin *m.* bad or ham actor. SEE: *acteuse / panne / ringard / théâtreux, euse.*

casser la baraque *exp.* to bring the house down • (lit); to break the house. NOTE: **baraque** *f.* house.

casserole *f.* projector, spotlight • (lit); casserole.

chauffer une salle/auditoire *exp.* to warm up an audience. • (lit); to warm up a room.

chahuter *v.* **1.** to boo. *L'acteur, y s'est fait chahuter;* The actor got himself booed (off the stage) • **2.** to make a lot of noise. *Arrêtez d'chahuter!;* Stop making such a racket! SEE: *se faire cueillir.*

couteau *m.* lead role • (lit); knife. NOTE: **couteau** *m.* head surgeon.

cueillir (se faire) *exp.* **1.** to get booed, hissed • **2.** to get arrested • (lit); to get oneself picked (over). SEE: *se faire chahuter.*

emboîter qqn. *v.* to boo, hiss (s.o.) • (lit); to box up (in a coffin) • *L'acteur, y s'est fait emboîter;* The actor got himself booed at (or "put into a coffin since he died a miserable death on stage").

éreinter *v.* to pan (an author, actor, book, etc.) • (lit); to exhaust • *L'auteur, y s'est fait éreinter par les critiques;* The author got raked over the coals by the critics.

faire de la frime *exp.* to have walk-on parts • (lit); to make pretense • *Y fait d'la frime;* He's a bit player. SEE: *frimant(e) / jouer les utilités / marcheuse / servir la soupe.*

faire des kilos (en) *exp.* to overact, to be going at it too strongly • (lit); to make a lot of kilos out of something (that should be "lighter") • *Elle en fait des kilos, c't' acteuse;* This actress is really overdoing it.

faire un bide *exp.* to flop (on stage). • (lit); to do a belly (flop) • *Y a fait un bide;* He really flopped.

faire un malheur *exp.* to be a big hit • (lit); to do a misfortune • *Y a fait un malheur!;* He was a smash! SEE: *faire un tabac.*

faire un tabac *exp.* to be a big hit • (lit); to do a tabacco • *Y a fait un tabac hier soir;* He was a big hit last night. SEE: *faire un malheur.*

flop *m.* flop. *La pièce, elle a fait flop;* The play was a total flop.
SEE: *four.*

four *m.* flop. *J'ai fait four;* I totally flopped
SEE: *flop.*

frimant(e) *f.* bit player
• (lit); show-off.
SEE: *faire de la frime / jouer les utilités / marcheuse / servir la soupe.*

guignol *m.* prompt box
• (lit); theater of puppets.

jouer avec ses tripes *exp.* to act with guts and feeling. • (lit); to act with one's guts.

jouer devant les banquettes vides *exp.* to play to an empty house • (lit); to play before empty seats.

jouer les utilités *exp.* to play bit parts • (lit); to play the utilities.
SEE: *faire de la frime / frimant(e) / marcheuse / servir la soupe.*

louper *v.* to flub a line or entrance
• (lit); to miss, to fail.
NOTE: **loup** *m.* flubbed line or entrance.

marcheuse *f.* walk-on, extra, bit player • (lit); walker.
SEE: *faire de la frime / frimant(e) / jouer les utilités / servir la soupe.*

navet *m.* lousy film • (lit); turnip
• *Quel navet!;* What a turkey!

panne *f.* **1.** small part. *Je r'fuse d'faire les pannes;* I refuse to do small parts • **2.** bad actor or actress.
SEE: *cabotin / acteuse / ringard / théâtreux, euse.*

pastille *f.* microphone
• (lit); lozenge.

poulaille *f.* audience.
NOTE: This refers to the people who sit in the *poulailler.*
SEE: *poulailler.*

poulailler *m.* cheap balcony seats • (lit); hen house
• *J'ai pris des places au poulailler;* I got some seats in the balcony.

projo *m.* projector in a movie theater.

recevoir des pommes cuites *exp.* to get "tomatoes" thrown at oneself • (lit); to receive cooked apples (thrown by the audience).

recevoir son morceau de sucre *exp.* to be applauded the moment one first appears on stage, to have one's moment of glory
• (lit); to receive one's piece of sugar.

ringard *m.* bad actor.
NOTE: **ringard** *m.* hopeless individual, a real zero
SEE: *cabotin / panne / acteuse / théâtreux, euse.*

servir la soupe *exp.* to take bit parts, to play small roles • (lit); to serve soup.
SEE: *faire de la frime / frimant(e) / jouer les utilités / marcheuse.*

télé *f.* Abbreviation of: *télévision.*
SEE: *Unit Three - Popular Abbreviations,* p. 217.

théâtreux, euse *n.* bad actor, bad actress • (lit); one who does theatrics.
SEE: *cabotin / panne / ringard / acteuse.*

trac *m.* stage fright. *Devant un public, j' commence à avoir le trac, moi!;* In front of an audience, I start to get stage fright!

PRACTICE USING SLANG MOVIE AND THEATER TERMS

A. Match the columns.

☐ 1. bad or ham actor

☐ 2. to get booed

☐ 3. to be a complete flop

☐ 4. lead role

☐ 5. to be a big hit

☐ 6. to play bit parts

☐ 7. to bring the house down

☐ 8. audience

☐ 9. microphone

☐ 10. turkey of a film

☐ 11. to get "tomatoes" thrown at oneself

☐ 12. stage fright

A. **poulaille**

B. **navet**

C. **cabotin**

D. **trac**

E. **se faire chahuter**

F. **recevoir des pommes cuites**

G. **couteau**

H. **faire un bide**

I. **jouer les utilités**

J. **casser la baraque**

K. **pastille**

L. **faire un tabac**

− 8 −

L'Invité

(The Houseguest)

Leçon Huit

L'INVITÉ...

DIALOGUE

Robert et Anne ont des ennuies avec leur invité.

Anne: Alors, y a fait quoi aujourd'hui, Henri?

Robert: Ben, y **s'baquait** pendant toute une heure, pis y a **joué des badigoinces** comme d'habitude. Y est **porté sur la bouffe**, c'ui-là! J'ai l'idée d'tout **caroubler**.

Anne: Ça m'étonn'rait pas qu'y **chatouille la serrure**!

Robert: Ensuite, y **s'est écroulé** dans mon fauteuil. Maintenant, y **pique une ronflette**. Y **les a à l'envers**! **A lui l'pompon**!

Anne: Tu commences à **perd'les pédales, mon chou**! Faut pas **t'biler** pour ça. Tu penses pas qu'tu **cherches la p'tite bête**, non?

Robert: Mais y nous **essore**, tu **mords**? Y a **attaqué** son frère au **flubard** aujourd'hui et y **niche à l'étranger**! C'est pas **au châsse** un **coup d'fil** comme ça, remarque, et c'est toujours moi qui **casque**! J'veux pas **cirer toujours l'même bouton**, mais **au prix où est l'beurre**, ça va pas, non! Là, j'dois **y mett'mon véto**. Oh, y commence à m'**asticoter**!

Anne: J'suppose qu'on doit **faire la loi** pour **l'étouffer dans l'œuf** le plus vite possible. Ah, non! Y est encore au flubard!

Robert: **Ça, c'est l'bouquet**! J'le **balanstique** dehors tout d'suite! J'**en ai soupé**!

Anne: Vas-y **mollo-mollo**, hein? Mais **serre les fesses**!

Robert: T'en fais pas. Ça va être une **promenade**!

Lesson Eight

THE HOUSEGUEST...

DIALOGUE

Robert and Anne are having troubles with their houseguest.

Anne: So, what did Henri do today?

Robert: Well, he took a bath for an entire hour, then stuffed his face as usual. That guy really has a thing for food! I have a notion to put everything under lock and key.

Anne: It wouldn't surprise me if he picked the lock!

Robert: Then, he flopped into my chair. Now, he's taking a nap. He is so unbelievably lazy! He really takes the cake!

Anne: I think you're starting to lose it, Sweetheart. You don't have to get yourself all worked up over it. Don't you think you're nitpicking?

Robert: He's squeezing us dry, don't you understand? He called his brother on the phone today and he lives abroad! A phone call like that isn't free, ya know, and I'm the one who's ends up paying for it! I don't mean to harp, but with the cost of living today, you just don't do that! I've got to draw the line. Oh, he's starting to bug me!

Anne: I suppose we do have to lay down the law and nip it in the bud as soon as possible. Oh, no! He's on the phone again!

Robert: Oh, that's the last straw! I'm throwing him out right now! I've had just about all I can take!

Anne: Go at it gently, okay? But hang in there!

Robert: Don't worry. This is going to be a picnic!

VOCABULARY

à l'envers (les avoir) *exp.* to be extremely lazy • (lit); to have them (hands) inside out.
SYNONYM: **les avoir à la retourne** *exp.* • (lit); to have them (hands) turned inside out.
ANTONYM: **être d'attaque** *adj.* to be very energetic, "rarin' to go" • (lit); to be (full) of attack.

à lui/elle le pompon *exp.* he/she takes the cake • (lit); to him/her the pom-pom.

asticoter *v.* to annoy greatly. *Arrête d'asticoter ta sœur;* Stop bugging your sister.
NOTE: **s'asticoter** *v.* to fight. *Arrêtez d'vous asticoter!;* Stop quarrelling!
SYNONYM: **assommer** *v.* • (lit); to knock (s.o.) out • NOTE: **assommeur, euse** *n.* annoying person, pain in the neck.

attaquer *v.* to telephone (s.o.) • (lit); to attack • *Attaque-moi d'main;* Give me a ring tomorrow.
SYNONYM: **bigophoner** *v. J'te bigophone ce soir;* I'll call you tomorrow • NOTE: **bigophone** *m.* telephone.

au châsse *adv.* free • (lit); at the eye • *On peut pas y entrer au châsse;* We can't go in there for free.
NOTE: *châsse* is slang for *œil* meaning "eye." In slang, *au châsse* means "free" or "nothing" since the eye has the same shape as zero.
SYNONYM: **à l'œil** *adv.*

au prix où est le beurre *exp.* with the cost of living • (lit); with the price of butter where it is • *Au prix où est l'beurre, c'est pas facile d'joindre les deux bouts;* With the cost of living today, it isn't easy to make ends meet.

balanstiquer *v.* to throw, to toss • (lit); to balance, to swing • *Y m'a balanstiqué l'ballon;* He threw me the football.
NOTE: This is a slang variation of the verb *balancer.*

baquer (se) *v.* to take a bath • (lit); to "tub" oneself • *Baque-toi avant de t'pieuter;* Take a bath before going to bed.
NOTE: This comes from the masculine noun *baquet* meaning "tub" or "bucket."

biler (se) *v.* to worry oneself, to get all worked up • (lit); to make oneself bile (from worrying too much) • *Pourquoi tu t'biles pour ça?;* What are you getting so worked up over that for?
NOTE: **se faire de la bile** *exp.* to worry oneself, to get all worked up.
SYNONYM: **se faire du mauvais sang** *exp. Y s'fait du mauvais sang pasque sa fille, elle est en r'tard;* He's all worked up because his daughter is late.

ça, c'est le bouquet *exp.* that's the last straw • (lit); that's the bouquet.
SYNONYM: **c'est la fin des haricots!** *exp.* • (lit); that's the end of the beans!

caroubler *v.* to put something under lock and key.
NOTE (1): This comes from the feminine noun *carouble* meaning "duplicate or skeleton key."
NOTE (2): **caroubler** *v.* to break into a house.
SYNONYM: **mettre qqch. sous clé** *exp.* to put something under lock and key • (lit); to put something under key.

casquer *v.* to pay, to cough up (money). *Pourquoi c'est toujours moi qui casque?;* Why am I always the one who ends up forking out the money?
SYNONYM: **douiller** *v.*

chatouiller une serrure *exp.* to pick a lock • (lit); to tickle a lock • *Le cambrioleur, y a chatouillé la serrure;* The burglar picked the lock.
SYNONYM: **crocher** *v.* to pick a lock with a hook *(un crochet).*

chercher la petite bête *exp.* to nitpick • (lit); to look for the little animal • *Tu cherches toujours la p'tite bête, toi;* You're always nitpicking.
SYNONYM: **chercher des poils sur l'œuf** *exp.* • (lit); to look for hairs on the egg.

cirer toujours le même bouton *exp.* to harp on a subject • (lit); always to wax the same button.
SYNONYM: **c'est toujours la même rengaine** *exp.* it's always the same old (repetitive) story.

coup de fil *m.* telephone call • (lit); wire call • *Passe-moi un coup d'fil, d'main;* Give me a call tomorrow.
NOTE: In the above expression, *fil* may be replaced with any number of slang synonyms for the word, "telephone" e.g., *bigophone, bigorneau, cornichon, escargot, phonard, ronfleur, télémuche, etc.*

écrouler dans un fauteuil (s') *exp.* to flop into an armchair • (lit); to crumble or collapse into a chair • *Ce soir, j'ai envie d'm'écrouler dans un fauteuil et regarder la télé;* Tonight, I feel like flopping into a chair and watching T.V.
SYNONYM: **s'affaler dans un fauteuil** *exp.* • (lit); to fall or drop into a chair.

essorer qqn. *exp.* to squeeze s.o. dry of money • (lit); to wring or spin dry s.o. (of all his money) • *Tu m'essores d'tout mon fric!;* You're draining me of all my cash!

étouffer qqch. chose dans l'œuf *exp.* to nip something in the bud • (lit); to smother something in the egg (so that it can never become full grown) • *Y prend mes affaires sans m'demander? On étouffe ça dans l'œuf tout d'suite!;* He's taking my stuff without asking me? We'll nip that in the bud right away!

faire la loi *exp.* to lay down the law • (lit); to make the law • *T'es rentré à 2h du matin?! Bon, j'fais la loi maintenant!;* You got home at 2:00 in the morning?! Fine, I'm laying down the law now!

flubard *m.* telephone.

   NOTE: **flubards** *m.pl.* legs.

   SYNONYM: **cornichon** *m.* telephone • (lit); pickle (since its shape resembles that of a telephone receiver).

jouer des badigoinces *exp.* to eat well • (lit); to play the lips • *Tu viens jouer des badigoinces chez nous ce soir?;* You wanna come over to our house and eat tonight?

   NOTE: **badigoinces** *m.pl.* lips.

   SYNONYM: **se taper la cloche** *exp.* • (lit); to cause one's bell to ring with joy (from eating).

mettre son véto sur qqch. *exp.* to draw the line, to put one's foot down • (lit); to put one's veto on something • *Si mes gosses, y commencent à rentrer après minuit, j'devrai y mett' mon véto;* If my kids start coming home after midnight, I'll have to draw the line.

mollo-mollo *adv.* carefully, cautiously. *Vas-y mollo-mollo;* Easy does it.

   SYNONYM: **tout doucement** *adv.* very carefully • (lit); all sweetly.

mon chou *exp.* sweetheart • (lit); my cabbage.

   SEE: *Inside Info - The Many Slang Terms of Affection,* p. 107.

mordre *v.* to understand, to get it • (lit); to bite • *Tu mords c' que j'veux dire?;* Are you getting what I'm trying to say?

   SYNONYM: **piger** *v.* to understand. *J'pige que dalle, moi!;* I don't understand a thing!

   NOTE: **que dalle** *adv.* nothing, "zip."

perdre les pédales *exp.* to lose control of one's temper • (lit); to lose (control of) the pedals • *J'peux pu t'parler; t'as perdu les pédales!;* I just can't talk to you anymore; you've flown off the handle!

   SYNONYM: **voir rouge** *exp.* to become extremely angry • (lit); to see red.

piquer une ronflette *exp.* to take a nap • (lit); to take a little snore • *J' suis crevé. J'vais aller piquer une ronflette;* I'm wiped out. I'm gonna go take a little nap.

   NOTE (1): **piquer** *v.* to take, to grab. *Y a piqué mon portefeuille!;* He grabbed my wallet!

   NOTE (2): The feminine noun *ronflette* comes from the verb *ronfler* meaning "to snore."

porté(e) sur la bouffe (être) *exp.* to be driven by food • (lit); to be carried by food • *Y est porté sur l'sexe;* He's driven by sex.

   NOTE: **bouffe** *f.* food / **bouffer** *v.* to eat.

   SYNONYM: **raffoler de qqch.** *exp.* to be wild for something. *J'raffole du chocolat!;* I'm nuts about chocolate!

promenade *f.* something easy to do, a cinch, a snap, a piece of cake • (lit); a (cake)walk • *C't'exam', c't'une promenade;* This test is a piece of cake.

serrer les fesses *exp.* to have courage, to hang in there • (lit); to squeeze the cheeks of one's buttocks • *Bon courage! Serre les fesses!;* Good luck! Hang in there!

soupé (en avoir) *exp.* to be fed up, to have taken all one can • (lit); to have eaten (all one can).

NOTE: **souper** *v.* to eat supper / **souper** *m.* supper. Commonly heard as: *A la soupe!;* Come and get it!

SYNONYM: **en avoir ras le bol** *exp.* to have had it, to be fed up • (lit); to have had it to the brim of the bowl • *J'en ai ras l'bol, moi!;* I've had it up to here!

PRACTICE THE VOCABULARY

[Answers to Lesson 8, p. 135]

A. Replace the following italicized word(s) with the appropriate slang synonym(s) from the right column.

1. Tu commences à m'*énerver* _____ .   A. **flubard**

2. J'en ai *jusque-là* _____ !   B. **attaque**

3. Ça va êt'*facile* _____ .   C. **au châsse**

4. Tu *comprends* _____ c'que j'te dis?   D. **les pédales**

5. Y commence à perd'*contrôle* _____ .   E. **soupé**

6. C'est Thomas au *téléphone* _____ .   F. **chou**

7. C'est toujours moi qui *paie* _____ .   G. **asticoter**

8. Y m'a *jeté* _____ dehors!   H. **biler**

9. Faut pas t'*inquiéter* _____ pour ça!   I. **une promenade**

10. J't'*appelle* _____ vers 10h.   J. **mords**

11. Comment ça va, mon *chéri* _____ ?   K. **casque**

12. Le musée, c'est *gratuit* _____ aujourd'hui. L. **balanstiqué**

B. Underline the word(s) in parentheses that best complete(s) the sentence.

1. Elle est pas croyable! A elle l'(**casque, pompon, flubard**)!

2. A cause de toi, j'suis dans la dèche! Tu m'as (**casqué, soupé, essoré**)!

3. Mon neveu, y fouine toujours dans mes affaires. Quand y vient nous rend'visite, j'suis obligé d'tout (**caroubler, essorer, écrouler**).

4. Robert, y a cassé mon ordinateur?! Ça, c'est l'(**coup d'fil, bouquet, châsse**)!

5. Y est (**mordu, caroublé, porté**) sur la bouffe, c'ui-là.

6. C'est toujours moi qui (**casque, étouffe, baque**).

7. J'vais m'(**mordre, piquer une ronflette, baquer**) avant d'me pieuter.

8. Y fait rien toute la journée. Faut dire qu'y les a à (**l'envers, souper, écrouler**).

9. Vas-y... serre les (**coups d'fil, châsses, fesses**)!

10. Quel dîner! On a bien (**essoré, serré les fesses, joué des badigoinces**).

11. Attention! Vas-y (**vite, mollo-mollo, à la six-quat'-deux**)!

12. Le cambrioleur, y a (**chatouillé, mordu, caroublé**) la serrure.

C. Match the English with the French equivalents.

☐ 1. You're losing control, pal.

☐ 2. She's on the phone.

☐ 3. I feel like taking a little nap.

☐ 4. Now, I'm laying down the law.

☐ 5. That's a piece of cake.

☐ 6. When I got home, I collapsed into the chair.

☐ 7. I'm drawing the line right there.

☐ 8. That's the last straw!

☐ 9. I'm gonna nip that in the bud right now!

☐ 10. I've had it!

☐ 11. The boss kicked me out.

☐ 12. With the cost of living today, I can't buy a new car just now.

☐ 13. You're always nitpicking.

☐ 14. You're always harping on the same thing.

A. **C't'une promenade, ça.**

B. **J'en ai soupé!**

C. **J'mets mon véto là-d'ssus.**

D. **Tu cires toujours l'même bouton.**

E. **Au prix où est l'beurre, j'peux pas acheter une nouvelle bagnole en c'moment.**

F. **C'est elle au flubard.**

G. **Y m'a balanstiqué dehors, l'chapeau.**

H. **Ça, c'est l'bouquet!**

I. **Tu perds les pédales, mon vieux.**

J. **Maintenant, j'fais la loi.**

K. **Tu cherches toujours la p'tite bête.**

L. **J'vais l'étouffer dans l'œuf tout d'suite!**

M. **J'ai envie d'piquer une ronflette.**

N. **En rentrant, je m'suis écroulé dans l'fauteuil.**

INSIDE INFO: *SLANG TERMS OF AFFECTION*

Throughout the world, the French are well known for being hopeless romantics. In fact, I don't know of any other language that has such a variety of slang terms of endearment. All of the words in the main list below are used to mean "my sweetheart." However, for added passion, you may insert *petit(e)* before any one of these nouns:

ma poule ➡ *ma p'tite poule*

my hen ➡ my little hen

If you want to get even "mushier," you may rearticulate the first syllable of the noun (the more common ones are given in the main list below):

ma p'tite poule ➡ *ma p'tite poupoule*

my little hen ➡ my little "henny-wenny"

You can even take this sweetness one step further by adding *en sucre* (of sugar) to any of these:

ma p'tite poupoule ➡ *ma p'tite poupoule en sucre*

my little "henny-wenny" ➡ my little sugar "henny-wenny"

Now, if you want to get positively saccharine, you can use the "mushier" form of *sucre* which becomes *susucre:*

ma p'tite poupoule en sucre ➡ *ma p'tite poupoule en susucre*

my little sugar "henny-wenny" ➡ my little "sugary-wugary henny-wenny"

If your teeth managed to survive all that sweetness, you're ready to delve right in. Remember, any one of the following terms can be custom tailored:

mon bellot *m.* • (lit); my pretty one.
NOTE: This comes from the feminine adjective *belle* meaning "pretty."

ma bellotte *f.* the feminine form of *mon bellot.*

ma biche *f.* my sweetheart • (lit); my doe.

ma bibiche *f.* my sweetie pie.
NOTE: *bibiche* is an affectionate variation of the feminine noun *biche* meaning "doe."

mon biquet *m.* • (lit); my young (male) goat, kid.

ma biquette *f.* • (lit); my young (female) goat, kid.

ma bobonne *f.* • (lit); my goody-good.
NOTE: This comes from the feminine adjective *bonne* meaning "good."

mon canard *m.* • (lit); my duck.

mon chien *m.* • (lit); my dog.

ma chochotte *f.* my sweety pie.

mon chou *m.* • (lit); my cabbage.

mon chou en sucre *m.* • (lit);
my sugar cabbage.

mon chou en susucre *m.*
• (lit); my sugar cabbage.
NOTE: *susucre* is an affectionate variation of the
masculine noun *sucre*
meaning "sugar."

mon chouchou *m.* • (lit); my
cabbage.
NOTE: *chouchou* is an affectionate variation of the
masculine noun *chou*
meaning "cabbage."

ma chouchoute *f.* This is the
feminine form of: *mon
chouchou.*

ma choute *f.* This is the
feminine form of: *mon chou.*

mon coco *m.* my sweetheart.

ma cocotte *f.* This is the
feminine form of: *mon coco.*

mon lapin *m.* • (lit); my rabbit.

mon loulou *m.* my sweetheart.

ma louloute *f.* This is the
feminine form of: *mon loulou.*

mon mimi *m.* my sweetheart.

ma mimine *f.* This is the
feminine form of: *mon mimi.*

mon minet *m.* • (lit); my
pussycat.

ma minette *f.* This is the
feminine form of: *mon minet.*

ma minoche *f.* • (lit); my
pussycat.
NOTE: This is a slang
variation of *minet* since
minoche was created by
using the slang suffix *-oche.*

ma poule *f.* • (lit); my hen.

mon poulet *m.* • (lit); my
chicken.

ma poulette *f.* • (lit); my
little hen.

ma poupoule *f.* • (lit); my
little hen.
NOTE: *poupoule* is an affectionate variation of the
feminine noun *poule*
meaning "hen."

mon poussin *m.* • (lit); my chick.

ma puce *f.* • (lit); my flea.

mon rat *m.* • (lit); my rat.

mon raton *m.* • (lit); my little rat.

ma totoche *f.* my sweetie pie.

mon trésor *m.* • (lit); my
treasure.

PRACTICE THE SLANG TERMS OF AFFECTION

A. Give the feminine form of each.

1. *mon bellot:*

_____

2. *mon biquet:*

_____

3. *mon chou:*

_____

4. *mon chouchou:*

_____

5. *mon coco:*

_____

6. *mon loulou:*

_____

7. *mon mimi:*

_____

8. *mon poulet:*

_____

– 9 –

Au Gymnase

(At the Gym)

AU GYMNASE...

DIALOGUE

Kim et Liz sont en train d'faire du sport.

Kim: Mais qu'est-c'que t'as, toi? T'as l'air **déphasée**. **T'en as gros sur la patate**?

Liz: Non, c'est pas ça. La semaine dernière, j'étais **au bout du rouleau**. Maintenant, j'essaie d'**me rebecter**. Oh, j'suis **vannée**, moi.

Kim: Tu f'rais mieux d'y aller mollo-mollo aujourd'hui. Après tout, tu veux pas **t'claquer un muscle**.

Liz: **Sans rigoler**! Et toi, ça **boume**?

Kim: Ouais, j'**me porte comme un charme**. T'as même pas r'marqué qu'j'ai **fondu** un peu – deux kilos!

Liz: Ben, ouais! C'est vrai qu'tu d'viens **hyper** p'tite! **Comment t'as fait pour** les perdre? C'était **coton**, non?

Kim: Mais, c'était **simple comme bonjour**. J'faisais des **pompes** tous les jours.

Liz: Quelle horreur! Non, merci. Tiens! **Vise** un peu les **sapes** qu'è porte la p'tite **frimeuse** sur l'aut'vélo. Elle est toujours à **montrer sa boutique**.

Kim: Oh, è m'**tape sur l'système**. Quand j'ui dis salut, è m'**rebiffe**. E **s'prend pas pour d'la p'tite bière**. J'peux pas l'**encadrer** avec c'te **cancérette** toujours dans la **gargoulette**. Et t'as pas vu comme è **s'déhanche** en marchant?

Liz: Et avec **les jambes en parenthèses** qu'elle a, on **s'rince pas l'œil**. Oh, la **vache**! Regarde c'ui-là qui **roule les biscottos**. Quelle **carrosserie**!

Kim: Mais, t'as des **lanternes esquintées** ou quoi? C't'un grand **patapouf**, lui! T'as **décroché**, non? J'pense que t'es plus malade que tu n'le pensais!

Lesson Nine

AT THE GYM...

DIALOGUE

Kim and Liz are working out.

Kim: What's wrong with you? You look out of it. You have a lot on your mind?

Liz: No, it's not that. Last week, I was practically at death's door. Now, I just have to get back into it. Oh, I'm wiped out!

Kim: You'd better take it easy today. After all, you don't want to screw up a muscle.

Liz: You're not kidding! So, you doing okay?

Kim: Yep, I feel absolutely fantastic. You didn't even notice I've lost some weight – two kilos!

Liz: Well, yeah! You really are getting slender! How did you go about losing them? Wasn't it hard?

Kim: It was easy as pie. I've been doing push-ups every day.

Liz: Gimme a break! No, thank you. Hey! Get a load of the clothes that little show-off on the other bike is wearing. She's always strutting her stuff.

Kim: Oh, does she ever get on my nerves. When I say hi to her, she totally snubs me. She thinks she's too cool. I can't stand her with that cancer stick always hanging from her mouth. And did you see how she throws her hips when she walks?

Liz: And with those bowlegs of hers, it's not a real pretty sight. Wow! Look at that guy with those biceps. What a bod!

Kim: Are your eyes wrecked or what? He's a fat tub of lard! Have you lost it? I think you're sicker than you thought!

VOCABULARY

au bout du rouleau (être) *exp.* to be at death's door • (lit); to be at the end of the roller.
NOTE: **être au bout de sa corde** *exp.* • (lit); to be at the end of one's cord.
SYNONYM: **être à l'article de la mort** *exp.* • (lit); to be at the critical moment of death.

boumer *v.* to be going very well • (lit); to be booming • *Ça boum?;* How's it going?
SYNONYM: **carburer** *v.* • (lit); to carburate.

cancérette *f.* cigarette • (lit); cancer stick.
SYNONYM: **clope** *f.*

carrosserie *f.* build (of person) • (lit); body (of car) • *Elle a une sacrée carrosserie, c'te fille-là;* That girl's got one helluva body.
SYNONYM: **châssis** *m.* • (lit); chassis (of car).

claquer un muscle (se) *exp.* to pull a muscle • (lit); to use up, to burn out (a light bulb, etc.) a muscle.

comment faire pour *exp.* how to go about doing something • (lit); how to do for • *Comment tu fais pour garder ta ligne;* How do you go about keeping your figure?
SYNONYM: **comment ça se fait que** *exp.* how is it that • (lit); how does it do that • *Comment ça s'fait qu'tu parles si bien français?;* How is it that you speak such good French?

coton (c'est) *adv.* it's difficult • (lit); it's cotton.
SYNONYM: **c'est duraille** *adv.* • (lit); it's hard • NOTE: This is a slang transformation of the adverb and adjective *dur(e)* meaning "hard."

décrocher *v.* to crack up, to go crazy • (lit); to take (a telephone, a towel, etc.) off the hook, to unhook • *T'as décroché, toi;* You've lost your mind.
SYNONYM: **dérailler** *v.* • (lit); to derail.

déhancher (se) *v.* to wiggle one's hips • (lit); to dislocate one's hips • *Regarde comme è s'déhanche;* Look how she wiggles those hips.

déphasé(e) (avoir l'air) *adj.* to be/to feel out of it • (lit); to be out of phase (of electrical current) • *Je m'sens déphasé aujourd'hui;* I feel out of it today.
SYNONYM: **ne pas être dans son assiette** *exp.* not to be in one's plate.

encadrer qqn. (ne pas pouvoir) *v.* to be unable to stand s.o. • (lit); to be unable to put s.o. into a frame (as one would a painting).
NOTE: This is actually a parody of the expression, *ne pas pouvoir voir qqn. en peinture* meaning "to be unable to see a painting of s.o. (since just the mere sight would be too much to bear)."
SYNONYM: **ne pas pouvoir blairer qqn.** *exp.* • (lit); to be unable to smell s.o. • *J'peux pas l'blairer!;* I can't stand him! • NOTE: **blair** *m.* nose, "schnozzola."

esquinter *v.* to ruin, to hurt • (lit); to exhaust • *Tu vas t'esquinter les yeux si tu regardes la télé d'si près;* You're gonna hurt your eyes if you watch T.V. that close.
SYNONYM: **bousiller** *v.* • (lit); to break.

fondre *v.* to lose weight • (lit); to melt.
ANTONYM: **prendre de la brioche** *exp.* to get a gut • (lit); to take on brioche (bread).

frimeur, euse *n.* showoff. *Quel frimeur!;* What a show-off!
SYNONYM: **crâneur, euse** *n.*

gargoulette *f.* **1.** mouth • **2.** throat • (lit); the gargler.
NOTE: This comes from the verb *se gargariser* meaning "to gargle."
SYNONYM: **égout** *m.* • (lit); sewer.

gros sur la patate (en avoir) *exp.* to have a lot on one's mind • (lit); to have a large amount on the heart.
NOTE: **patate** *f.* **1.** heart • **2.** head • **3.** big nose • **4.** peasant • **5.** punch (to the face).

hyper *adv.* extremely • (lit); hyper • *Ton frère, y est hyper beau;* Your brother's really handsome.
SYNONYM: **archi** *adv.*

jambes en parenthèses (avoir les) *exp.* to be bowlegged • (lit); to have legs shaped like parentheses.
NOTE: Any number of slang synonyms for "legs" could certainly replace *jambes* in this expression such as: *(m.pl.) bâtons, bégonias, bouts de bois, compas, flubards, gigots, nougats, piliers, pivots, etc.* • *(f.pl.) baguettes, béquilles, cannes, gambettes, gambilles, guibolles, quilles, etc.*
SYNONYM: **avoir les jambes Louis XV** *exp.* • (lit); to have legs like Louis XV.
ANTONYM: **avoir les jambes en X** *exp.* to be knock-kneed.

lanterne *f.* eye • (lit); lantern.
SYNONYM: **mirette** *f.* This comes from the verb *mirer* meaning "to see."

montrer (toute) sa boutique *exp.* to expose oneself, to flash • (lit); to show (all) of one's goods • *Tu risques de t'faire sauter si tu montres ta boutique comme ça;* You're liable to get raped if you expose yourself like that.

patapouf *m.* fatso.
SYNONYM: **bouboule** *m. & f.*
ANTONYM: **planche** *f.* very thin person • (lit); board.

pompes (faire des) *f.pl.* to do push-ups • (lit); to do pumps • *J'fais des pompes tous les jours;* I do push-ups every day.

porter comme un charme (se) *exp.* to be fit as a fiddle • (lit); to carry oneself like a charm.
ANTONYM: **se sentir patraque** *adj.* to feel sick.

prendre pour de la petite bière (ne pas se) *exp.* to think highly of oneself, to be conceited • (lit); not to take oneself for a little beer.
SYNONYM: **se croire sorti(e) de la cuisse de Jupiter** *exp.* • (lit); to think of oneself as having come from Jupiter's thigh.

rebecter (se) *v.* to start feeling better (after an illness), to pick oneself back up. *J'étais malade la semaine dernière, mais maintenant j'commence à m'rebecter;* I was sick last week, but now I'm starting to feel better.
SYNONYM: **se refaire la cerise** *exp.* • (lit) to redo one's face • NOTE: **cerise** *f.* • (lit); cherry • **1.** face • **2.** head.

rebiffer *v.* to snub s.o. *E m'a rebiffé à la soirée;* She snubbed me at the party.
SYNONYM: **snober** *v.* / **snobinard(e)** *n.* snob • NOTE: This is taken from the English noun "snob" • SEE: *Street French - English Words That Are Commonly Used in Colloquial French,* p. 157.

rincer l'œil (se) *exp.* to enjoy looking at something provocative • (lit); to rince one's eye • *Quelle beauté! J'me rince l'œil;* What a beauty! I'm relishing this.

rouler les biscottos *exp.* to swagger, to strut (said of a bodybuilder) • (lit); to roll one's biceps • *Mais regarde un peu comme y roule les biscottos, c'mec;* Just look at that guy strut his stuff.
NOTE: **biscotto** *m.* bicep.

sans rigoler *exp.* no kidding • (lit); without laughing • *Tu lui as dit ses quat' vérités? Sans rigoler?;* You told him exactly what you thought of him? No kidding?
NOTE: **rigoler** *v.* to laugh.
SYNONYM: **sans blague** *exp.* • (lit); without a joke.

sapes *f.pl.* clothes, "threads." *Y est arrivé à la soirée dans des sapes tout à fait bizarres!;* He came to the party in the weirdest clothes!.
NOTE: **se saper** *v.* to get dressed.
SYNONYM: **fringues** *f.pl.* • NOTE: **se fringuer** *v.* to get dressed.

simple comme bonjour (c'est) *exp.* it's easy as pie • (lit); it's easy as hello • *T'en fais pas. C'est simple comme bonjour!;* Don't get so worked up. It's a snap!
SYNONYM: **c'est bête comme chou** *exp.* • (lit); it's silly as cabbage.

taper sur le système *exp.* to annoy (s.o.) • (lit); to hit on the system • *Tu m'tapes sur l'système, toi!;* You're really getting on my nerves!
SYNONYM: **casser les pieds à qqn.** *exp.* • (lit); to break s.o.'s feet.

vache (oh, la) *exclam.* wow! • (lit); oh, the cow (American equivalent: holy cow!) • *Oh, la vache! Elle est belle!;* Wow! She's beautiful!
SYNONYM: **ça alors!** *exp.* • (lit); that then!

vanné(e) (être) *adj.* to be exhausted • (lit); to be winnowed • *J'suis complètement vanné aujourd'hui;* I'm totally wiped out today.
SYNONYM: **être lessivé(e)** *adj.* • (lit); to be washed out (of all energy).

viser *v.* to get a look at (something) • (lit); to take aim (at something) • *Vise-moi c'te fille-là!;* Get a load of that girl!
SYNONYM: **gaffer** *v.*

PRACTICE THE VOCABULARY

[Answers to Lesson 9, p. 135]

A. Complete the sentences by choosing the appropriate word from the list below. Make any necessary changes.

boumer	claquer	viser
rincer	taper	vache
biscottos	rebecter	hyper
parenthèses	déphasé	coton

1. Oh, c'est _____ ces d'voirs! J'ai du mal à les faire.

2. Salut, Cécile! Ça _____ ?

3. Mais qu'est-c'que t'as, toi? T'as l'air _____ .

4. Attention! Tu veux pas t' _____ un muscle.

5. Oh, la _____ ! Elle est énorme!

6. Mon prof d'anglais, y est _____ beau!

7. Arrête! Tu commences à m' _____ sur l'système!

8. Regarde comme è marche. Elle a les jambes en _____ .

9. J'commence à m'_____ après avoir été malade quat'jours.

10. _____ un peu c'qu'è porte! C't'affreux!

11. Elle est belle, celle-là. J'me _____ l'œil.

12. Regarde comme y roule les _____ en marchant, c'mec.

B. Underline the correct synonym.

1. **vanné:**   a. fatigué   b. énergique

2. **sapes:**   a. chaussures   b. vêtements

3. **biscotto:**   a. biscuit   b. biceps

4. **lanterne:**   a. œil   b. phare

5. **gargoulette:**   a. gorge   b. ventre

6. **fondre:**   a. grossir   b. perdre du poids

7. **décrocher:**   a. devenir fou   b. partir

8. **cancérette:**   a. jambe   b. cigarette

9. **c'est coton:**   a. c'est simple   b. c'est difficile

10. **viser:**   a. partir   b. regarder

11. **hyper:**   a. extrêmement   b. un peu

12. **esquinter:**   a. ruiner   b. réparer

C. Match the columns.

☐ 1. He flashed me!

☐ 2. No kidding?

☐ 3. It's simple as pie.

☐ 4. She's at death's door.

☐ 5. I hate doing push-ups.

☐ 6. What a bod!

☐ 7. I'm feeling fit as a fiddle.

☐ 8. How did you go about inventing it?

☐ 9. He ignored me, the snob.

☐ 10. Look how she throws her hips.

☐ 11. That guy's a big tub of lard.

☐ 12. I have a lot on my mind.

☐ 13. What a show-off!

☐ 14. I can't stand him!

A. **Elle est au bout du rouleau.**

B. **Quelle carrosserie!**

C. **Comment t'as fait pour l'inventer?**

D. **Regarde comme è s'déhanche.**

E. **Quel frimeur!**

F. **J'en ai gros sur la patate.**

G. **Y m'a montré toute sa boutique!**

H. **C't'un grand patapouf, c'ui-là.**

I. **J'ai horreur d'faire des pompes.**

J. **J'me porte comme un charme.**

K. **Y m'a rebiffé, l'snobinard.**

L. **J'peux pas l'encadrer.**

M. **Sans rigoler?**

N. **C'est simple comme bonjour.**

INSIDE INFO: *SLANG TERMS USED IN MUSIC*

As discussed in Lesson 7, the television, movie, and theater industries have given birth to an enormous wealth of imaginative slang terms and expressions. Another facet of the entertainment industry that has one of the most creative "languages" all its own is music.

The music world has not only come up with slang that pertains solely to its own craft, but has provided us with several words and expressions having nothing to do with music at all.

The following is a list destined to help you understand any conversation among musicians or simply among music lovers.

assassiner une chanson *exp.* to butcher a song • (lit); to assassinate a song.

bêler *v.* to sing badly • (lit); to bleat.

beuglante *f.* song.
NOTE: This comes from the verb *beugler* meaning "to low (of cattle), to bellow (of bull)."

beugler *v.* **1.** to sing badly. *J' l' ai écouté beugler pendant toute une heure!;* I listened to her screech out a song for an entire hour! • **2.** to yell. *Arrêtez d' vous beugler!;* Stop screaming at each other • (lit); to low (of cattle), to bellow (of bull).

biniou *m.* **1.** musical instrument (in general) • **2.** telephone • (lit); Breton bagpipes.

bœuffer *v.* to have a jam session, to jam.
SYNONYM: **faire un bœuf** *exp.* to have a jam session.

canard *m.* wrong note, klinker • (lit); duck.

chaudron *m.* tiny old piano, worn-out instrument • (lit); cauldron.

commode *f.* piano • (lit); chest of drawers.

connaître la musique *exp.* to know the score • (lit); to know the music.

crincrin *m.* screechy violin, fiddle. *Râcler le crincrin;* To scrape on the fiddle.
NOTE: This comes from the masculine noun *crin* meaning "horsehair."

écraser de l'ivoire *exp.* to play the piano, to tickle the ivories • (lit); to crush ivory.

en balancer une *v.* to sing • (lit); to toss one off.

faire de la sauce *exp.* to improvise • (lit); to make sauce.

faire des poussières *exp.* to play false notes, to play klinkers • (lit); to make dust clouds.

gig *m.* a music gig.

goualante *f.* song. *Pousser une goualante;* To sing a song.

goualer *v.* to sing.
NOTE: **goualeur, euse** *n.* (bad or noisy) singer.

grand-mère *f.* double bass • (lit); grandmother.

gratouille *f.* maraca.
NOTE: This comes from the verb *gratter* meaning "to scratch" since the maraca makes a "scratching" sound.

gratte *f.* guitar • (lit); scratcher (since the player looks as though he/she is scratching the strings) • *Y joue d' la gratte;* He plays the guitar.

gratter/râcler du jambon *exp.* to play the guitar, banjo, etc. • (lit); to scratch the ham (since the guitar, banjo, etc. all have the shape of a ham hock).
ALSO: **jambonner** *v.* to play the guitar, etc. • (lit); to "ham" or play the ham.

marteler un air *exp.* • (lit); to hammer out a tune (on the piano, etc.) • *J'essaierai d'marteler un air mais j'te préviens qu'je joue pas bien;* I'll try to hammer out a tune but I'm warning you that I don't play well.

musicien *m.* **1.** flatterer • **2.** crook • **3.** beans • (lit); musician.

musico *m.* **1.** musician • **2.** flatterer • **3.** crook • **4.** beans.

pibouic *m.* clarinet.

poireau *m.* clarinet • (lit); leek (since this vegetable is long and slender like the body of a clarinet).

réglé comme du papier à musique *exp.* regular as clockwork • (lit); regular or ruled like music paper.

ritournelle *f.* musical jingle.
ALSO: *C'est toujours la même ritournelle;* It's always the same old story.

s'emmêler les paluches *exp.* to play piano badly • (lit); to tangle up the hands.
NOTE: **paluche** *f.* hand.

saxo *m.* Abbreviation of: *saxophone.*

seringue *f.* trombone • (lit); syringe (since its shape resembles that of a trombone).

soufflante *f.* trumpet • (lit); blower.

tapeur, euse *n.* third-rate pianist • (lit); one who strikes (something), striker.

taquiner l'ivoire *exp.* to tickle the ivories • (lit); to tease the ivory.

touches de piano *f.pl.* teeth • (lit); piano keys.

tourtières *f.pl.* cymbals • (lit); pie dish, baking tin (that which is used for making pies or *tourtes*).

tube *m.* hit song. *Son dernier tube, ça arrache!;* His latest hit is running off the charts!

violon *m.* prison, jail • (lit); violin • *On l'a jeté au violon;* He got thrown into the slammer.

zicmu *m.* music.
NOTE: This is a verlan (SEE: ***Street French***, *Lesson 13*, p. 130) transformation of the feminine noun *musique.*
SYNONYM: **zic** *f.*

PRACTICE USING SLANG TERMS IN MUSIC

A. Underline the correct definition of the given slang term.

1. **bœuffer:**
   a. to have a jam session   b. to sing   c. to hit a klinker

2. **canard:**
   a. song   b. klinker   c. guitar

3. **commode:**
   a. violin   b. guitar   c. piano

4. **en balancer une:**
   a. to sing   b. to play the cello   c. to play the piano

5. **marteler un air:**
   a. to hammer out a tune   b. to play the maraca   c. to sing badly

6. **seringue:**
   a. trombone   b. trumpet   c. violin

7. **soufflante:**
   a. trombone   b. trumpet   c. violin

8. **crincrin:**
   a. trombone   b. trumpet   c. violin

9. **goualer:**
   a. to tickle the ivories   b. to sing   c. to play the guitar

10. **violon:**
    a. prison   b. house   c. car

11. **musicien:**
    a. idiot   b. crook   c. policeman

12. **touches de piano:**
    a. fingers   b. toes   c. teeth

13. **tube:**
    a. hit song   b. flop   c. clarinet

14. **gratte:**
    a. violin   b. cello   c. guitar

15. **poireau:**
    a. trombone   b. saxophone   c. clarinet

– 10 –

Le Nouveau Bébé

(The New Baby)

LE NOUVEAU BÉBÉ...

DIALOGUE

Essie découvre que Debbie est récemmement dev'nue maman.

Essie: Salut, Debbie. T'as fait un **fondu**! Ben, **quoi d'neuf**?

Debbie: Mais, ça **crève les yeux**! J'ai eu un p'tit **gluant**. Y s'appelle Eric. Dans trois mois, y aura un **balai**.

Essie: Oh! C'qu'y est **trognon**! **Borgnote** ses p'tites **menottes**... et c'te **fraise** adorable! Et quel **mouchodrome**! Y a pas encore d'**plumes** sur la **cafetière**. Y a pas d'**pavé dans la cour**, non plus. Tu sais, c'est l'**portrait tout craché** d'son **dabuche**.

Debbie: Ouais, t'as raison. Michel et Eric, y z'ont l'même **tarbouif**.

Essie: Alors, comment y était, l'accouchement?

Debbie: Quelle aventure! On **s'est aboulé** à l'**hosto** avec juste **dix minutes de bon** à cause d'un **bouchon** sur la route. Pis, **pour éponger le r'tard**, Michel, y a dû conduire **à toute barde**. T'aurais dû voir comme on **prenait les virages sur les chapeaux d'roues**! J'étais **blanche comme un cachet d'aspirine**. Et pour comble d'malheur, y a failli **s'faire coffrer**. Heureusement qu'le **maton**, y a vu qu'j'étais **grosse à pleine ceinture** et nous a laissé **décamper**. A part ça, **tout s'est passé comme une lettre à la poste**.

Essie: J'parie qu'Michel, y **faisait les cent pas** dans la salle d'attente.

Debbie: Ah, ouais! Y avait une **peur bleue** que j'fasse un **doublé**!

THE NEW BABY...

DIALOGUE

Essie finds out that Debbie has recently become a mother.

Essie: Hi, Debbie. You've dropped out of sight! So, what's new?

Debbie: It's staring you in the face! I had a little baby. His name is Eric. In three months, he'll be a year old.

Essie: Oh! Is he ever cute! Get a load of his tiny hands... and that adorable little face! And what a chrome dome! He doesn't have a single hair on his head. He doesn't have any teeth, either. You know, he's the spittin' image of his father.

Debbie: Yeah, you're right. Michel and Eric have the same nose.

Essie: So, how did labor go?

Debbie: What an adventure! We finally made it to the hospital with just ten minutes to spare because of a traffic jam on the road. Then, in order to make up for lost time, Michel had to put the pedal to the metal. You should have seen us screeching around turns! I was white as a ghost. And to make matters worse, he almost got himself arrested. Fortunately, the cop saw that I was going to give birth any second and let us get out of there fast. Aside from that, everything went smooth as silk.

Essie: I bet Michel was pacing around in the waiting room.

Debbie: I'll say! He was scared out of his mind that I'd have twins!

VOCABULARY

à toute barde *adv.* very quickly. *J'ai couru à toute barde pour n'pas être en r'tard;* I ran like a maniac in order not to be late.
SYNONYM: **à toute pompe** *adv.*

abouler (s') *v.* to arrive, to show up, to come along • (lit); to hand over oneself • *Y s'est aboulé en r'tard;* He showed up late • *Aboule-toi!;* Come on!
NOTE: **abouler** *v.* to hand over. *Aboule-moi ça!;* Hand it over!
SYNONYM: **se pointer** *v.* • (lit); to point oneself • *E s'est pointée chez moi à midi;* She showed up at my house at noon.

balai *m.* year • (lit); broom • *Ça fait deux balais qu'on s'connaît;* We've known each other for two years.
SYNONYM: **pige / pigette** *f.*

blanc(he) comme un cachet d'aspirine (être) *exp.* to be white as a ghost • (lit); to be white as an aspirin tablet.

borgnoter *v.* to look. *Borgnote un peu c'te chemise!;* Get a load of that shirt!
NOTE: This comes from the adjective *borgne* meaning "blind in one eye."

bouchon *m.* traffic jam • (lit); stopper of wine bottle which prohibits any liquid (or in this case, cars) from getting through • *J'm'excuse d'être en r'tard mais y'avait un bouchon sur l'autoroute;* I'm sorry to be late but there was a tie-up on the freeway.

ça passe comme une lettre à la poste *exp.* Said of anything that is easy to do • (lit); to go through like a letter in the post office.
SYNONYM: **ça va comme sur des roulettes** *exp.* • (lit); it's going (smoothly) as if it were on rollers.

cafetière *f.* head • (lit); coffeepot • *J'ai mal à la cafetière!;* I've got such a headache!
SYNONYM: **caillou** *m.* • (lit); pebble.

cent pas (faire les) *exp.* to pace • (lit); to do the one hundred steps • *Arrête d'faire les cent pas!;* Stop pacing!

coffrer (se faire) *v.* to get arrested • (lit); to get oneself put into a safe.
NOTE: **coffre** *m.* prison • (lit); safe.
SYNONYM: **se faire épingler** *v.* • (lit); to get oneself pinned.

crever les yeux *exp.* to be under one's nose • (lit); to be killing one's eyes • *Mais, ça crève les yeux!;* It's right under your nose!
SYNONYM: **sauter aux yeux** *exp.* • (lit); to jump to the eyes • *Mais, ça saute aux yeux!;* It's jumping right at you!

dabuche *m.* father. *Y est gentil, ton dabuche;* Your dad's a nice guy.
NOTE: The slang suffix *-uche* was added to the slang masculine noun *dab* to further intensify its slang connotation.
SYNONYM: **vieux** *m.* • (lit); old man.
ANTONYM: **vieille** *f.* mother • (lit); old lady.

décamper *v*. to leave quickly, to clear out • (lit); to decamp • *Les flics! On décampe!;* The cops! Let's scram!
SYNONYM: **prendre la tangente** *exp*. • (lit); to take the tangent (and slip away quickly).
ANTONYM: **se pointer** *v*. to show up • (lit); to point oneself.

dix minutes de bon (avec) *exp*. with ten minutes to spare • (lit); with ten minutes that are (still) good • *J' suis arrivé avec 5, 10, 15 minutes de bon!;* I made it with 5, 10, 15 minutes to spare.

doublé (faire un) *m*. to have twins • (lit); to do a double.

éponger le retard *exp*. to make up for lost time • (lit); to sponge up the delay.

fondu (faire un) *m*. to drop out of the picture, to fade away • (lit); to do a dissolve (as in the movie industry).

fraise *f*. face • (lit); strawberry.
SYNONYM: **citron** *m*. **1.** face • **2.** head • (lit); lemon.

gluant *m*. baby • (lit); sticky, gummy (since a baby is always stuck to its mother's breast).
SYNONYM: **criard** *m*. • (lit); screamer.

grosse à pleine ceinture (être) *exp*. to be in an advanced state of pregnancy • (lit); to be fat to the point of filling an entire belt (on its last notch).

hosto *m*. Abbreviation of: *hôpital* meaning "hospital."
SEE: *Unit Three - Popular Abbreviations*, p. 217.

maton *m*. policeman, cop • (lit); looker.
NOTE: This comes from the verb *mater* meaning "to look carefully."
SYNONYM: **flic** *m*.

menottes *f.pl.* child's little hands • (lit); handcuffs.
NOTE: Other words used in a child's language are: **lolo** *m*. milk / **peton** *m*. foot / **quenotte** *f*. tooth.

mouchodrome *m*. bald head • (lit); a launching pad for flies • Also seen as: **piste d'envol pour mouches** *f*. • (lit); launching pad for flies.
SYNONYM: **un genou** *m*. • (lit); a knee.

pavé dans la cour (n'avoir plus de) *exp*. to be toothless • (lit); to have no more pavement in the courtyard • *Y a pu d' pavé dans la cours, c' ui-là;* That guy doesn't have a single tooth in his mouth.

peur bleue *f*. intense fear • (lit); blue fear.
SYNONYM: **la trouille** *f*. *J' avais la trouille, moi;* I was scared shitless.

plumes *f.pl.* hair • (lit); feathers • *Elle a pleine d' plumes, c' te fille-là;* That girl's got piles of hair.
SYNONYM: **tignasse** *f*.

portrait tout craché (c'est le) *m.* the spittin' image • (lit); the portrait completely spit
• *C'est l'portrait tout craché d'son père / C'est son père tout craché;* He's the spittin'
image of his father.

pour comble de malheur *exp.* to make matters worse • (lit); as an overflowing of
misfortune.
ANTONYM: **mettre du beurre dans les épinards** *exp.* to make matters easier • (lit);
to put butter in the spinach • *Ça mettra du beurre dans les épinards;* That'll make it
easier for me.

prendre les virages sur les chapeaux de roues *exp.* to screech around bends (in the
road) • (lit); to take bends on the hats of the wheels.

quoi de neuf? *exp.* • (lit); what's new?
SYNONYM: **qu'est-ce qu'il y a de nouveau?** *exp.*

tarbouif *m.* nose, honker, "schnozzola."
SYNONYM: **tarrin** *m.*

trognon *n. & adj.* sweet, cute • *n. Qu'y est mignon, ce p'tit trognon;* This little sweetheart is so cute • *adj. Y est trognon, ce p'tit;* This little boy is cute.

PRACTICE THE VOCABULARY

[Answers to Lesson 10, p. 136]

A. Write the letter of the word(s) that best complete(s) the sentence.

1. Y s'est ____ chez moi à midi .
   a. **épongé**   b. **aboulé**   c. **fondu**

2. J'avais une peur ____ qu'y pleuve le jour d'mon mariage.
   a. **orange**   b. **rouge**   c. **bleue**

3. Faut ____ not'retard.
   a. **essuyer**   b. **salir**   c. **éponger**

4. J'ai couru ____ pour n'pas être en r'tard.
   a. **à pleine ceinture**   b. **à toute barde**   c. **un doublé**

5. Demain, j'aurai 21 ____ .
   a. **balais**   b. **dabuches**   c. **trognons**

6. J'avais tellement peur qu'j'étais blanc comme un ____ .
   a. **cachet d'aspirine**   b. **mouchodrome**   c. **tarbouif**

7. C'est l' ____ d'sa mère.
   a. **portrait tout craché**   b. **maton**   c. **bouchon**

8. On est en r'tard. Faut ____ tout d'suite!

   a. **crever les yeux**   b. **borgnoter**   c. **décamper**

9. Y en était tellement nerveux qu'y faisait les ____ pas pendant deux heures.

   a. **dix**   b. **cent**   c. **mille**

10. Y a pas d'cheveux sur la cafetière du tout! Mais quel ____ !

   a. **tarbouif**   b. **trognon**   c. **mouchodrome**

11. E prend toujours les virages sur les ____ .

   a. **plumes**   b. **menottes**   c. **chapeaux d'roues**

12. Y a pu d' _____ sur la cafetière.

   a. **bouchons**   b. **plumes**   c. **balais**

B. Match the English with the French.

☐ 1. She's due any moment.   A. **Elle a fait un doublé.**

☐ 2. Look at that sunset.   B. **Ça crève les yeux.**

☐ 3. What a traffic jam!   C. **Elle a fait un fondu.**

☐ 4. I have a headache.   D. **Elle a une jolie fraise.**

☐ 5. It's right under your nose.   E. **Borgnote c'coucher d'soleil.**

☐ 6. I had two minutes to spare.   F. **J'avais deux minutes de bon.**

☐ 7. She had twins.   G. **C'est ça ton nouveau gluant?**

☐ 8. She faded out of the picture. H. **Elle est grosse à pleine ceinture.**

☐ 9. She has a pretty face.   I. **J'ai mal à la cafetière.**

☐ 10. Is that your new baby?   J. **Quel bouchon!**

☐ 11. Your father is handsome.   K. **Y a un tarbouif gigantesque.**

☐ 12. He has a huge nose.   L. **Y est beau, ton dabuche.**

C. Complete the following sentences by using the word list below.

coffrer	comble	neuf
trognon	hosto	maton
menottes	pavé	doublé
aboulé	lettre à la poste	tarbouif

1. Elle a pas d' _____ dans la cour.

2. Tu t'es _____ sur l'clou.

3. Quel grand _____ qu'il a!

4. Ce bébé, y a d'petites _____ .

5. T'as deux bébés? J'savais pas qu't'as fait un _____ .

6. Alors, quoi d' _____ ?

7. Y s'est fait _____ par les flics.

8. Y est _____ , c't'enfant.

9. Le malade, y a passé trois jours à l' _____ .

10. Y est _____ , ton père? C't'un travail dang'reux, ça.

11. Et pour _____ d'malheur, le patron, y m'a mis à la porte!

12. Ça passe comme une _____ .

INSIDE INFO: *SLANG TERMS FOR PLAYING CARDS*

Any foreigner who has a good working knowledge of standard French slang is bound to raise an eyebrow or two upon sitting down with other avid card players and discovering that there is yet another slang that must be covered.

This would be just as confusing for a student of English hearing for the first time expressions like: *Hit me, I fold, pair of deuces, card shark, to bust, etc.* Thanks to the following list, should one of the players at the table say he's going to "stand by the window," you'll know he's planning to take in the "view" of your hand!

avoir la matraque *exp.* to hold a winning hand • (lit); to have the bludgeon or club.
NOTE: *avoir la matraque* refers to a hand of kings since they are the face cards that hold bludgeons.

barbichonner *v.* to win at cards.
NOTE: The verb *barbichonner* comes from the feminine noun *barbiche* meaning "small beard" or "goatee" and refers to a hand of kings since they all wear beards.

bauches *f.pl.* playing cards.

brêmes *f.pl.* playing cards • (lit); breams.
NOTE (1): A bream is a fish that is flat like a playing card.
NOTE (2): **maquiller les brêmes** *exp.* to mark cards • (lit); to put makeup on the breams (or cards).

carré *m.* four of a kind • (lit); a square • *un carré de valets;* four jacks.

carton *m.* playing card • (lit); cardboard • *Battre les cartons;* To shuffle the cards.

cartouse *f.* card.
NOTE: The slang suffix *-ouse* was used to create a slang word out of the feminine noun *carte* meaning "card."

chpile *m.* a hand (of cards) • (lit); play (from German) • *Avoir beau chpile;* To have a good hand at cards.

cornanche *f.* marked playing card • (lit); a horn.

courrier *m.* jack • (lit); courier, messenger.

faire la barbe *exp.* to win at cards (by having kings in one's hand) • (lit); to make the beard.
NOTE: This expression refers to a hand of kings since they all wear beards.

faire le mort *exp.* to play dummy, to have a poker face • (lit); to play dead.

faire valser la dame de pique *exp.* to enjoy playing cards • (lit); to make the queen of diamonds dance.

femme *f.* queen • (lit); the woman.

flamber *m.* to play cards • (lit); to burn (or get hot at playing cards).

flambeur *m.* card player • (lit); the burner (one who is hot at playing cards).

les barbus *m.pl.* the four king cards • (lit); the bearded ones.

les papiers *m.pl.* playing cards • (lit); the papers.

les puces *f.pl.* the three aces • (lit); the fleas.

les putes *f.pl.* the queen cards • (lit); the whores.

les quatre papas *exp.* the four kings • (lit); the four dads.

lessive *f.* heavy loss (at cards, etc.) • (lit); washing • *Je m' suis fait lessiver au poker;* I got cleaned out during poker.

lorgne *f.* ace.
NOTE: This comes from the verb *lorgner* meaning "to make eyes at, to ogle, to leer" since it is the ace that everyone has his eye on.

misti *m.* jack of clubs.

mouiller *v.* to bet • (lit); to make wet.

niçois(e) (être) *adj.* not to increase one's stake, to stand • (lit); to be a native of Nice.

poke *m.* Abbreviation of: *poker. Taper un poke jusqu' à l' aube;* To play poker till dawn.

requin *m.* • (lit); (card-)shark.

se mettre à la fenêtre *exp.* to try to see the opponent's cards • (lit); to place oneself at the window.

taper la carte *exp.* to play cards • (lit); to tap the card.

tourne *f.* turned-up card.
NOTE: This comes from the verb *tourner* meaning "to turn (up)."

valdingue *m.* This is a slang creation of the masculine noun *valet* meaning "jack."

PRACTICE USING SLANG TERMS WHEN PLAYING CARDS

A. Match the columns.

☐ 1. playing cards   A. **femmes, putes**

☐ 2. to hold a winning hand   B. **taper la carte**

☐ 3. to mark the cards   C. **cartons, cartouses, bauches**

☐ 4. jacks   D. **mouiller**

☐ 5. queens   E. **avoir la matraque**

☐ 6. kings   F. **courriers, valdingues**

☐ 7. four of a kind   G. **papas, barbus**

☐ 8. to bet   H. **un carré**

☐ 9. to play cards   I. **maquiller les brêmes**

ANSWERS TO LESSONS 6-10

LESSON SIX - *Rien Que Des Racontars*

Practice the Vocabulary

A.
1. quat', réveil
2. poudre, tissu
3. dessus
4. gueule
5. bouché
6. à la coule
7. peau neuve
8. carafe
9. fréquenter
10. sceau

B.
1. à trois on s'ennuie
2. tombé
3. échappe
4. dépourvu
5. étoffe
6. déclaration
7. moins
8. fous
9. coule douce
10. tissu
11. faire la grimace
12. air

C.
1. K
2. B
3. J
4. F
5. L
6. E
7. H
8. G
9. C
10. I
11. A
12. D

INSIDE INFO:

Practice Expressions That Contain Numbers

A. 1. b.   7. a
    2. c   8. a
    3. a   9. c
    4. b   10. a
    5. c   11. b
    6. a   12. c

LESSON SEVEN - *Les Nouveaux Voisins*

Practice the Vocabulary

A. 1. C   8. L   B. 1. c   9. a
    2. E   9. I   2. c   10. c
    3. F   10. N   3. a   11. b
    4. K   11. M   4. a   12. c
    5. H   12. B   5. b   13. a
    6. J   13. D   6. a   14. c
    7. A   14. G   7. b   15. b
                                 8. b

C. 1. b   7. b
    2. a   8. b
    3. a   9. b
    4. a   10. a
    5. b   11. b
    6. b   12. b

INSIDE INFO

Practice Using Slang Movie and Theater Terms

A. 1. C   7. J
    2. E   8. A
    3. H   9. K
    4. G   10. B
    5. L   11. F
    6. I   12. D

LESSON EIGHT - *L'Invité*

Practice the Vocabulary

A.
1. G
2. E
3. I
4. J
5. D
6. A
7. K
8. L
9. H
10. B
11. F
12. C

B.
1. pompon
2. essoré
3. caroubler
4. bouquet
5. porté
6. casque
7. baquer
8. l'envers
9. fesses
10. joué des badigoinces
11. mollo-mollo
12. chatouillé

C.
1. I
2. F
3. M
4. J
5. A
6. N
7. C
8. H
9. L
10. B
11. G
12. E
13. K
14. D

INSIDE INFO:

Practice Using Slang Terms of Affection

A.
1. ma bellotte
2. ma biquette
3. ma choute
4. ma chouchoute
5. ma cocotte
6. ma louloute
7. ma mimine
8. ma poulette

LESSON NINE - *Au Gymnase*

Practice the Vocabulary

A.
1. coton
2. boume
3. déphasé
4. claquer
5. vache
6. hyper
7. taper
8. parenthèses
9. rebecter
10. Vise
11. rince
12. biscottos

B.
1. a
2. b
3. b
4. a
5. a
6. b
7. a
8. b
9. b
10. b
11. a
12. a

C. 1. G   8. C
   2. M   9. K
   3. N   10. D
   4. A   11. H
   5. I   12. F
   6. B   13. E
   7. J   14. L

INSIDE INFO:

Practice Using Slang Terms in Music

A. 1. a   9. b
   2. b   10. a
   3. c   11. b
   4. a   12. c
   5. a   13. a
   6. a   14. c
   7. b   15. c
   8. c

LESSON TEN - *Le Nouveau Bébé*

Practice the Vocabulary

A. 1. b   7. a   B. 1. H   7. A
   2. c   8. c   2. E   8. C
   3. c   9. b   3. J   9. D
   4. b   10. c   4. I   10. G
   5. a   11. c   5. B   11. L
   6. a   12. b   6. F   12. K

C. 1. pavé   7. coffrer
   2. aboulé   8. trognon
   3. tarbouif   9. hosto
   4. menottes   10. maton
   5. doublé   11. comble
   6. neuf   12. lettre à la poste

INSIDE INFO:

Practice Using Slang Terms When Playing Cards

A. 1. C   6. G
    2. E   7. H
    3. I   8. D
    4. F   9. B
    5. A

REVIEW EXAM
FOR LESSONS 6-10

[Answers to Review, p. 142]

A. Underline the synonym of the word(s) in bold:

1. **fraise:**
   a. visage   b. jambe   c. bras

2. **mordre:**
   a. partir   b. arriver   c. comprendre

3. **déboisé:**
   a. fatigué   b. chauve   c. grand

4. **flubard:**
   a. téléphone   b. maison   c. voiture

5. **lanterne:**
   a. tête   b. œil   c. ventre

6. **mollo-mollo:**
   a. vite   b. doucement   c. malade

7. **fouetter:**
   a. puer   b. sentir bon   c. arriver

8. **viser:**
   a. crier   b. pleurer   c. regarder

9. **piquer une ronflette:**
   a. faire un doublé   b. faire le ménage   c. faire la popote

10. **plumes:**
   a. doigts   b. cheveux   c. pieds

11. **presto:**
   a. lentement   b. rapidement   c. largement

12. **sapes:**
   a. idiots   b. chemises   c. vêtements

13. **tire-au-flanc:**
   a. paresseux   b. idiot   c. voiture

14. **vanné:**
   a. parti   b. ivre   c. fatigué

B. Complete the following sentences by choosing the appropriate word from the list below.

rigoler	côtelettes	soupé
système	tarbouif	douce
biscottos	promenade	éponger
dabuche	craspèque	badaboum

1. T'as trouvé cents francs? Sans _____ ?

2. Mais, c'est pas dure. Ça va être une _____ .

3. Ah, la bonne vie. Je m'la coule _____ .

4. Arrête! Tu commences à m'taper sur l' _____ !

5. J'connais ta mère, mais j'connais pas ton _____ .

6. Comme on est pas arrivé à l'heure, faut _____ not'retard.

7. Jimmy Durante, y était connu pour son grand _____ .

8. T'as entendu l' _____ chez les voisins?

9. Y roule les _____ c'mec.

10. Mais pourquoi tu m'as menti encore une fois?! J'en ai _____ !

11. Je r'fuse d'entrer dans ta chambre. Elle est _____ !

12. Voilà ta mère qui arrive! Sauve-toi les _____ !

C. Match the English with the French.

☐ 1. You've made your bed, now lie in it.

    A. **C'est moi qui ai l'dessus, maintenant.**

☐ 2. It's right in front of your face.

    B. **Arrête d'faire les cent pas.**

☐ 3. There are my parents.

    C. **J'te passe un coup d'fil ce soir.**

☐ 4. I've had it with all these traffic jams.

    D. **Comme on fait son lit, on s'couche.**

☐ 5. I'll give you a call tonight.

    E. **J'dois m'cavaler.**

☐ 6. You're nitpicking.

    F. **Voilà mes croulants.**

☐ 7. I got here with one minute to spare.

    G. **Y est au bout du rouleau.**

    H. **Ça crève les yeux.**

☐ 8. I'm always the one who pays.

    I. **J'suis arrivé avec une minute de bon.**

☐ 9. Stop pacing.

☐ 10. I've got to get out of here.

    J. **J'en ai assez de tous ces bouchons.**

☐ 11. He's at death's door.

    K. **C'est toujours moi qui casque.**

☐ 12. I have the upper hand now.

    L. **Tu cherches la p'tite bête.**

D. Underline the appropriate word(s) that best complete(s) the sentence.

1. J'viens d'(**casquer, briquer, asticoter**) toute la maison.

2. Je m'suis (**coffré, caroublé, claqué**) un muscle.

3. Y s'est fait (**coller, coffrer, boumer**) par l'flic.

4. Elle est belle, c'te fille-là! Quelle (**carrosserie, baraque, cancérette**)!

5. J'ai l'coup d'(**coton, bouboule, pompe**), moi.

6. On peut entrer au (**balai, châsse, bouboule**) aujourd'hui.

7. Son père, y lui a collé une (**gargoulette, pâtée maison, fraise**).

8. Arrête de (**fouiner, esquinter, fouetter**) dans mes affaires.

9. T'as bien dormi, mon (**onion, chou, concombre**)?

10. Tu sais pas c'qui s'est passé? J'te met à la (**froide, chaude, coule**).

11. J'viens d'm'installer dans un nouveau (**lardu, maton, gourbi**).

12. On apprend pas à un vieux singe à faire la (**barraque, grimace, bouboule**).

E. Underline the correct definition of the word(s) in italics.

1. Une *lanterne* se trouve sur la:
   a. figure
   b. voiture
   c. table

2. Les *menottes* se trouve sur les:
   a. chaussures
   b. chaussettes
   c. bébés

3. Une *fraise* se trouve sur une:
   a. une chaise
   b. maison
   c. personne

4. Un *mouchodrome* se trouve sur un:
   a. avion
   b. aéroport
   c. homme chauve

5. Un *tarbouif* sur trouve sur le:
   a. visage
   b. dos
   c. pieds

6. Les *sapes* se trouvent sur une:
   a. personne
   b. voiture
   c. bouteille

7. Les *plumes* se trouvent sur la:
   a. voiture
   b. chaise
   c. tête

8. Un *dabuche* se trouve dans une:
   a. bouche
   b. envelope
   c. famille

9. Un(e) *bouboule* est une personne:
   a. maigre
   b. stupide
   c. grosse

10. La *cafetière* se trouve sur les:
    a. pieds
    b. épaules
    c. mains

ANSWERS TO REVIEW FOR LESSONS 6-10

A.
1. a
2. c
3. b
4. a
5. b
6. b
7. a
8. c
9. b
10. b
11. b
12. c
13. a
14. c

B.
1. rigoler
2. promenade
3. douce
4. système
5. dabuche
6. éponger
7. tarbouif
8. badaboum
9. biscottos
10. soupé
11. craspèque
12. côtelettes

C.
1. D
2. H
3. F
4. J
5. C
6. L
7. I
8. K
9. B
10. E
11. G
12. A

D.
1. briquer
2. claqué
3. coffrer
4. carrosserie
5. pompe
6. châsse
7. pâtée maison
8. fouiner
9. chou
10. coule
11. gourbi
12. grimace

E.
1. a
2. c
3. c
4. c
5. a
6. a
7. c
8. c
9. c
10. b

SPECIAL NOTE FROM THE AUTHOR

Some of the terms and expressions in the following unit are vulgar and/or sexual in nature. Although it is not necessary and indeed frequently inadvisable to employ such language in one's own use of slang, it is crucial to have an understanding of popular obscenities, as they pepper the daily communication of the living French language.

– 11 –

Derrière Le Volant

(Behind the Wheel)

DERRIÈRE LE VOLANT...

DIALOGUE

Jean conduit tout doucement avec son copain Marc. Tout d'un coup, Mimi leur rentre dedans.

Jean: Oh, **putain** d'**bordel** d'**merde**! T'es **siphonnée**, non?

Mimi: Tu **foutais** quoi derrière l'volant, **ordure**?!

Marc: Quelle **connasse**. E doit **avoir ses anglais**, l'**boudin**.

Mimi: J'parie qu't'es **bourré à bloc**, en plus. J'peux pas **renifler** des **couillons** comme toi! **J'en ai ras l'cul**!

Marc: Qu'è **boucle son égout**, celle-là.

Jean: Faut pas **déconner**, non?! Mais regarde c'que t'as fait d'ma **tire**!

Mimi: J'**m'en branle**! D'ailleurs, y **vaut pas un pet d'lapin**, c'te **saloperie**-là.

Jean: Oh, la vieille **garce**! E commence à m'**casser les couilles**!

NOTE: THE ABOVE IS ONLY A HYPOTHETICAL SITUATION TO ILLUSTRATE THE DIALOGUE AND IS NOT MEANT TO SUGGEST THAT DRIVERS IN FRANCE HAVE THE HABIT OF SPEAKING TO EACH OTHER IN SUCH VEHEMENT TERMS. HOWEVER, IT MUST BE MENTIONED THAT THE FRENCH ARE UNDENIABLY MORE EMOTIONAL BEHIND THE WHEEL THAN AMERICANS.

BEHIND THE WHEEL...

DIALOGUE

Jean is driving along with his friend, Marc. All of a sudden, Mimi plows right into them.

Jean: Holy shit! Are you nuts?

Mimi: What the hell were you doing behind the wheel, you jerk?!

Marc: What a bitch. That fatso must be on the rag.

Mimi: I bet you're bombed out of your mind, too. I can't stand idiots like you! I've had it!

Marc: I wish that lady would shut her trap.

Jean: Gimme a break, huh?! Look what you did to my car!

Mimi: I couldn't give a shit! Besides, that piece of crap isn't worth a damn.

Jean: That old bitch! She's really starting to get on my nerves!

VOCABULARY

avoir ses anglais *exp.* to menstruate, to have one's period, "to be on the rag" • (lit); to have one's English • *Elle doit avoir ses anglais;* She must be on the rag.
NOTE: This expression most likely comes from English history when the British were called "Red Coats."
SYNONYM: **avoir ses angliches** *exp.* The noun *Angliches* is slang for *anglais* meaning "English."

bordel *m. & expl.* • (lit); brothel, whorehouse • **1.** When followed by *de, bordel* is used to intensify the expletive that it precedes: *Merde!;* Shit! / *Bordel de merde!;* Holy shit! *Bordel de* may also be used along with other intensifiers: *Bordel de putain de...* SEE: *putain* • **2.** a "fucking" mess. *Quel bordel, c'te maison!;* This house is a fuckin' mess!
NOTE: **foutre le bordel** *exp.* (pronounced: *fout' le bordel*) to make a fucking mess SEE: *foutre.*

boucler son égout *exp.* to shut one's mouth • (lit); to shut one's sewer • *Boucle ton égout!;* Shut your trap!
NOTE (1): **boucler** *v.* to shut • (lit); to buckle or fasten.
NOTE (2): **égout** *m.* mouth, trap, kisser • (lit); sewer.
SYNONYM: *La boucle!;* Can it! • Here, *la* represents *la bouche* meaning "the mouth."

boudin *m.* **1.** fat woman • **2.** prostitute, whore • **3.** tire (of car) • **4.** penis • (lit); blood sausage.

bourré(e) (être) *adj.* to be dead drunk, ripped • (lit); to be stuffed or packed tightly (with alcohol) • *J'en ai marre! Y rentre bourré tous les soirs;* I've had it! He comes home plastered every night.
NOTE: **être bourré(e) à bloc , à zéro;** to be bombed out of one's mind / **à bloc, à zéro;** completely.
SYNONYM: **être poivré(e)** *adj.* • (lit); to be peppered.

branler *v.* **1.** *se branler;* to masturbate, to beat off. *Y s'branle;* He's beating off • **2.** *s'en branler;* not to give a damn. *J'm'en branle royalement!;* I don't give a flying fuck! • (lit); to jiggle, to shake.

casser les couilles *exp.* to annoy (s.o.) greatly • (lit); to break one's balls • *Y m'casse les couilles, c'ui-là!;* He bugs the crap out of me!
NOTE (1): **casse-couilles** *m.* an annoying person, one who bugs the crap out of others • (lit); ball-breaker.
NOTE (2): **en avoir plein les couilles** *exp.* to be fed up • (lit); to have had it up to one's balls • SEE: *ras le cul (en avoir).*
SEE: *couillon.*

connasse *f.* **1.** bitch, "cunt" • **2.** stupid woman • (lit); female genitals, cunt.
NOTE (1): The difference between definition **1.** and **2.** simply depends on the context and manner in which the word is used: *J' veux pas l'inviter. C' t'une vraie connasse!;* I don't want to invite her! She's a real cunt! / *Je l'aime bien mais c' t'une vraie connasse;* I like her but she's a real idiot.
NOTE (2): *connasse* comes from the masculine noun *con* which literally means "cunt."
NOTE (3): Also spelled *conasse.*

couillon *m. & adj.* **1.** *m.* idiot, jerk, fool. *Quel couillon, c' mec!;* This dude's a real jerk! • **2.** *adj.* silly, foolish, dumb. *Y est un peu couillon, c' ui-là;* That guy's a little stupid.
NOTE: *couillon* comes from the feminine noun *couille* which means "testicle." Perhaps it could be best compared to the American slang word "dickhead," which is used to refer to someone who is a real jerk. In French, they simply go a little bit lower.

déconner *v.* **1.** to talk absolute nonsense, to "bullshit." *T' as perdu dix livres en trois jours?! Arrête de déconner!;* You lost ten pounds in three days?! Get outta here! • **2.** to act silly and goofy. *Arrête de déconner! C' t'une cérémonie sérieuse!;* Stop goofing around! This is a serious ceremony!
NOTE (1): The verb *déconner* comes from the masculine noun *con* meaning "cunt."
NOTE (2): **Sans déconner?** *exp.* No fooling? (extremely popular).
SYNONYM: **déjanter** *v.*

foutre *v.* This is an *extremely* popular verb with many different meanings, all of which are harsh since its literal translation is "to fuck." **1.** to fuck. *Va t'faire foutre!;* Fuck you! / *Fous l' camp!;* Fuck off! • **2.** to fuck something up. *Ça marche plus! C' est tout à fait foutu!;* It won't work any more! It's totally fucked up! • *Tu l' as foutu en l'air!;* You fucked it all up (you broke it)! • **3.** to do, to make. *Qu' est-c' que tu fous là?;* What the hell are you doing there? • **4.** to put. *Fous-le sur la table;* Chuck it on the table • **5.** to give. *Fous-moi ça tout d' suite!;* Hand that over right now!
NOTE (1): **s'en foutre** *exp.* not to give a damn. *Mais, j' m' en fous d' c' y pense!;* I don't give a damn what he thinks! / *J' m' en fous comme de ma première chaussette!* (very popular expression); I give a fuck as much as I do about my first sock! • *J' m' en fous et m' en contrefous!;* I couldn't give a flying fuck!
NOTE (2): **foutre** *interj. Foutre! J' ai paumé mes clés!;* Fuck! I lost my keys!
NOTE (3): **foutrement** *adv. C' est foutrement loin!;* That's fucking far!

garce *f. & adj.* **1.** *f.* bitchy woman or girl, bitch. *C' t'une vraie garce, sa mère!;* Her mother's a real bitch! • **2.** *adj.* bitchy. *C' qu' è peut êt' garce!;* Can she ever be a bitch! ALSO: *Quelle garce de vie!;* What a bitch of a life!

merde *f. & expl.* • (lit); shit • **1.** *f.* shit. *Attention à la merde de chien!;* Watch out for the dog shit! • **2.** *expl.* shit. *Oh, merde!;* Oh, shit! • **3.** good luck. *Merde pour ton examen;* Good luck on your test • **4.** "No." *Tu vas m' aider. Oui ou merde?;* Are you going to help me? Yes or no? • **5.** *Y s'prend pas pour d' la merde;* He thinks he's hot shit • **6.** *être dans la merde;* to be in hot water • **7.** *avoir un œil qui dit merde à l' autre;* to be cross-eyed (lit); to have one eye that says shit to the other.

NOTE (1): **merder à** *v.* to screw up. *J'ai complètement merdé à l'examen;* I totally screwed up the test.

NOTE (2): **un(e) petit(e) merdeux, euse** *m. & f.* little squirt • (lit); a little shit • *J'suis obligé d'rester avec le p'tit merdeux d'ma sœur pendant qu'elle est en vacances;* I have to stay with my sister's little brat while she's on vacation.

NOTE (3): **merdique** *adj.* shitty. *Y est merdique, c'te film!;* This film is shitty!

ordure *f.* • (lit); dirt, filth, trash • This is commonly used as an expletive to refer to a thoroughly contemptible person. *Qu'est-c'que tu fous là, ordure?!;* What the hell are you doing there, you scum bag?!

pet de lapin (ne pas valoir un) *exp.* said of something worthless • (lit); not to be worth a rabbit's fart • *C'te télévision, ça vaut pas un pet d'lapin;* This television isn't worth a damn.

putain *f., expl. & adj.* **1.** *f.* whore, prostitute. *Y'en a, des putains dans c'quartier;* There sure are a lot of whores in this neighborhood • **2.** *expl.* Used to denote surprise, amazement. *Putain! J'ai jamais rien vu d'pareil!;* Wow! I've never seen anything like it! • **3.** *expl.* Also, used to signify anger, frustration. *Putain! Ça marche pas, c'te truc!;* Damn! This thing's not working!

NOTE: **putain de** *adj.* damn, fucking. *J'en ai marre d'c'te putain d'bagnole!;* I've had it with this fucking car! *Putain de* is often used in conjunction with *bordel de* to further condemn the noun that it modifies: *Cette putain de bordel de voiture!;* This goddamn fucking car!

ras le cul (en avoir) *exp.* to be fed up • (lit); to have had it up to the brim of one's ass • *J'en ai ras l'cul d'ces d'voirs!;* I've had it with this homework!

SYNONYM: **en avoir ras le bol** *exp.* to have had it up to the rim of the bowl. *J'en ai ras l'bol de lui!;* I've had it with him!

renifler *v.* • (lit); to sniff • *J'peux pas la renifler!;* I can't stand (even smelling) her!

saloperie *f.* **1.** junk, trash. *C'est d'la vraie saloperie;* That's absolute junk • **2.** dirty language, smut. *Arrête de dire des saloperies comme ça!;* Stop talking such filth! • **3.** a dirty trick. *Y m'a fait une saloperie;* He did a real rotten thing to me.

ALSO: **saloperie de** *adj.* filthy, junky, disgusting. *Quelle saloperie de temps!;* What lousy weather!

siphonné(e) (être) *adj.* to be nuts, crazy • (lit); to be siphoned (of all sanity) • *J'pense qu'y est carrément siphonné, lui!;* I think he's really out of his mind!

SYNONYM: **être cinglé(e)** *adj.*

tire *f.* car • (lit); puller • *Félicitations! J'ai entendu dire qu't'as acheté une nouvelle tire!;* Congratulations! I heard you bought a new car!

NOTE: This comes from the verb *tirer* meaning "to pull."

SYNONYM: **bagnole** *adj.* (very popular).

PRACTICE THE VOCABULARY

[Answers to Lesson 11, p. 209]

A. Underline the synonym.

1. **couillon:** a. beau b. idiot c. fatigué

2. **tire:** a. pneu b. femme c. voiture

3. **boudin:** a. chemise b. grosse femme c. voiture

4. **bourré:** a. ivre b. fatigué c. content

5. **siphonné:** a. fou b. étonné c. en retard

6. **boucler:** a. parler b. fermer c. regarder

7. **putain:** a. fenêtre b. livre c. prostitué

8. **foutre:** a. marcher b. mettre c. chanter

B. Complete the sentence by choosing the appropriate word from the list below. Make any necessary changes.

merde	égout	bordel
renifler	pet	garce
anglais	branler	couilles
déconner	cul	saloperie

1. J'm'en _____ d'c'qu'y pense!

2. Laisse-moi tranquille! Tu m'casses les _____ !

3. Arrête de _____ ! C'est pas possible c'que tu racontes.

4. J'peux pas la _____ ! E m'énerve.

5. Pourquoi t'as acheté, ça? Ça vaut pas un _____ d'lapin.

6. _____ ! J'ai oublié mon portefeuille!

7. J'en ai ras l' _____ d'ces _____ de d'voirs!

8. Ma sœur, è peut pas aller nager aujourd'hui pasqu'elle a ses _____ .

9. J'ui parle pu pasqu'y m'a fait une _____ .

10. Boucle ton _____ ! C't'un mensonge!

C. Fill in the crossword puzzle by using the word list below.

anglais	ordure	siphonné
branler	pet	tire
connasse	putain	renifler
foutre	ras	
garce	saloperie	

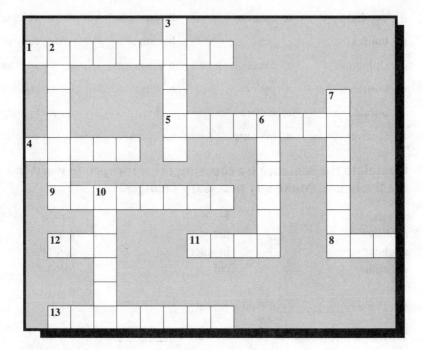

ACROSS

1 junk, dirty trick
4 bitchy woman or girl
5 *J' peux pas la _____ !*
8 *J' en ai _____ l' cul!*
9 crazy, nuts
11 car
12 *Ça vaut pas un _____ d' lapin!*
13 bitch, stupid woman

DOWN

2 woman's period
3 contemptible person
6 to fuck, to do, to make, to give
7 not to give a damn: *s' en _____*
10 whore, "wow!"

INSIDE INFO (1): *OFFENSIVE NAME-CALLING*

Certainly, one of the best ways to learn offensive name-calling is to hop a cab in Paris, sit back, and just listen. Within minutes, you will have heard some of the most "earthy" words and imaginative expressions soar out of the cabby's mouth.

Whenever I go back to Paris to visit my family, I am fortunate to be the passenger of a driver who surely gives name-calling lessons to the cabbies; a driver who makes even the most foulmouthed trucker cringe with fear – my Aunt Mimi. Since I've gotten into the habit of carrying a pen and paper with me whenever I go driving with her, over the years I've managed to pick up some very colorful and commonly used terms guaranteed to make any visitor fit right in.

A. Offensive Name-Calling: *For a man*

bordille *f.* bastard, piece of junk.

bourdille *f.* Variation of: *bordille.*

charognard *m.* bastard.

charogne *f.* Variation of: *charognard.*

con *m.* **1.** bastard (very popular) • **2.** *adj.* stupid, silly • (lit); cunt.

con(n)ard *m.* Variation of: *con.*

couillon *m.* idiot.
NOTE: This is from *couilles* meaning "testicles, balls."

fils de pute *m.* son of a bitch • (lit); son of a whore.

fumier *m.* bastard, "piece of shit" • (lit); manure.

ordure *f.* bastard • (lit); trash.

peau de vache *f.* bastard • (lit); cow skin.

pourriture *f.* bastard • (lit); rotting trash.

raclure *f.* bastard • (lit); scrapings.
NOTE: **raclure de bidet** *f.* • (lit); bidet scrapings.

salaud *m.* bastard (very popular).

saligaud *m.* Variation of: *salaud.*

salopard *m.* Variation of: *salaud.*

trou du cul *m.* • (lit); asshole.

trouduc *m.* Abbreviation of: *trou du cul.*

troufignard *m.* Variation of: *trou du cul.*

troufignon *m.* Variation of: *trou du cul.*

vache *m.* bastard • (lit); cow.

Now that you've learned some useful words for driving the streets of Paris, you are ready to create some of your own personalized insults.

Simply choose an item from each column in the following chart to form a series of handy phrases to draw upon for those unexpected traffic emergencies.

NAME-CALLING CHART: *FOR A MAN*

		bordille *f.*
		bourdille *f.*
		charognard *m.*
		charogne *f.*
		con *m.*
		con(n)ard *m.*
	sale	couillon *m.*
	(dirty)	fils de pute *m.*
espèce de	**grand(e)**	fumier *m.*
("you....")	*(big)*	ordure *f.*
putain de	**gros(se)**	peau de vache *f.*
("you fucking...")	*(fat)*	pourriture *f.*
	vieux, vieille	raclure *f.*
	(old)	salaud *m.*
		saligaud *m.*
		salopard *m.*
		trou du cul *m.*
		trouduc *m.*
		troufignard *m.*
		troufignon *m.*
		vache *f.*

EXAMPLES

Espèce de vieux salaud!   *Putain d' gros con!*

You old bastard!   You fucking fat asshole!

B. Offensive Name-Calling: *For a woman*

boude *m.* Variation of: *boudin.*

boudin *m.* ugly and fat woman
• (lit); blood sausage.

con(n)arde *f.* Variation of: *connasse.*

con(n)asse *f.* bitchy • (lit); cunt.

copaille *f.* bitch.

fumelle *f.* broad.

garce *f.* bitch.

gale *f.* bitch • (lit); mange.

grognasse *f.* bitchy woman.
NOTE: **grogner** *v.* to grumble.

limace *f.* bitch • (lit); slug.

mistonne *f.* bitch.

ordure *f.* bitch • (lit); trash.

peau de vache *f.* bitch • (lit); cow skin.

pétasse *f.* (lit); fart.

pouffiasse *f.* fat slob of a woman, "blimp."

pourriture *f.* bitch • (lit); rotting trash.

raclure *f.* bitch • (lit); scrapings. ALSO: **raclure de bidet** *f.* bidet scrapings.

rombière *f.* bitch.

saloparde *f.* Variation of: *salope.*

salope *f.* bitch (very popular).

tarderie *f.* old hag.

tartavelle *f.* ugly woman.

vache *f.* bitch • (lit); cow.

Once again, simply match up the columns and *voilà!* You're ready to get behind the wheel!

NAME-CALLING CHART: *FOR A WOMAN*

espèce de *("you...")* putain de *("you fucking...")*	sale *(dirty)* grand(e) *(big)* gros(se) *(fat)* vieille, vieux *(old)*	boude *f.* boudin *m.* con(n)arde *f.* con(n)asse *f.* copaille *f.* fumelle *f.* garce *f.* gale *f.* grognasse *f.* limace *f.* mistonne *f.* ordure *f.* peau de vache *f.* pétasse *f.* pouffiasse *f.* pourriture *f.* raclure *f.* rombière *f.* saloparde *f.* salope *f.* tarderie *f.* tartavelle *f.* vache *f.*

EXAMPLES

Espèce de vieille salope!   *Putain d' gros boudin!*
You old bitch!   You fucking fat pig!

You are now armed with the essentials of proper name-calling for any given situation. Of course, there are certainly other names that are *less* insulting and which you may find appropriate as well. The following words mean "idiot":

abruti *m.*

andouille *f.*
• (lit); sausage.

ballot *m.* • (lit); bundle.

baluchard *m.*

barjot 1. *m.* idiot
• **2.** *adj.* crazy.

bécasse *f.* stupid woman.

bêtasse *f.* stupid woman.

bourrique *f.*
• (lit); (jack)ass.

braque *m.*
• (lit); hound.

buse *f.* • (lit); buzzard.

cave *m.*

chonosof *m.*

cornichon *m.*
• (lit); pickle.

cruche *f.*
• (lit); pitcher.

cruchon *m.*
• (lit); small pitcher.

dinde *f.* • stupid woman
• (lit); turkey.

dingo 1. *m.* idiot
• **2.** *adj.* crazy.

évaporé(e) *m. & f.*

ganache *f.*

gourde *f.* • (lit); gourd.

huître *f.* dope
• (lit); oyster.

job *m.*

jobard *m.*

moule *f.* • (lit); mussel.

phénomène *m.*
• (lit); phenomenon.

pocheté(e) *m. & f.*

saucisse *f.*
• (lit); sausage.

schnock *m.*

souche *f.* • (lit); stump.

triple buse *f.* big idiot.

tourte *f.* • (lit); tart.

INSIDE INFO (2): *OBSCENE GESTURES*

Sometimes we can't seem to find just the right words that express our true feelings about a driver that just cut us off, a rude salesclerk, or an unfriendly bank teller. No problem! We simply call upon the ol' middle finger, and all our thoughts are immediately conveyed in one quick maneuver.

A. "The Finger"

The French, as well, use a gesture that is quite similar and means exactly the same thing. In English, this gesture is referred to in a few ways: "the finger," "the bird," and "to flip someone off." Oddly enough, the French don't seem to have a name for this. Perhaps the action speaks for itself.

• *With the palm of your hand facing upward, raise your middle finger at a
   90°angle. Now, with a quick and deliberate motion, lift your hand straight
   up about a foot or so.*

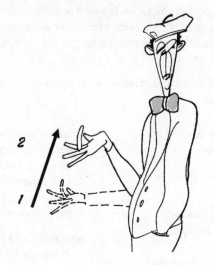

B. The "Arm of Honor" *(Le Bras d'Honneur)*

This gesture requires a little more effort than the previous one, since it involves
both arms, but there are those who feel that it's definitely worth it.

• *Clenching your fist, raise your arm as if you were saluting but stop your
   fist even with your nose. At the same time your fist stops, take your other
   hand and slap it against the bicep of the "saluting" arm.*

INSIDE INFO (3): *SLANG DRIVING TERMS*

To complete your indoctrination into the artful world of driving, let us take an in-depth look at the language of the motorist. It would be difficult to find an American driver who isn't familiar with expressions like: *to cut someone off, to floor it, to run a light, to put the pedal to the metal, to hang a left or right, to punch it, to tailgate, a set of wheels, etc.*

The following is a list of terms and expressions to help you converse with any car buff or mechanic in France:

à plat (être) *exp.* • (lit); to be flat (said of a tire).

à plein gaz *adv.* at full speed • (lit); at full gas.

accidenter *v.* **1.** to damage another car • **2.** to injure s.o. in an accident.
NOTE: This comes from the masculine noun *accident* meaning "accident."

aller aux fraises *exp.* to go off the road (by accident) • (lit); to go to the strawberries.

aller aux pâquerettes *exp.* to go off the road (by accident) • (lit); to go to the daisies.

bousculer les bornes *exp.* to speed along • (lit); to push along the kilometers.

bouzine *f.* **1.** old car • **2.** computer.

c'est de la belle mécanique *exp.* that's a nice-looking machine • (lit); it's a pretty (piece of) mechanics.

caisse *f.* car • (lit); crate.

caler *v.* to stall (a car) • (lit); to chock (up), to wedge (up).

caramboler *v.* to plough into a car • (lit); to cannon (in billiards) • *Dix voitures, è se sont carambolées sur l'autoroute;* There was a ten-car pileup on the freeway.

casserole *f.* old banger of a car • (lit); saucepan.

cerceau *m.* steering wheel • (lit); hoop.

chandelle *f.* spark plug • (lit); candle.

charrette *f.* car • (lit); cart.

chaussette *f.* tire (of car) • (lit); sock.

chignol(l)e *f.* car.

chiotte *f.* (vulgar) car • (lit); shithouse, can, bathroom.

coccinelle *f.* beetle, bug, Volkswagen • (lit); ladybird.

coller derrière *exp.* to tailgate • (lit); to stick behind.
ALSO: **coller au cul** *exp.* • (lit); to stick to the ass (of s.o.).

coucou *m.* old car, jalopy • (lit); cowslip.

couiner *v.* to squeal, screech (of brakes, tires) • (lit); to squeak, to squeal.

crayonner *v.* to accelerate, to use one's leg or *crayon*.
NOTE: This comes from the masculine noun *crayon* meaning "pencil" or "leg."

démonté(e) (être) *adj.* temporarily without a car • (lit); to be dismounted.

dépoter *v.* to drop off a passenger (said of a taxi).
NOTE: This comes from the masculine noun *dépôt* meaning "deposit."

deuche *f.* two horsepower.
NOTE: Abbreviation of: *deux cheveaux.*

embrasser un platane *exp.* to wrap one's car around a tree • (lit); to kiss a plane tree.

emplafonner *v.* to collide with another car • (lit); to go through a ceiling.

encadrer un arbre *exp.* to wrap one's car around a tree • (lit); to frame a tree.

esquinter une voiture *exp.* to run a car into the ground • (lit); to ruin a car.

faire des appels de phare à qqn. *exp.* to flash one's headlights at s.o. • (lit); to make headlight calls to s.o.

faire la figue à qqn. *exp.* to make an obscene gesture at s.o. • (lit); to make the fig at s.o.

faire un panache complet *exp.* to overturn • (lit); to do a complete panache.
NOTE: This expression comes from the days of knights who wore an ornamental tuft of feathers called a *panache*. When a knight was overturned from his horse during jousting, this was called *faire un panache complet.*

faire un tonneau *exp.* to roll over • (lit); to do a barrel.

freiner à mort *exp.* to slam on the brakes • (lit); to brake to death.

gondole *f.* taxi • (lit); gondola.

gratter *v.* to overtake or pass another car • (lit); to scratch.

griller le feu *exp.* to run a light • (lit); to grill the light.

hotte *f.* car • (lit); basket (carried on the back).

Jag *m.* Abbreviation of: *Jaguar.*

la place du mort *exp.* passenger seat • (lit); the death seat.

macaron *m.* steering wheel • (lit); macaroon.

mettre le pied sur la planche *exp.* to put the pedal to the metal • (lit); to put the foot to the board.

mob *f.* Abbreviation of: *Mobylette* meaning "motor bike."

moteur gonflé *exp.* souped up engine • (lit); swollen motor.
NOTE: **gonfler un moteur** *exp.* to soup up an engine.

motorisé(e) (être) *adj.* to have wheels • (lit); to be motorized.

moulin *m.* motor (of car) • (lit); windmill.

papillon *m.* parking ticket • (lit); butterfly.

pelures *f.pl.* tires (of racing cycle) • (lit); skins (of apple, onion, etc.).

péniche *f.* large car • (lit); canal boat, coal barge.

pissette *f.* windshield washer • (lit); the pisser.
NOTE: This comes from the verb *pisser* meaning "to piss."

poubelle *f.* old car, jalopy • (lit); trash can.

prendre l'orange bien mûre *exp.* to jump the lights • (lit); to take the rather ripe orange light (or yellow light).

prendre un virage/un tournant à la corde *exp.* to cut a corner close • (lit); to take a curve/turn like a rope.

prendre un virage sur les chapeaux de roue(s) *exp.* to screech around a bend at full speed • (lit); to take a curve on the hats of the wheels.

rajouter de la sauce *exp.* to step on it • (lit); to add sauce.
NOTE: **sauce** *f.* gasoline.

ratatouiller *v.* to misfire, to sputter • (lit); to stew.
NOTE: This comes from the feminine noun *ratatouille* meaning "stew."

rétro *m.* Abbreviation of: *rétroviseur* meaning "rear-view mirror."

rideau *m.* **1.** (of car) *tomber en rideau;* to break down • **2.** (of person) *J' suis en rideau;* I've come up against a wall, a stand still • (lit); curtain.

roulant *m.* taxi • (lit); roller.
NOTE: This comes from the verb *rouler* meaning "to roll."

roulante *f.* car (in general) • (lit); roller.
NOTE: This comes from the verb *rouler* meaning "to roll."

rouler pied au plancher *exp.* to drive with the pedal floored • (lit); to roll foot to the board.

rouler en limande *exp.* to ride crouched forward on one's bike • (lit); to roll (along) like a straight-edged ruler.

sapin *m.* taxi • (lit); coffin.

sauce *f.* gasoline • (lit); sauce.

savonnette *f.* bald tire • (lit); cake of soap.

super *m.* Abbreviation of: *supercarburant* meaning "four-star gasoline."

tac *m.* Abbreviation of: *taxi.*

taper *exp.* • (lit); to hit (a speed). *C'te bagnole, è peut taper du cent bornes en deux secs!;* This car can hit one hundred kilometers in two seconds!

taquemar *m.* taxi

tas de boue / merde / ferraille / tôle *m.* old car • (lit); pile of mud / shit / scrap iron / sheet metal.

taxi *m.* car (in general).

teuf-teuf *m.* old car, "putt-putt." NOTE: This is an onomatopoeia for the sound that an old broken-down car makes.

tenir la mer *exp.* to hold the road well • (lit); to hold the sea.

tinette *f.* old car, jalopy, broken-down vehicle.

tire *f.* car • (lit); puller. NOTE: This comes from the verb *tirer* meaning "to pull."

veau *m.* slow car, broken-down vehicle • (lit); calf.

virage à mort *exp.* dangerous bend in the road • (lit); curve of death.

PRACTICE USING SLANG DRIVING TERMS

A. Match the terms with the appropriate definition.

☐ 1. **caisse**

☐ 2. **aller aux fraises**

☐ 3. **chandelle**

☐ 4. **rajouter d'la sauce**

☐ 5. **être démonté**

☐ 6. **embrasser un platane**

☐ 7. **chaussette**

☐ 8. **faire un panache complet**

☐ 9. **griller un feu**

☐ 10. **moteur gonflé**

☐ 11. **moulin**

☐ 12. **ratatouiller**

☐ 13. **tomber en rideau**

☐ 14. **savonnette**

☐ 15. **tenir la mer**

A. souped up engine

B. bald tire

C. car

D. to overturn

E. to misfire, to sputter

F. to break down

G. to give it gas

H. to go off the road by accident

I. motor

J. tire

K. to be without a car

L. to run a light

M. spark plug

N. to wrap one's car around a tree

O. to hold the road

– 12 –

Le Dîner Habillé

(The Formal Dinner)

LE DÎNER HABILLÉ...

DIALOGUE

Gina et Michel assistent à une grande soirée. Gina crie aux hôtes qui sont parmis la foule à l'aut'côté d'la salle.

Gina:	Nancy et Georges! Merci tellement d'nous avoir invités. On s'amuse super bien!!
	(Puis, à voix basse…)
	On **s'fait chier** dans c'te **trou**.
Michel:	Et la **ragoûgnasse**, elle est **gerbosse**! J'ai failli **dégueuler mes tripes** quand j'ai goûté d'c'te **barbaque**-là!
Gina:	On aurait pas dû **s'morfaler** comme ça. **J'ai les dents du fond qui baignent**, moi.
Michel:	T'arrives à croire comment è **jacasse** sans arrêt, Nancy? C't'une vraie **mitrailleuse**, celle-là. Tiens! T'as **châssé** un peu les **écrases-merde cradocs** du gros **patapouf**-là?
Gina:	J'le connais. Y **tue les mouches à quinze pas**, c'ui-là. C'est normal qu'y **rougnotte** pasqu'y **s'décrotte** jamais! Et sa **tignasse** – berk! Et c't'un **béni-bouftou** en plus.
Michel:	Au moins, c'est pas un **ballot** comme celui à côté d'l'**asperge**-là.
Gina:	Non, mais c't'un beau **lèche-cul**, c'ui-là. Et tu sais, y m'a dit qu'y a mis une **pouliche** en **cloque** mais, à mon avis, ce sont qu'des **couillonnades**.

THE FORMAL DINNER...

DIALOGUE

Gina and Michel are attending a big party. Gina yells to the hosts who are with the crowd at the other end of the room.

Gina: Nancy and George! Thank you so much for inviting us. We're having such a great time!!

         (Then, under her breath...)

         I'm bored shitless in this place.

Michel: And the food sucks! I almost puked my guts out when I tasted that meat stuff!

Gina: We shouldn't have pigged out like that. I'm so stuffed I could practically heave.

Michel: Can you believe how Nancy just keeps blabbing nonstop? She's got a mouth like a machine gun. Hey! Did you get a load of the dirty shit-kickers of that fatso over there?

Gina: I know him. That guy's got breath that could kill from fifteen feet away. It figures he stinks cause he never bathes! And his hair – yuck! And he's a total pig, too.

Michel: At least, he's not an idiot like that guy next to that stick of a lady.

Gina: No, but he's a real kiss-ass. And you know, he told me that he knocked up some chick but in my opinion, it's just a big bunch of bull.

VOCABULARY

asperge *f.* very thin and tall person • (lit); asparagus.
ANTONYM: **bouboule** *m. & f.* fatso • SEE: *patapouf.*

ballot *m.* idiot, jerk.
NOTE: This comes from the verb *ballotter* meaning "to shake up, to toss about."
Therefore, *un ballot* might be loosely translated as "one who has had his brains
shaken around."
SYNONYM: **cave** *m.*

barbaque *f.* poor quality meat. *Comment tu veux qu'je bouffe c'te barbaque?;* How
do you expect me to eat this leathery stuff?
NOTE: *barbaque* is also used to refer to human skin, e.g., *Amène ta barbaque!;* Get
your butt over here! / **sac à barbaque** *m.* sleeping bag • (lit); meat sack.
SYNONYM: **bidoche** *f.*

béni-bouftou *m.* one who eats constantly, "a pig" • (lit); a blessed eater of everything.
NOTE: The masculine word *bouftou* is actually a contraction of the slang verb *bouffer*
meaning "to eat" and the masculine noun *tout* meaning "everything." Also spelled
béni-bouffe-tout.
SYNONYM: **bâfreur** *m.* This comes from the slang verb *bâfrer* meaning "to eat a lot."

châsser *v.* to look, to get a load at (something or someone) • (lit); to eye • *Châsse-moi
ça!;* Get a load of that!
NOTE: This comes from the masculine noun *châsse* which literally means "a frame
or mounting (of a pair of glasses)." However, in French slang, *châsse* is commonly
used to mean "eye."
SYNONYM: **zieuter** *v.* This comes from the plural masculine noun *yeux* meaning
"eyes" since *les yeux* is pronounced "les **z**'yeux." Hence the verb, *zyeux-ter* or *zieuter.*

chier (se faire) *v.* to be bored shitless • (lit); to cause oneself to shit • *Je m'fais chier
dans c'te cours!;* I'm bored shitless in this class!
SYNONYM: **s'emmerder** *v.* This comes from the feminine noun *merde* meaning
"shit." *J'm'emmerde dans c'te cours!;* I'm bored shitless in this class! • NOTE: The
verb *emmerder* is not quite as strong as the verb *chier.*
SEE: *chier (faire),* p. 194.

cloque (être en) *adj.* to be knocked up • (lit); to have a lump or swelling (from an insect
bite, etc.)
NOTE: **mettre en cloque** *exp.* to knock up (s.o.) • (lit); to put s.o. in a swollen state •
Henri, y a mis Sophie en cloque!; Henry knocked up Sophia!

couillonnades *f.pl.* nonsense, crap, bullshit. *Y m'a raconté des couillonnades;* He told
me nothing but bullshit.
NOTE: This comes from the plural feminine noun *couilles* meaning "testicles, balls."
SYNONYM: **merde** *f.* • (lit); shit • *C'est d'la merde, ça!;* That's a bunch of (bull) shit!
ALSO: **couillonnerie** *f.*

cradoc *adj.* dirty, filthy. *C' te baraque, elle est cradoc;* This house is filthy.
NOTE: There are several variations of the adjective *cradoc* which are: *cracra* / *crade* / *cradeau* (sometimes *crado*) / *cradingue* / *crados*.

décrotter (se) *v.* to clean oneself • (lit); to "un-dung" oneself • *T' es tout sale! Va te décrotter tout d' suite!;* You're all dirty! Go clean yourself off right now!
NOTE: This comes from the feminine noun *crotte* meaning "dung, droppings (from a rabbit, horse, etc.)."
SYNONYM: **se décrasser** *v.* This comes from the feminine noun *crasse* meaning "(body) dirt."

dégueuler ses tripes *exp.* to puke one's guts up • (lit); to "un-mouth" one's guts.
NOTE (1): This comes from the feminine noun *gueule* (literally meaning "the mouth of an animal") which is used in a derogatory matter to refer to the mouth of a person.
NOTE (2): **dégueulasse** *adj.* disgusting, that which makes one want to throw up. *C' est dégueulasse, c' te dîner!;* This dinner is disgusting! • SEE: *gerbosse.*
SYNONYM: **dégobiller ses tripes** *exp.*

dents du fond qui baignent (avoir les) *exp.* to be stuffed to the gills • (lit); to have back teeth that are floating.

écrases-merde *m.pl.* big shoes, "shit-kickers" • (lit); shit smashers.

gerbosse *adj.* disgusting, that which makes one throw up. *Mais, c' est gerbosse, c' te sandwich!;* This sandwich is gross!
NOTE: **gerber** *v.* to throw up.

jacasser *v.* to chatter, to talk a lot. *Y arrête pas d' jacasser!;* He doesn't stop blabbing!
NOTE (1): **jacasserie** *f.* endless chatter.
NOTE (2): **jacasseur, euse** *n.* chatterbox • SEE: *mitrailleuse.*
SYNONYM: **bavasser** *v.* This comes from the verb *baver* meaning "to drool."

lèche-cul *m.* kiss-ass • (lit); lick-ass.
NOTE: **faire du lèche-cul** *exp.* to kiss ass. *Si l' patron, y s' attend à c' que j' fasse du lèche-cul pour réussir dans c' boulot, j' rends mon tablier tout d' suite;* If the boss expects me to kiss ass in order to make it in this job, I'm throwing in the towel right now.

mitrailleuse *f.* chatterbox • (lit); machine gun • *Quelle mitrailleuse, celle-là!;* Is she ever a blabbermouth!
SYNONYM: **tapette** *f.* 1. blabbermouth • 2. gay man, "fag" • (lit); tongue.
SEE: *jacasser.*

morfaler (se) *v.* to stuff oneself with food.
NOTE: **morfale** *m.* / **marfalou** *m.* glutton, pig.
SYNONYM: **s'empiffrer** *v.* This comes from the slang masculine noun *pif* meaning "nose, schnozzola." Therefore, *s' empiffrer* might loosely be translated as "to eat until it's coming out of one's nose."

patapouf *m.* fatso (used only for men).
SYNONYM: **bouboule** *m. & f.*

pouliche *f.* young girl, chick.
    SYNONYM: **nana** *f.* (very popular).

ragoûgnasse *f.* low quality food, grub.
    SYNONYM: **graillon** *m.* • (lit); burned fat.

rougnotter *v.* to stink, to smell to high heaven. *Ça rougnotte dans c'te trou!;* It stinks
    in this place!
    SYNONYM: **schlinguer** *v.* / **schlingotter** *v.*

tignasse *f.* insulting term for "hair." *Regarde un peu sa tignasse!;* Look at that mop!
    SYNONYM: **tifs** *m.pl.* hair • NOTE: *Tifs* is a non-insulting slang synonym for *tignasse*.

trou *m.* place, dive • (lit); hole • *Ça fait une heure bien tassée qu'j't'attend dans c'te
    trou;* I've been waiting for you in this hole for a solid hour.
    SYNONYM: **bled** *m.*

tuer les mouches à quinze pas *exp.* to have bad breath • (lit); to kill flies fifteen paces
    away.
    SYNONYM: **repousser du goulot** *exp.* • (lit); to repel from the mouth.
    NOTE: **goulot** *m.* mouth, gullet.

PRACTICE THE VOCABULARY

[Answers to Lesson 12, p. 210]

A. Complete the sentence by choosing the appropriate word(s) from the list below. Make any necessary changes.

tignasse	asperge	jacasser
trou	à quinze pas	ballot
dents du fond	cradoc	décrotter
gerbosse	couillonnades	châsser

  1. Elle est mince, c't' _____ -là.

  2. Faut pas l'croire. Y t'raconte que des _____ .

  3. Tu _____ c'te fille-là? C'qu'elle est belle!

  4. Pourquoi tu voulais v'nir dîner dans c'te _____ ?

  5. Quelle halaine! Y tue les mouches _____ , c'ui-là.

  6. Y est stupide, c'te mec. Quel _____ !

  7. Elle a d'beaux yeux et un beau sourire. Mais sa _____ – n'en
     parlons pas!

8. Y m'casse les oreilles! Y arrête pas d' _____ .

9. J'ai pu faim, moi. J'ai les _____ qui baignent.

10. T'es tout sale! Va te _____ tout d'suite!

11. T'es tout _____ ! Va t'laver tout d'suite!

12. C'est _____ , c'te dîner! J'peux pu l'manger.

B. Underline the synonym.

1. **barbaque:**	a. vieille voiture	b. mauvaise viande	c. maison
2. **rougnotter:**	a. conduire	b. sentir mauvais	c. arriver
3. **en cloque:**	a. enceinte	b. fatigué	c. content
4. **patapouf:**	a. idiot	b. gros	c. individu
5. **cradoc:**	a. sale	b. propre	c. neuf
6. **pouliche:**	a. agent de police	b. voiture	c. jeune fille
7. **se morfaler:**	a. courir	b. manger	c. se taire
8. **tignasse:**	a. cheveux	b. yeux	c. jambes
9. **jacasser:**	a. sentir mauvais	b. parler beaucoup	c. partir
10. **gerbosse:**	a. dégoûtant	b. agréable	c. gentil

C. Underline the appropriate word(s) that best complete(s) the sentence.

1. Ça (**morfale, rougnotte, châsse**) dans c'te (**tignasse, ballot, trou**)!

2. J'ai (**châssé, jacassé, dégueulé**) mes tripes tellement j'étais malade.

3. Tu connais c'te (**pouliche, ragoûgnasse, barbaque**)-là?

4. Quel béni-(**ballot, barbaque, bouftou**)! Y arrête pas d'manger, c'ui-là!

5. Elle est (**pouliche, cradoc, gerbosse**), c'te (**couillonnade, lèche-cul, ragoûgnasse**)-là.

6. Mais, j'te comprends pas du tout. Qu'est-c'que tu (**jacasses, rougnottes, châsses**)?

7. Le patron, y aime bien Henri pasque c't'un beau (**ballot, lèche-cul, trou**).

8. Quel gros (**cradoc, cloque, patapouf**)!

9. J'mets toujours mes (**barbaques, bouboules, écrases-merde**) quand y pleut.

10. Méfie-toi d'lui. Y raconte que des (**écrases-merdes, mitrailleuses, couillonnades**).

INSIDE INFO: *SEXUAL SLANG TERMS*

Although many people prefer to ignore sexual slang, it regularly creeps into the very unrestricted books and movies of France.

If you are a high school or college student who hooks up with other young people in France, rest assured that you'll eventually be tested on your knowledge of these kinds of words and expressions.

Penis

andouille à col roulé *f.*
• (lit); sausage with a rolled-down collar.

anguille de calecif *f.*
• (lit); underwear eel.

arbalète *f.* • (lit); crossbow.

asperge *f.* • (lit); asparagus.

baigneur *m.* • (lit); bather.

baïonnette *f.* • (lit); bayonet.

baisette *f.*
NOTE: This comes from the slang verb *baiser* meaning "to fuck."

balayette *f.* • (lit); small broom.

baveuse *f.* • (lit); drooler.

béquille *f.* • (lit); crutch.

berloque *f.* • (lit); charm, trinket.

biroute *f.* • (lit); wind sock.

bitte *f.* (very popular)
• (lit); bitt, bollard (on ship).

boudin blanc *m.* • (lit); white blood sausage.

bout *m.* • (lit); end.

braquemard *m.*
NOTE: This comes from the verb *braquer* meaning "to aim or point a gun (at something or someone)."

canne *f.* • (lit); cane.

carabine *f.* • (lit); rifle.

Charles-le-Chauve *m.*
• (lit); Charles the Bald.

chose *f.* • (lit); thing.

cigare à moustache *m.*
• (lit); cigar with a moustache.

clarinette *f.* • (lit); clarinet.

colonne *f.* • (lit); column.

cornemuse *f.* • (lit); bagpipe.

cyclope *m.* • (lit); cyclops.

dard *m.* • (lit); javelin.

dardillon *m.* • (lit); small dart.

défonceuse *f.* • (lit); penetrator.

doigt du milieu *m.*
• (lit); middle finger.

flageolet *m.* • (lit); flageolet.

flûte *f.* • (lit); flute.

frétillante *f.* • (lit); wagger.
NOTE: This comes from
the verb *frétiller* meaning
"to wag."

frétillard *m.* • (lit); wagger.
NOTE: This comes from
the verb *frétiller* meaning
"to wag."

gaule *f.* • (lit); (long, thin) pole,
stick.

goupillon *m.* • (lit); sprinkler
(for holy water).

gourde à poils *f.* • (lit); gourd
with hairs.

gourdin *m.* • (lit); club,
bludgeon.

instrument *m.* • (lit); instrument.

jambe du milieu *f.*
• (lit); middle leg.

macaroni *m.* • (lit); macaroni.

machin *m.* • (lit); thing.

mandrin *m.* • (lit); bandit,
ruffian.

marsouin *m.* • (lit); porpoise.

morceau *m.* • (lit); morsel, piece.

nœud *m.* • (lit); knot.

os à moelle *m.* • (lit); marrow
bone.

outil *m.* • (lit); tool.

panais *m.* • (lit); parsnip.

père frappart *m.* • (lit); father
hitter.
NOTE: This comes from the
verb *frapper* meaning "to hit,
strike, knock."

petit frère *m.* • (lit); little
brother.

pine *f.*

pointe *f.* • (lit); point.

poireau *m.* • (lit); leek.

Popaul *m.* Also: *Popol.*

quéquette *f.*

queue *f.* • (lit); tail.

quille *f.* • (lit); pin.

quiquette *f.*

quiqui *m.*

sabre *m.* • (lit); saber.

tracassin *m.* • (lit); worrier.

tringle *f.* • (lit); rod.

trique *f.* • (lit); heavy stick.

troisième jambe *f.* • (lit); third
leg.

verge *f.* • (lit); rod, wand, cane.

zeb *m.*

zigouigoui *m.*

zizi *m.*

zob *m.*

zobi *m.*

Vagina

abricot *m.* • (lit); apricot.

baba *m.*

baisoir *m.* • (lit); place where
one has sex, e.g., bedroom,
brothel, etc.
NOTE: This comes from the
slang verb *baiser* meaning
"to fuck."

barbu *m.* • (lit); the bearded one.

baveux *m.* • (lit); drooler.

bénitier *m.* • (lit); (holy water)
basin.

berlingot *m.* • (lit); carton.

bijou de famille *m.*
• (lit); family jewel.

boîte à ouvrage *f.* • (lit); work box.

bonbonnière *f.*
• (lit); sweetmeat box.

bonnet à poils *m.* • (lit); hair bonnet.

bréviaire d'amour *m.*
• (lit); breviary of love.

centre *m.* • (lit); center.

chagatte *f.* • (lit); cat, "pussy."
NOTE: This is a javanais transformation of the feminine word *chatte* meaning "cat" or "pussy."
SEE: *Street French, javanais,* p. 144.

chat *m.* • (lit); cat, "pussy."

chatte *f.* • (lit); cat, "pussy."

cheminée *f.* • (lit); chimney.

cicatrice *f.* • (lit); scar.

con *m.* • (lit); cunt.

connasse *f.* • (lit); cunt.

crac *m.* • (lit); crack.

cramouille *f.*

craque *f.* • (lit); crack.

craquette *f.* • (lit); little crack.

crevasse *f.* • (lit); crevice.

étau *m.* • (lit); vice.

fente *f.* • (lit); crack, crevice, split.

figue *f.* • (lit); fig.

greffier *m.* • (lit); cat, scratcher, "pussy."
NOTE: This comes from the verb *griffer* meaning "to scratch."

grippette *f.* • (lit); pouncer.
NOTE: This comes from the verb *gripper* meaning "to seize, pounce upon."

mille-feuille *m.* • (lit); Napoleon pastry.

mimi *m.*

minet *m.* • (lit); kitty, "pussy."

minou *m.* • (lit); kitty, "pussy."

motte *f.* • (lit); mound of dirt.

moule *f.* • (lit); mussel.

nénuphar *m.* • (lit); water lily.

panier d'amour *m.* • (lit); love basket.

pâquerette *f.* • (lit); daisy.

pince *f.* • (lit); holder, gripper.

portail *m.* • (lit); portal.

tire-lire *f.* • (lit); piggy bank.

Breasts

amortisseurs *m.pl.* • (lit); shock absorbers.

ananas *m.pl.* • (lit); pineapples.

avant-postes *m.pl.*
• (lit); outposts.

avant-scènes *f.pl.* • (lit); apron (of stage).

avantages *m.pl.* • (lit); advantage.

balcon *m.* • (lit); balcony.

ballons *m.pl.* large breasts
• (lit); balloons.

blagues à tabac *f.pl.*
• (lit); tobacco pouches.

boîtes à lait *f.pl.*
• (lit); milk cans.

bossoir *m.* • (lit); bow (of ship).

devanture *f.* • (lit); front (of building, etc.).

flotteurs *m.pl.* • (lit); floaters.

globes *m.pl.* • (lit); globes, spheres.

il y a du beau monde *exp.* Said of a woman with large breasts • (lit); there are a lot of people up there.

il y a du monde au balcon *exp.* Said of a woman with large breasts • (lit); there are people on the balcony.

il y a de quoi s'amuser *exp.* Said of a woman with large breasts • (lit); there's something to have fun with.

lolos *m.pl.* • (lit); little milkers. NOTE: **lolo** *m.* Child's language for "milk."

mamelles *f.pl.* large breasts • (lit); mammae (anatomy).

mappemonde *f.* • (lit); map of the world in two hemispheres.

melons *m.pl.* large breasts • (lit); melons.

Testicles

balloches *f.pl.* • (lit); balls.

ballustrines *f.pl.* • (lit); balls.

bibelots *m.pl.* • (lit); trinkets.

bijoux de famille *m.pl.* • (lit); family jewels.

billes *f.pl.* • (lit); (small) balls.

bonbons *m.pl.* • (lit); goodies.

breloques *f.pl.* • (lit); charms, trinkets.

burettes *f.pl.* • (lit); oilcans.

burnes *f.pl.*

couilles *f.pl.* (very popular)

nénés *m.pl.*

nibards *m.pl.*

nichons *m.pl.* (very popular)

oranges *f.pl.* • (lit); oranges.

pare-chocs *m.pl.* • (lit); bumpers.

pelotes *f.pl.* • (lit); balls (of wool, string, etc.).

rebelles *f.pl.* • (lit); rebels.

roberts *m.pl.*

rondins *m.pl.* • (lit); round post, log.

roploplos *m.pl.*

rotoplots *m.pl.*

tétés *m.pl.* NOTE: This comes from the verb *téter* meaning "to suck (a mother's breast)."

tétons *m.pl.* NOTE: This comes from the verb *téter* meaning "to suck (a mother's breast)."

couillons *m.pl.* This is a masculine variation of the feminine plural noun: *couilles*.

croquignoles *f.pl.* • (lit); biscuits.

joyeuses *f.pl.* • (lit); the joyful ones, the ones that cause great joy.

noisettes *f.pl.* • (lit); hazelnuts.

noix *f.pl.* • (lit); nuts.

olives *f.pl.* • (lit); olives.

pendeloques *f.pl.* • (lit); **1.** pendants • **2.** jewels (of drop earring).

pendentifs *m.pl.*
• (lit); pendentives, "hangers."

petits oignons *m.pl.* • (lit); little onions.

précieuses *f.pl.* • (lit); precious ones.

Posterior

abat-jour *m.* • (lit); lamp shade.

arrière-boutique *m.*
• (lit); back-shop.

ballon *m.* • (lit); **1.** balloon • **2.** rubber ball.

bottom *m.* (Americanism).

cadran solaire *m.* • (lit); sundial.

contrebasse *m.* • (lit); tuba.

croupion *m.* • (lit); rump (of bird).

cul *m.* (very popular) • (lit); ass.

demi-lunes *f.pl.* • (lit); half moons.

der *m.* Abbreviation of: *derrière* meaning "backside."

derche *m.* Slang variation of: *derrière* meaning "backside."

derge *m.* Slang variation of: *derrière* meaning "backside."

derjeot *m.* Slang variation of: *derrière* meaning "backside."

deux frangines *f.pl.* • (lit); two sisters.

discret *m.* • (lit); the discreet one.

disque *m.* • (lit); record, disc.

faubourg *m.* • (lit); suburb, outlying part (of town).

fiacre *m.* • (lit); cab.

fion *m.* • (lit); end or finish (of an article).

rognons *m.pl.* • (lit); kidneys.

rouleaux *m.pl.* • (lit); rollers.

roustons *m.pl.*

valseuses *f.pl.* • (lit); waltzers.

fouettard *m.* • (lit); spanker. NOTE: This comes from the verb *fouetter* meaning "to spank."

joues *f.pl.* • (lit); cheeks.

jumelles *f.pl.* • (lit); (female) twins.

lune *f.pl.* • (lit); moon.

médaillon *m.* • (lit); medallion.

meules *f.pl.* • (lit); stacks, piles (of hay, etc.).

miches *f.pl.* • (lit); loaves.

montre *f.pl.* • (lit); watch.

moutardier *m.* • (lit); mustard pot.

n'a qu'un œil *m.* • (lit); only one eye.

noix *f.* • (lit); nut.

pains au lait *m.pl.* • (lit); white breads.

panier à crottes *m.* • (lit); shit basket.

panier *m.* • (lit); basket.

pastèque *f.* • (lit); watermelon.

pendule *f.* • (lit); **1.** pendulum • **2.** clock.

père fouettard *m.* • (lit); father spanker. NOTE: This comes from the verb *fouetter* meaning "to spank."

petits pains *m.pl.* • (lit); little
rolls.

pétoulet *m.* • (lit); farter.
NOTE: This comes from the
verb *péter* meaning "to fart."

pétrus *m.* • (lit); farter.
NOTE: This comes from the
verb *péter* meaning "to fart."

pont arrière *m.* • (lit); rearaxle.

postère *m.* Abbreviation of:
postérieur meaning
"posterior, buttocks."

pot à crottes *m.* • (lit); shit pot.

salle de danse *f.* • (lit); dance
hall.

soufflet *m.* • (lit); whistle.

tambour *m.* • (lit); drum.

train *m.* • (lit); train.
ALSO: **arrière-train** *m.*
• (lit); caboose.

valseur *m.* • (lit); waltzer.

vase *m.* • (lit); vessel, receptacle.

To Have an Erection

air (l'avoir en l') *exp.* • (lit); to
have it in the air.

arquer *v.* • (lit); to bend.

balle dans le canon (avoir une)
exp. • (lit); to have a ball in
the cannon.

bandaison (avoir une) *f.*
• (lit); to have a boner.
SEE: *bander.*

bander *v.* • (lit); to tighten.

bandocher *m.* Slang variation
of: *bander.*

bâton (avoir le) *m.* • (lit); to
have the club.

canne (avoir la) *exp.* • (lit); to
have the cane.

dure (l'avoir) *exp.* • (lit); to
have it hard.

garde-à-vous (être au) *exp.*
• (lit); to be at attention.

gaule (avoir la) *f.* • (lit); to have
the pole.

goder *v.* • (lit); to pucker
(of trousers).

gourdin (avoir le) *m.* • (lit); to
have the club or bludgeon.

lever *v.* • (lit); to raise.

manche (avoir le) *m.* • (lit); to
have the sleeve.

marquer midi *exp.* • (lit); to be
hitting straight up at noon.

os (avoir l') *m.* • (lit); to have
the bone.

**porte-manteau dans le
pantalon (avoir un)** *exp.*
• (lit); to have a coatrack in
the pants.

redresser *v.* • (lit); to set
(something) upright again,
to reerect.

rouleau (avoir le) *m.* • (lit); to
have the roller.

tendre pour *exp.* • (lit); to
tighten for (s.o.).

tringle (avoir la) *f.* • (lit); to
have the rod.

triqué(e) (être) *adj.* • (lit); to be
"sticked."
SEE: *avoir la trique.*

trique (avoir la) *f.* • (lit); to
have the heavy stick.
SEE: *être triqué(e)*

To Masturbate

achever à la manivelle (s') *exp.*
• (lit); to reach completion of
the pedal crank.

agacer le sous-préfet *exp.*
• (lit); to excite the subprefect.

agiter le poireau (s') *exp.*
• (lit); to agitate the leek.

allonger la couenne (s') *exp.*
• (lit); to lengthen one's skin.
NOTE: **couenne** *f.* skin.

allonger le macaroni (s') *exp.*
• (lit); to lengthen one's
macaroni.

allonger (se l') *exp.* • (lit); to
lenghten it.

amuser tout seul (s') *exp.*
• (lit); to have fun alone.

astiquer (s') *v.* • (lit); to polish
oneself.

astiquer la baguette (s') *exp.*
• (lit); to polish one's baguette.

astiquer le fourniment (s') *exp.*
• (lit); to polish one's
equipment.

battre une (s'en) *exp.* • (lit); to
beat one.

branler (se) *v.* (very popular)
• (lit); to shake oneself.

chatouiller le poireau (se) *exp.*
• (lit); to tickle one's leek.

cinq contre un (faire) *exp.*
• (lit); to do five against one.

douce (se faire une) *exp.*
• (lit); to do oneself a sweet
thing.

écrémer (se faire) *exp.* • (lit); to
make oneself cream.

épouser la veuve Poignet *exp.*
• (lit); to marry the Widow
Wrist.

étrangler Popaul *exp.* • (lit); to
strangle Popaul.
NOTE: Also spelled *Popol.*

**faire sauter la cervelle à
Charles-le-Chauve** *exp.*
• (lit); to blow out the brains
of Charles the Bald.

fréquenter (se) *v.* • (lit); to
frequent oneself.

glouglouter le poireau (faire)
exp. • (lit); to make one's
leek gurgle.

gonfler son andouille *exp.*
• (lit); to swell one's sausage.

griffer (se) *v.* • (lit); to scratch
oneself.

grimper au mât de cocagne
exp. • (lit); to climb up the
greasy pole.

mettre la main à la pâte *exp.*
• (lit); to put the hand to
the dough.

mousser le créateur (se faire)
exp. • (lit); to make one's
creator foam.

palucher (se) *v.* • (lit); to give
oneself a hand job.
NOTE: **paluche** *f.* hand.

pogne (se faire une) *exp.*
  • (lit); to give oneself a
  hand job.
  NOTE: **pogne** *f.* hand.

pogner (se) *v.* • (lit); to have
  oneself a hand job.
  NOTE: **pogne** *f.* hand.

reluire (se faire) *exp.* • (lit); to
  make oneself glisten.

secouer le bonhomme (se) *exp.*
  • (lit); to shake one's
  good-natured man.

soulager (se) *v.* • (lit); to relieve
  oneself.

taper sur l'os (se) *exp.* • (lit); to
  tap on one's bone.

taper sur la colonne (se) *exp.*
  • (lit); to tap on one's column.

taper une (s'en) *exp.* • (lit); to
  treat oneself to one.

touche (se faire une) *exp.*
  • (lit); to give oneself a touch.

toucher (se) *v.* • (lit); to touch
  oneself.

tripoter (se) *v.* • (lit); to play
  around with oneself.

tutoyer (se) *v.* • (lit); to be on
  familiar terms with oneself.

venir aux mains (en) *exp.*
  • (lit); to end up taking it out
  with the hands (as in a fight).

To Perform Fellatio

allonger (se le faire) *exp.*
  • (lit); to get it laid out.

asperge (faire un) *exp.* • (lit); to
  do an asparagus.

brouter la tige *exp.* • (lit); to
  graze the stem.

croquer (se faire) *exp.* • (lit); to
  get oneself eaten or munched.

dents (se laver les) *exp.*
  • (lit); to wash one's teeth.

dévorer *v.* • (lit); to devour.

manger *v.* • (lit); to eat.

pipe (faire une) *exp.* • (lit); to
  do a pipe.

pomper *v.* • (lit); to pump.

pompier (faire un) *exp.*
  • (lit); to do (like) a fireman
  and pump (water).

pomplard (faire un) *exp.*
  Variation of: *faire un*
  pompier.
  NOTE: **pomplard** *m.* fireman.

ronger l'os *exp.* • (lit); to gnaw
  at the bone.

souffler dans la canne *exp.*
  • (lit); to blow in the cane.

souffler dans le mirliton *exp.*
  • (lit); to blow in the toy flute.

sucer *v.* • (lit); to suck.

tailler une plume *exp.* • (lit); to
  trim a pen.

tailler une pipe *exp.* (very
  popular) • (lit); to trim a pipe.

To Menstruate

affaires (avoir ses) *f.pl.*
- (lit); to have one's business.

alliés (avoir ses) *f.pl.* • (lit); to have one's relations.

anglais (avoir ses) *f.pl.* • (lit); to have one's English.

argagnasses (avoir ses) *f.pl.*

cardinales (avoir ses) *f.pl.*
- (lit); to have one's cardinals.

coquelicots (avoir ses) *m.pl.*
- (lit); to have one's red poppies.

drapeau-rouge (avoir son) *m.*
- (lit); to have one's red flag.
SEE: **pavoiser.**

époques (avoir ses) *exp.*
- (lit); to have one's epoch or era.

histoires (avoir ses) *exp.*
- (lit); to have one's stories.

marquer *v.* • (lit); to mark.

ours (avoir ses) *m.pl.* • (lit); to have one's bears.

pavoiser *v.* • (lit); to deck (house, etc.) with flags, in this case, red flags.
SEE: *avoir son drapeau-rouge.*

ramiaous (avoir ses) *m.pl.*

recevoir sa famille *exp.*
- (lit); to receive one's family.

recevoir ses cousins *exp.*
- (lit); to receive one's cousins.

repeindre sa grille en rouge *exp.* • (lit); to repaint one's grill red.

rue barrée (avoir sa) *f.*
- (lit); to have one's street closed • *Rue barrée;* No Thoroughfare.

sauce-tomate (avoir sa) *f.*
- (lit); to have one's tomato sauce.

tomates (avoir ses) *f.pl.*
- (lit); to have one's tomatoes.

trucs (avoir ses) *m.pl.* • (lit); to have one's things.

visite (avoir de la) *f.* • (lit); to have visitors.

– 13 –

Une Balade Dans le Quartier

(A Stroll in the Neighborhood)

UNE BALADE DANS LE QUARTIER...

DIALOGUE

Douglas et Martine font une balade après l'dîner.

Douglas: Y fait beau ce soir! Si on faisait une balade à la Place Pigalle?

Martine: A la place Pigalle? Pour quoi faire – regarder les **bisenesseuses** qui **font l'tapin**?! Faut pas exagérer, non! C't'un quartier pour les **macs** et les **michés**. J'veux rien à voir avec ça, moi!

Douglas: Ah, ouais, t'as raison. La dernière fois qu'j'y suis passé, tu vas pas croire c'que j'ai vu! J'suis tombé sur Etienne avec une des **fenêtrières** – une vraie **bandeuse**. J'parie qu'è peut **faire flasher** les mecs, facile.

Martine: J'parie qu'y t'aurais **foutu en l'air** s'y savait qu'tu l'as vu!

Douglais: Comme tu dis. Y était en train d'lui **rouler une pelle**! J'savais pas qu'il y allait pour **draguer**.

Martine: Bof, ça m'étonne pas tellement. Y a toujours été **chaud d'la pince**, lui.

Douglas: Mais, j'savais pas qu'y était **porté sur la bagatelle** à c'point-là!

Martine: Ah, ouais! J'espère qu'il est prudent, au moins. Avec une nana comme ça qui a **la cuisse légère**, y risque de **ramasser la chtouille** s'y **michetonne** sans **capote**.

Douglas: Non, j'suppose qu'y veut juste **mett'la louche au panier**, c'est tout. C'est bizarre – rien qu'l'idée d'aller dans un **boxif**, j'me sentirais tellement mal à l'aise que je s'rais **constipé d'l'entre-jambe**.

A STROLL IN THE NEIGHBORHOOD...

DIALOGUE

Douglas and Martine take a stroll after dinner.

Douglas: It's really a nice night out. What if we take a stroll to la Place Pigalle?

Martine: To Place Pigalle? What for – to watch the hookers walk the streets?! Get outta here! That's a neighborhood for pimps and johns. I'll have nothing to do with that!

Douglas: Oh, yeah, you're right. The last time I went by there, you won't believe what I saw! I ran into Etienne with one of the window hookers – a real pricktease. I bet she can turn guys on with no problem.

Martine: I bet he would have fuckin' killed you if he knew you saw him!

Douglas: You're not kidding. He was right in the middle of French-kissing her! I didn't know he went there to cruise.

Martine: Oh, that doesn't really surprise me. He's always been hot for women.

Douglas: But I didn't know he had sex on the brain to that degree!

Martine: Oh, yeah! At least, I hope he's careful. With a girl like that who has sex at the drop of a hat, he's liable to get a good case of the clap if he tricks without a rubber.

Douglas: No, I suppose he just wants to feel her up, that's all. It's weird – just the idea of going into a whorehouse, I'd get so nervous that I wouldn't be able to even get it up.

VOCABULARY

bandeuse *f.* pricktease • (lit); a woman who makes men get hard-ons.
NOTE: **bander** *v.* to get a hard-on • (lit); to tighten.

biseneusseuse *f.* prostitute, whore • (lit); businesswoman.

boxif *m.* brothel, whorehouse.

capote *f.* condom, rubber • (lit); bonnet.
SYNONYM: **capote anglaise** *f.* • (lit); English bonnet.

chaud de la pince (être) *exp.* to be hot for women • (lit); to be hot for a woman's vagina.
NOTE: **pince** *f.* vagina • (lit); the gripper.

constipé de l'entre-jambe (être) *exp.* to be unable to get an erection, to be unable to get it up • (lit); to have a constipated middle leg.

cuisse légère (avoir la) *exp.* to be loose, easy • (lit); to have a light thigh (that goes up at the drop of a hat).

draguer *v.* to cruise (s.o.) • (lit); to dredge (a river, etc.).
NOTE: **dragueur** *m.* skirt chaser.

fenêtrière *f.* prostitute who hangs out the window.
NOTE: This comes from the feminine noun *fenêtre* meaning "window."

flasher (faire) *exp.* to turn (s.o.) on • (lit); to make one's lights turn on.

foutre en l'air *exp.* **1.** to chuck or get rid of something. *C' te carrière d' malheur, j' l' ai foutue en l' air!;* You can take this career and shove it! • **2.** to kill, to do away with.
Y s' est foutu en l' air; He killed himself.
NOTE (1): **foutre** *v.* • (lit); "to fuck" • Therefore, *foutre en l' air* might be literally translated as "to fuck it all."
NOTE (2): **fiche(r) en l'air** *exp.* A less strong variation of: *foutre en l' air.*

mac *m.* pimp.
SYNONYM: **macquereau** *m.*

mettre la louche au panier *exp.* to feel up a girl • (lit); to put the ladle in the basket.
NOTE (1): **louche** *f.* hand • (lit); (soup)ladle.
NOTE (2): **panier** *m.* vagina • (lit); basket.

miché *m.* prostitute's client, john.

michetonner *v.* to pay for sex • (lit); to be a *miché.*

porté(e) sur la bagatelle (être) *exp.* to have sex on the brain • (lit); to be carried (away) on lovemaking.

ramasser la chtouille *exp.* to get the clap • (lit); to gather venereal disease.

rouler une pelle à qqn. *exp.* to French kiss • (lit); to roll s.o. a shovel.

tapin (faire le) *m.* to work the streets (as a prostitute).
NOTE: **tapineuse** *f.* prostitute, hooker.

PRACTICE THE VOCABULARY

[Answer to Lesson 13, p. 210]

A. Underline the appropriate word(s) that best complete(s) the sentence.

1. Jean-Pierre, y va toujours au quartier chaud pour (**bomber, griller l'feu, michetonner**).

2. Dans un (**livre, piano, boxif**), y'a des prostitués.

3. Un (**mac, patapouf, bouquin**), c'est l'souteneur d'la prostitué.

4. Si tu portes pas d'(**mac, capote, boxif**), tu risques de ramasser la (**bagnoles, chtouille, mirette**).

5. Méfie-toi d'lui! Y veut toujours mett'la louche au (**pif, bigophone, panier**).

6. C'te prostitué là-haut, c't'une (**cuisse légère, capote, fenêtrière**).

7. Le client d'une prostitué, y s'appelle un (**miché, mac, boxif**).

8. C't'une vraie (**capote, bandeuse, cuisse légère**)! E peut faire (**draguer, rouler, flasher**) les mecs, facile.

B. Fill in the blanks by choosing the appropriate word(s) from the list below.

draguer	pince	pelle
bandeuse	entre-jambe	mac
cuisses	bagatelle	capote

1. Elle est sexy, c'te fille! Quelle _____ !

2. Y est v'nu à la soirée pour _____ les nanas.

3. C'mec-là, c'est l' _____ de toutes les prostitués dans l'quartier.

4. Y est constipé d'l' _____ .

5. Une _____ , c't'un préservatif.

6. Elle a les _____ légères.

7. Y est porté sur la _____ .

8. Y est chaud d'la _____ .

9. E m'a roulé une _____ .

INSIDE INFO: *MORE SEXUAL SLANG*

Prostitute

amazone *f.* high-class prostitute.

béguineuse *f.* • (lit); a woman who causes men to have the *béguin.*
NOTE: **avoir le béguin** *exp.* to have a crush (on s.o.) / *avoir le béguin* has been replaced with *en pincer pour qqn.*

bisenesseuse *f.* • (lit); business-woman, working girl.

boudin *m.* • (lit); blood sausage.

bourrin *m.* prostitute, loose woman • (lit); horse or nag.

catin *f.*

chamelle *f.* • (lit); camel.

chèvre *f.* • (lit); goat.

crevette *f.* • (lit); shrimp.

dossière *f.* • (lit); a woman who lies on her back a lot.
NOTE: This comes from the masculine noun *dos* meaning "back."

essoreuse *f.* a prostitute who squeezes her client dry of all his money • (lit); spin dryer.

étoile filante *f.* • (lit); shooting star.

fille *f.* • (lit); girl.

frangine *f.* • (lit); sister.

frangipane *f.* Variation of: *frangine.*

gagneuse *f.* • (lit); girl who earns money.

garce *f.* • (lit); (insulting) bitch.

gonzesse *f.* • (lit); girl.

grue *f.* • (lit); a crane (which refers to a woman who causes a man's penis to lift).

guenon *f.* • (lit); long-tailed monkey, ugly woman.

julie *f.* • (lit); girlfriend.

horizontale *f.* • (lit); a horizontal (because of the position she frequently assumes).

langouste *f.* • (lit); lobster.

marcheuse *f.* a girl who walks the streets • (lit); walker.

morue *f.* • (lit); cod.

moukère *f.* • (lit); woman.

nana *f.* • (lit); girl.

pépée *f.* • (lit); girl.

persilleuse *f.*
NOTE: **persil** *m.* pubic hair • (lit); parsley.

ponette *f.* • (lit); poney.

pouffiasse *f.* low-class prostitute • (lit); woman (insulting).

poule *f.* girl • (lit); hen.

pouliche *f.* young girl • (lit); young hen.

punaise *f.* • (lit); bedbug.

putain *f.* (very popular) whore.

pute *f.* Abbreviation of: *putain.*

raccrocheuse *f.* • (lit); woman who accosts men.

racoleuse *f.* • (lit); woman who recruits or solicits men.

respectueuse *f.* • (lit); woman who is respectful.

roulure *f.* insulting term for "prostitute," whore.

sauterelle *f.* • (lit); grasshopper.
NOTE: This is actually a play on words since the verb *sauter* (literally meaning "to jump") has the slang meaning of "to jump sexually."

sœur *f.* • (lit); sister.

souris *f.* • (lit); mouse.

To Hustle

aller au turf *exp.* • (lit); to go to the turf.
SEE: *turf (faire le)*

aller aux asperges *exp.* to go to (find) some penis.
NOTE: **asperge** *f.* penis • (lit); asparagus.

arpenter le bitume *exp.*
• (lit); to survey the asphalt.

bitume (faire le) *m.* • (lit); to do the asphalt.

business (faire le) *m.* • (lit); to do business.

chasser le mâle *exp.* • (lit); to chase the male (species).

défendre (se) *v.* • (lit); to make a living.

dérouiller *v.* to get the first client of the day • (lit); to take the rust off (something).

draguer *v.* • (lit); to cruise (s.o.).

emballer *v.* • (lit); to excite (s.o.).

tapin *f.*
NOTE: **faire le tapin** *exp.* to solicit men.
SEE: *tapineuse*.

tapineuse *f.*
SEE: *tapin*.

traînée *f.* • (lit); one who loiters (on the sidewalk, etc.).
NOTE: This comes from the verb *traîner* meaning "to dawdle, to loiter."

travailleuse *f.* • (lit); working girl.

grue (faire la) *f.* • (lit); to do like a crane (and lift a man's penis).

levage (faire un) *m.* • (lit); to make a pickup.

lever un client *exp.* • (lit); to pick up a client.

macadam (faire le) *exp.*
• (lit); to do the macadam or sidewalk.

moudre (en) *v.* • (lit); to grind some.

pavé (faire le) *m.* • (lit); to do the pavement.

persil (faire son) *m.* • (lit); to do one's parsley.
NOTE: **persil** *m.* pubic hair • (lit); parsley.

persiller *v.* • SEE: *faire son persil*.

quart (faire le) *m.* • (lit); to keep watch.

raccrocher *v.* • (lit); to accost (men).
SEE: *raccroc (faire le)*.

raccroc (faire le) *m.*
SEE: *raccrocher.*

rade (faire le) *m.* • (lit); to do
the road.

retape (faire la) *f.*

retourner (en) *v.* • (lit); to turn
them over.

ruban (faire le) *m.* • (lit); to do
the road.
NOTE: **ruban** *m.* road
• (lit); ribbon.

tapin (faire le) *m.* to do the
street.
NOTE: **tapineuse** *f.* hooker,
prostitute.

tapiner *v.*
SEE: *tapin (faire le).*

tas (faire le) *m.* • (lit); to do
(a lot of) work.
NOTE: **tas** *m.* work
• (lit); heap, stack.

trottoir (faire le) *m.* • (lit); to
do the sidewalk.

turbin (faire le) *m.* • (lit); to do
hard work.
NOTE: **turbin** *m.* work, grind.

turbiner *v.* SEE: *turbin (faire le).*

turf (faire le) *m.* • (lit); to do the
turf • SEE: *turf (aller au).*

turfer *v.* •SEE: *turf (faire le).*

usiner *v.* • (lit); to work hard.

Pimp   (Note that many of the following slang synonyms
for "pimp" are, oddly, types of fish.)

alphonse *m.*

barbeau *m.*

broche *f.* • (lit); (barbecue) spit.

brochet *m.* • (lit); pike.

brocheton *m.* Variation of:
brochet.

croc *m.* • (lit); fang.

dos vert *m.* • (lit); green back.

estaffier *m.*

hareng *m.* • (lit); herring.

Jules *m.* • (lit); Julius.

Julot *m.* Diminutive of: *Jules.*

mac *m.* Abbreviation of:
macquereau.

mangeur de blanc *m.* pimp,
white slaver • (lit); eater of
white (flesh).

mangeur de brioche *m.*
• (lit); ass-eater.
NOTE: **brioche** *f.* buttocks,
"buns" • (lit); butter bread.

maquereau *m.* • (lit); mackerel.

marchand de barbaque *m.*
pimp, white slaver
• (lit); meat seller.
NOTE: **barbaque** *f.* (low
quality) meat.

marchand de bidoche *m.* pimp,
white slaver • (lit); meat
seller.
NOTE: **bidoche** *f.* (low
quality) meat.

marchand de viande *m.* pimp,
white slaver • (lit); meat
seller.

marle *m.* Abbreviation of:
marlou.

marlou *m.*

marloupin *m.* Variation of: *marlou.*

mec *m.* • (lit); guy, dude.

mecton *m.* • (lit); little guy.

merlan *m.* • (lit); whiting.

poiscaille *m.* • (lit); fish.

poiscal *m.* • (lit); fish.

poisson *m.* • (lit); fish.

proxémac *m.* Slang transformation of the masculine noun *proxénète* meaning "white slaver."

proxo *m.* Abbreviation of: *proxémac.*

sauré *m.* • (lit); smoked herring. NOTE: This comes from the adjective *saur* used in *hareng saur;* smoked herring.

sauret *m.* Variation of: *sauré.*

Condom

capote *f.* (very popular)
• (lit); bonnet.
SYNONYM: **capote anglaise** *f.*
• (lit); English bonnet.

chapeau *m.* • (lit); hat.

imper(méable) à Popol *m.*
• (lit); Popol's raincoat.
NOTE (1): **Popol** *m.* penis.
NOTE (2): Also spelled *Popaul.*

scaphandre de poche *m.*
• (lit); pocket-size diving suit.

To Ejaculate

balancer (se) *v.* • (lit); to sway and rock.

briller *v.* • (lit); to shine and glisten.

envoyer en l'air (s') *v.* • (lit); to send oneself into the air.

jouir *v.* • (lit); to enjoy.

juter *v.* (very popular) • (lit); to give off juice.

mettre les doigts de pieds en éventail *exp.* • (lit); to spread one's toes apart.

prendre son panard *exp.* to enjoy (something) greatly • (lit); to take one's foot.
NOTE: **panard** *m.* foot.

prendre son pied *exp.* to enjoy (something) greatly • (lit); to take one's foot.

rayonner *v.* • (lit); to beam, to shine, to radiate.

régaler (se) *v.* to enjoy oneself greatly.

reluire *v.* • (lit); to shine, to glisten.

vider ses burettes *exp.* • (lit); to empty one's testicles.
NOTE: **burettes** *f.pl.* testicles, balls • (lit); oilcans.

voir les anges *exp.* • (lit); to see the angels.

To Fornicate

abattre la quille *exp.* • (lit); to bring down the (bowling) pin. NOTE: **quille** *f.* penis, dick • (lit); (bowling) pin.

aiguiller *v.* to "dick" s.o. • (lit); to give the needle. NOTE: **aiguille** *f.* penis, dick • (lit); needle.

amener le petit au cirque *exp.* • (lit); to take the little one to the circus.

arracher son copeau *exp.* • (lit); to pull out one's (wood) shaving.

arracher son pavé *exp.* • (lit); to pull out one's (hard) pavement.

asperger le persil *exp.* • (lit); to put asparagus into the parsley. NOTE (1): **asperge** *f.* penis • (lit); asparagus. NOTE (2): **persil** *m.* vagina, pubic hair • (lit); parsley.

baiser *v.* to fuck.

baisouiller *v.* Slang variation of: *baiser.*

besogner *v.* • (lit); to work hard.

biter *v.* to "dick" s.o. NOTE: **bite** *f.* penis, dick.

bourre (aller à la) *f.* to screw. NOTE: **bourre** *f.* lay, screw. *C't'une bonne bourre!;* She's a good lay!

bourrer *v.* • (lit); to stuff.

bourriquer *v.* to screw like a donkey. NOTE: **bourrique** *f.* donkey, she-ass.

brosser *v.* to screw • (lit); to brush (one's penis up against a woman's vagina).

calecer *v.* to "dick" s.o., to use what is under one's shorts. NOTE: This comes from the masculine noun *caleçon* meaning "underwear."

caramboler *v.* • (lit); to push and shove.

caser *v.* • (lit); to put or stow (something) away.

casser la canne *exp.* • (lit); to break the cane. NOTE: **canne** *f.* penis, dick • (lit); cane.

chevaucher *v.* • (lit); to overlap.

coller *v.* • (lit); to stick.

coucher avec *exp.* • (lit); to sleep with.

cracher dans le bénitier *exp.* • (lit); to spit in the holy water basin. NOTE: **bénitier** *m.* vagina • (lit); holy water basin.

défoncer *v.* • (lit); to smash in (a box, etc.).

dérouiller *v.* • (lit); to rub the rust off (something).

dérouiller son petit frère *exp.* • (lit); to rub the rust off one's little brother. NOTE: **petit frère** *m.* penis, dick • (lit); little brother.

dérouiller Totor *exp.* • (lit); to rub the rust off Totor. NOTE: **Totor** *Prn.* penis, dick.

effeuiller la marguerite *exp.*
• (lit); to pluck the petals from the daisy, to play "she loves me, she loves me not."

égoïner *v.*
NOTE: This comes from the feminine noun *égoïne* meaning "handsaw."

en payer un petit coup (s') *exp.*
• (lit); to treat oneself to a little bit.

enfiler *v.* • (lit); to thread.

enfoncer (se l') *v.* • (lit); to drive it in.

enjamber *v.* • (lit); to put in one's "third leg."
NOTE: This comes from the feminine noun *troisième jambe* meaning "third leg" or "penis, dick."

envoyer en l'air (s') *exp.*
• (lit); to send oneself into the air.

faire ça *exp.* • (lit); to do it.

faire la bête à deux dos *exp.*
• (lit); to make like the beast with two backs (said of two people who are fused together during sex).

faire qqn. (se) *exp.* • (lit); to do s.o.

faire un carton *exp.* • (lit); to do some target practice.

faire une partie d'écarté *exp.*
This is a pun based on the expression *faire une partie de cartes* meaning "to play a hand of cards." However, in the above expression, the noun *cartes* has been replaced with the adjective *écarté,* meaning "spread apart" as in a woman's thighs.

faire une partie de balayette
exp. • (lit); to "play a hand of" small broom.
NOTE: **balayette** *f.* penis, dick • (lit); small broom.

faire une partie de jambes en l'air *exp.* to play a hand of "legs in the air."

farcir qqn. (se) *exp.* • (lit); to stuff oneself with s.o.

filer un coup d'arbalète *exp.*
• (lit); to give (s.o.) a shot with the crossbow.
NOTE: **arbalète** *f.* penis, dick • (lit); crossbow.

filer un coup de brosse *exp.*
• (lit); to give (s.o.) a shot of the brush.

filer un coup de sabre *exp.*
• (lit); to give (s.o.) a shot with the saber.
NOTE: **sabre** *m.* penis, dick • (lit); saber.

fourailler *v.* • (lit); to stuff.
NOTE: This is a variation of the verb *fourrer* meaning "to stuff."

fourrer *v.* • (lit); to stuff.

frotter *v.* • (lit); to rub.

goupilloner *v.* • (lit); to "dick" (s.o.).
NOTE: **goupillon** *m.* penis, dick • (lit); sprinkler (for holy water).

grimper *v.* • (lit); to climb up (on s.o.).

le faire *exp.* • (lit); to do it.

le mettre *exp.* • (lit); to put it (in).

limer *v.* • (lit); to polish.

mouiller le goupillon *exp.*
• (lit); to wet one's sprinkler.
NOTE: **goupillon** *m.* penis,
dick • (lit); sprinkler (for
holy water).

niquer *v.* • (lit); to fuck.

pinailler *v.* Variation of: *piner.*

piner *v.* • (lit); to "dick" (s.o.).
NOTE: This comes from the
feminine noun *pine* meaning
"penis, dick."

pinocher *v.* Variation of: *piner.*

planter *v.* • (lit); to plant.

pointer *v.* • (lit); to thrust, to
stab (with a sword).
NOTE: **pointe** *f.* penis, dick
• (lit); point.

pousser sa pointe *exp.* • (lit); to
push (in) one's point.
NOTE: **pointe** *f.* penis, dick
• (lit); point.

quener *v.* • (lit); to "dick" (s.o.).
NOTE: This comes from the
feminine noun *queue* which
literally means "tail" but has
taken the slang connotation of
"penis, dick."

ramer *v.* • (lit); to row.

ramoner *v.* (humorous)
• (lit); to sweep (a chimney).
NOTE: **cheminée** *f.* vagina
• (lit); chimney.

sabrer *v.* • (lit); to "dick" (s.o.).
NOTE: **sabre** *m.* penis, dick
• (lit); saber.

sauter *v.* • (lit); to jump
(one's bones).

taper (se) *v.* • (lit); to treat
oneself.

torcher *v.* • (lit); to wipe.

torpiller *v.* • (lit); to
torpedo (s.o.).

tremper son baigneur *exp.*
• (lit); to dip one's bather.
NOTE: **baigneur** *m.* penis,
dick • (lit); bather.

tremper son biscuit *exp.*
• (lit); to dip one's biscuit.

tremper son panais *exp.*
• (lit); to dip one's parsnip.
NOTE: **panais** *m.* penis, dick
• (lit); parsnip.

tringler *v.* • (lit); to "dick" (s.o.).
NOTE: This comes from the
feminine noun *tringle* which
literally means "rod" but has
taken the slang connotation
of "penis, dick."

verger *v.* • (lit); to "dick" (s.o.).
NOTE: This comes from the
feminine noun *verge* which
literally means "rod, wand,
cane" but has taken the slang
connotation of "penis, dick."

voir la feuille à l'envers *exp.* to
have sex under a tree
• (lit); to see the leaf (or
leaves) from underneath.

– 14 –

Au Métro

(In the Subway)

AU MÉTRO...

DIALOGUE

Paul et Richard, y z'attendent le train.

Paul:	Avant qu'on s'en aille, faut qu'j'**fasse pleurer mon colosse.**
Richard:	Mais, c'est **dégueu** dans ces **chiottes**-là! On dirait qu'on a **molardé** par terre. En plus, y'a jamais ni d'savon ni d'**torche-cul**. Que ça m'fait **chier**, ça! J'crois qu'tu f'rais mieux d'attend'qu'on arrive chez moi.
Paul:	Pas d'problème. Tiens! Regarde tous ces **morbacs** avec c'te bonne femme-là. Faut dire qu'y **pètent le feu**! Oh, les p'tits **emmerdeurs**!
Richard:	Ça doit êt'leur mère. Elle a pas bonne mine. On dirait qu'è va **débagouler**.
Paul:	Tu s'rais pareil, mon vieux, si t'avais une **chiée** d'enfants comme ça.
Richard:	Rien qu'd'y penser, ça m'fout la **chiasse**. J'pourrais jamais changer une couche d'bébé. Le **caca** et la **pisse**, ça m'dit pas grand' chose!

Lesson Fourteen

IN THE SUBWAY...

DIALOGUE

Paul and Richard are waiting for the train.

Paul: Before we leave, I gotta go take a leak.

Richard: But, it's gross in those bathrooms! It always looks like people have spit on the floor. Besides, there's never any soap or toilet paper in there. It really pisses me off! I think you'd be better off waiting till we get to my house.

Paul: No problem. Wow! Look at all those little brats with that lady over there. They sure are wild! Oh, what little pains in the neck!

Richard: That must be their mother. She doesn't look well. She looks like she's gonna puke.

Paul: You'd be the same, pal, if you had a shitload of kids like that.

Richard: Just thinking of it scares the crap out of me. I would never be able to change a baby's diaper. Poop and piss don't do a lot for me!

VOCABULARY

caca *m*. crap.

chiasse (avoir la) *f*. to be scared to death • (lit); **1.** to be scared shitless • **2.** to have diarrhea.
SEE: *chier*.

chiée *f*. a lot • (lit); a shitload.
SEE: *chier*.

chier (faire) *v*. to annoy greatly, to bug the shit out of s.o. • (lit); to cause to shit • *Tu m'fais chier!;* You drive me fuckin' crazy!
NOTE: **chiant(e)** *adj*. "fuckin'" annoying.
SYNONYM: **emmerder** *v*. This comes from the feminine noun *merde* meaning "shit."
Tu m'emmerdes!; You're buggin' the shit outta me! • NOTE: The verb *emmerder* is not quite as strong as the verb *chier*.
SEE: *chier (se faire)*, p. 166.

chiottes *f.pl*. bathroom • (lit); shithouse.
NOTE: This comes from the verb *chier* meaning "to shit."

débagouler *v*. to barf, to puke, to spew.

dégueu *adj*. disgusting, that which causes vomiting.
NOTE: This comes from the verb *dégueuler* meaning "to vomit, to barf."

emmerdeur *m*. annoying person, pain in the ass • (lit); one who bugs the shit out of others.
NOTE: This comes from the feminine noun *merde* meaning "shit."

molarder *v*. to spit, to hawk a loogie.
NOTE: **molard** *m*. gob of spit or phlegm, loogie.

morbac *m*. annoying little child, brat • (lit); crab(louse), pubic louse.

péter le feu *exp*. to be very energetic • (lit); to fart fire.
NOTE: **avoir la pétasse** *exp*. to be horribly frightened • (lit); to have the farts.

pisse *f*. urine • (lit); piss.

pleurer son colosse (faire) *exp*. to urinate, to take a leak • (lit); to make one's giant cry.

torche-cul *m*. toilet paper • (lit); ass-wipe.

PRACTICE THE VOCABULARY

[Answers to Lesson 14, p. 211]

A. Underline the correct definition.

1. **torche-cul:**   a. toilet paper   b. soap
2. **avoir la chiasse:**   a. to be scared "shitless"   b. to be energetic

3.	**débagouler:**	a. to urinate	b. to throw up
4.	**molarder:**	a. to spit	b. to defecate
5.	**morbac:**	a. urine, piss	b. brat
6.	**chiée:**	a. crap, turd	b. a "shitload"
7.	**péter le feu:**	a. to be energetic	b. to urinate
8.	**emmerdeur:**	a. enjoyable person	b. pain in the neck
9.	**pisse:**	a. rain	b. urine

B. Complete the crossword puzzle by using the list below.

caca	chiasse	colosse
emmerder	feu	morbac
pisse	molarder	torche

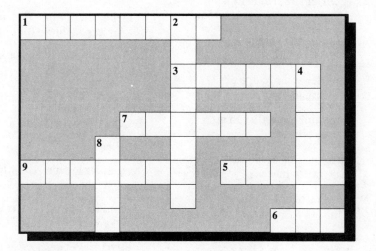

ACROSS

1. to spit
3. brat, crab(louse)
5. urine, piss
6. *péter le* _____
7. _____ - *cul*
9. *avoir la* _____ ; to be scared

DOWN

2. to annoy, to bug the shit out of s.o.
4. *faire pleurer son* _____
8. crap

INSIDE INFO: *BODILY FUNCTIONS IN SLANG*

To Urinate

aller faire sa petite commission
exp. • (lit); to go do one's
little job.

arroser les marguerites *exp.*
• (lit); to go water the daisies.

égoutter (se l') *exp.* • (lit); to
drain it.

égoutter Popol *exp.* • (lit); to
drain Popol.
NOTE (1): **Popol** *Prn.* penis,
dick.
NOTE (2): Also spelled *Popaul*.

égoutter sa sardine *exp.*
• (lit); to drain one's sardine.

égoutter son colosse *exp.*
• (lit); to drain one's giant.

égoutter son cyclope *exp.*
• (lit); to drain one's cyclops.

faire pipi *exp.* • (lit); to go
pee-pee.

faire pleurer le colosse *exp.*
• (lit); to make one's giant cry.

faire pleurer le costaud *exp.*
• (lit); to make the hefty
one cry.

faire pleurer le petit Jésus *exp.*
• (lit); to make the little
Jesus cry.

faire sa goutte *exp.* • (lit); to do
one's drop.

faire une vidange (se) *exp.*
• (lit); to do an emptying
of oneself.

glisser un fil *exp.* • (lit); to slip
(out) a thread (of urine).

jeter de la lance *exp.* • (lit); to
throw out urine.
NOTE: **lance** *f.* **1.** urine
• **2.** water.
SEE: *lancequiner*.

jeter sa goutte *exp.* • (lit); to
throw out one's drop.

lâcher l'eau *exp.* • (lit); to
release water.

lâcher l'écluse *exp.* • (lit); to
release the floodgate.

lâcher les vannes *exp.* • (lit); to
release the floodgates.

lâcher un fil *exp.* • (lit); to
release a thread (of urine).

lancecailler *v.* Slang variation
of: *lancequiner*.

lancequiner *v.* **1.** to urinate
• **2.** to rain.
SEE: *jeter de la lance*.

lisbroquer *v.*

mouiller le mur *exp.* • (lit); to
wet the wall.

mouiller une ardoise *exp.*
• (lit); to wet a slate.

ouvrir les écluses *exp.* • (lit); to
open the floodgates.

pisser *v.* • (lit); to piss.

pisser son coup *exp.* • (lit); to
piss one's shot.

renverser la vapeur *exp.*
• (lit); to turn over the steam.

tenir l'âne par la queue *exp.*
• (lit); to hold the donkey by
the tail.

To Defecate

chier *v.* • (lit); to shit.

couler un bronze *exp.* • (lit); to flow out a bronze (thing).

débloquer *v.* • (lit); to free, to unblock.

débonder *v.* • (lit); to burst forth, to gust out.

déboucher son orchestre *exp.* • (lit); to uncork one's orchestra (of farting sounds).

déposer sa pêche *exp.* • (lit); to deposit one's peach.

déposer une prune *exp.* • (lit); to deposit a plum.

faire caca *exp.* • (lit); to make caca.

faire sa grande commission *exp.* • (lit); to do one's big job.

faire ses affaires *exp.* • (lit); to do one's business.

faire ses grands besoins *exp.* • (lit); to do one's big needs.

faire son gros *exp.* • (lit); to do one's fat (job).

foirer *v.* • (lit); to have diarrhea.

fuser *v.* • (lit); to burst out.

mouler un bronze *exp.* • (lit); to mold a bronze (thing).

planter une borne *exp.* • (lit); to plant a boundary.

poser sa pêche *exp.* • (lit); to set down one's peach.

poser un rondin *exp.* • (lit); to set down a log.

poser une prune *exp.* • (lit); to set down a plum.

poser une sentinelle *exp.* • (lit); to set down a sentinel.

pousser le bouchon *exp.* • (lit); to push the cork.

(To) Fart

boule *f.* fart • (lit); ball.

cloque *m.* fart • (lit); blister.

cloquer *v.* • (lit); to blister.

déchirer la toile *exp.* • (lit); to rip the linen.

déchirer son false *exp.* • (lit); to rip one's pants.
NOTE: **false** *m.* Abbreviation of: *falzar* meaning "pants."

déchirer son froc *exp.* • (lit); to rip one's pants.
NOTE: **froc** *m.* pants.

détacher une pastille *exp.* • (lit); to detach a lozenge. SEE: *pastille.*

en écraser un *exp.* • (lit); to crush one.

en lâcher un *exp.* • (lit); to let one go.

flouser *y.*

flousse *m.* fart.

fusant *m.* • (lit); that which bursts out.

fuser *v.* • (lit); to burst out.

lâcher les gaz *exp.* • (lit); to
release the gases.

lâcher une louise *exp.* • (lit); to
release a louise.
SEE: *louise.*

lâcher une perle *exp.* • (lit); to
release a pearl.
SEE: *perle.*

lâcher une perlouse *exp.*
Variation of: *lâcher une
perle.*

louise *f.* fart

navet *m.* fart • (lit); turnip.

pastille *f.* fart • (lit); lozenge.
SEE: *détacher une pastille.*

pastoche *f.* Slang variation of:
pastille.

perle *f.* fart • (lit); pearl.

perlouse *f.* Slang variation of:
perle.

vesse *f.* silent fart, S.B.D. (silent
but deadly).

(To) Spit

glaviot *m.* spit wad, loogie.

glavioter *v.* to hawk a loogie.

gluau *m.* spit wad, loogie.

graillon *m.* spit wad, loogie.

graillonner *v.* to cough up
phlegm.

huître *f.* spit wad, loogie
• (lit); oyster.

molard *m.* spit wad, loogie.

molarder *v.* to spit, to hawk
a loogie.

postillon *m.* spit wad, loogie.

To Vomit

aller au refile *exp.*
SEE: *refiler.*

aller au renard *exp.* • (lit); to
go to the fox.

bader *v.*

débagouler *v.*

dégobiller *v.*
NOTE: This comes from the
verb *gober* meaning "to
gobble down (food, etc.)."

dégoupillonner *v.*

dégueuler *v.*
NOTE: This comes from
the feminine noun *gueule*
meaning "mouth."

évacuer le couloir *exp.* • (lit); to
evacuate the hall.

gerber *v.* • (lit); to sheave
(corn, etc.).

lâcher son goujon *exp.* • (lit); to
release one's bait.

lâcher une fusée *exp.* • (lit); to
release a rocket.

refiler *v.* • (lit); to give s.o.
something that one no longer
wants, to pawn off.

renarder *v.* Variation of: *aller
au renard.*

rendre ses comptes *exp.* • (lit);
to render one's accounts.

renvoyer la classe *exp.* • (lit); to
send back the class.

– 15 –

À la Boîte de Nuit

(At the Nightclub)

À LA BOÎTE DE NUIT...

DIALOGUE

Katherine et Adrienne, è z'ont pas d'chance en draguant les mecs.

Katherine: Tiens! Voilà Paul!

Adrienne: J'le trouve vachement beau, lui, mais y m'dit jamais salut. J'suppose qu'y s'intéresse pas à moi.

Katherine: T'as pas r'marqué qu'y fait très **chouquette**? J'parie qu'c't'un **pédé**.

Adrienne: Oh, j'en sais rien, moi. P't-êt'que c't'une **honteuse**.

Katherine: Tu crois pas qu'y est avec c'te **cuir**-là?

Adrienne: Où ça? Tu veux dire l'mec-là qui est **bien outillé**?

Katherine: Ouais! C'est sans doute son **papa gâteau**. Tu sais, on dit qu'la frangine d'Paul, c't'une **gousse**.

Adrienne: C'est du réchauffé, ça. Mais, ça fait longtemps qu'è **s'gouine** avec Sylvie.

Katherine: Remarque que Sylvie, è **marche à voile et à vapeur**.

AT THE NIGHTCLUB...

DIALOGUE

Katherine and Adrienne aren't having any luck picking up guys.

Katherine: Hey! There's Paul!

Adrienne: I think he's so handsome, but he never talks to me. I suppose he's not interested in me.

Katherine: Haven't you noticed he's a little swishy? I bet he's a fag.

Adrienne: Oh, I don't know about that. Maybe he's a closet queen.

Katherine: You don't think he's with that leather dude over there?

Adrienne: Where? You mean that guy over there who's well hung?

Katherine: Yeah! That's probably his sugar daddy. You know, they say Paul's sister is a dyke.

Adrienne: That's old news. She's been having a lesbian relationship with Sylvie for quite some time.

Katherine: Ya know, Sylvie is A.C.-D.C.

VOCABULARY

bien outillé (être) *adj.* to be well hung • (lit); to be well tooled.
  NOTE: **outil** *m.* penis, dick • (lit); tool.

chouquette *f.* effeminate, swishy. *Y fait très chouquette, lui;* He's real queeny.

cuir *m.* (especially homosexual) man who is into the leather scene, who wears leather • (lit); leather.

gouiner (se) *v.* to practice lesbianism, to make love between two women.
  NOTE: **gouine** *f.* lesbian, dyke.

gousse *f.* lesbian, dyke.
  NOTE: **se gousser** *v.* to practice lesbianism, to make love between two women.

honteuse *f.* homosexual man who has not yet come out of the closet, "closet queen" • (lit); ashamed.

marcher à voile et à vapeur *exp.* to be bisexual, to be A.C.-D.C. • (lit); to walk by sail and by steam.

papa gâteau *m.* man who takes care of a younger man or woman financially in exchange for sexual favors, sugar daddy • (lit); father cake.

pédé *m.* (very popular) pederast, fag.
  NOTE: This is an abbreviation of: *pédéraste,* which is sometimes seen as simply *P.D.* Although the noun *pédéraste* is not an insulting term, note that in its abbreviated form it becomes extremely derogatory.

PRACTICE THE VOCABULARY

[Answers to Lesson 15, p. 212]

A. Match the columns.

☐ 1. He's well hung.

☐ 2. That's his sugar daddy.

☐ 3. She's a dyke.

☐ 4. He's a fag.

☐ 5. He's a closet queen.

☐ 6. That guy's into leather.

☐ 7. He's bisexual.

☐ 8. They practice lesbianism together.

A. **Y marche à voile et à vapeur.**

B. **E s'gouinent, les deux.**

C. **Y est bien outillé.**

D. **C't'un cuir, lui.**

E. **C'est ça, son papa gâteau.**

F. **C't'un pédé.**

G. **C't'une gousse.**

H. **C't'une honteuse.**

B. Underline the word(s) that best complete(s) the sentence.

1. Y est efféminé, c'ui-là. Faut dire qu'y fait très (**gousse, bien outillé, chouquette**).

2. C't'une (**gousse, honteuse, bagnole**). Y a pas encore avoué qu'c't'un homosexuel.

3. Avec c'pantalon qu'y porte, c'est facile à voir qu'y est bien (**papa gâteau, pédé, outillé**).

4. Elle aime les garçons et les filles. Faut dire qu'è marche à (**voile, cuir, chouquette**) et à vapeur.

5. C't'une (**honteuse, chouquette, gousse**). E fréquente que les filles.

6. Regarde un peu c'qu'y porte, lui. C'est évident qu'c't'un (**plombard, papier, cuir**).

7. C't'un (**pédé, cuir, papa gâteau**). Y fréquente que les mecs.

8. Y vit avec son papa (**pédé, honteuse, gâteau**).

INSIDE INFO (1): *HOMOSEXUAL SLANG TERMS*

(To be) Homosexual

chochotte *f.* gay man who acts very effeminate.
NOTE: **chochotter** *v.* to put on airs, to act queer.

chouquette *f.* gay man who acts very effeminate, queer.

donner du rond *exp.* • (lit); to give some ass.
NOTE (1): **rond** *m.* ass • (lit); round (one).
NOTE (2): The masculine noun *rond* may be replaced by any number of synonyms for "posterior" • SEE: *Posterior,* p. 174

emmanché *m.*
NOTE: This comes from the verb *emmancher* meaning "to sodomize."

empaffé *m.*
NOTE: This comes from the verb *empaffer* meaning "to sodomize."

empalé *m.*
NOTE: This comes from the verb *empaler* meaning "to sodomize" or literally "to impale."

empapaouté *m.*
NOTE: This comes from the verb *empapouter* meaning "to sodomize."

empétardé *m.*
NOTE: This comes from the verb *empétarder* meaning "to sodomize."

emprosé *m.*
NOTE: This comes from the verb *emproser* meaning "to sodomize."

en donner *exp.* to be a passive homosexual • (lit); to give some (ass, in this case).

en être *exp.* • (lit); to be one of them.

en prendre *exp.* to be an active homosexual • (lit); to take some (ass, in this case).

encaldossé *m.*
NOTE: This comes from the verb *encaldosser* meaning "to sodomize."

enculé *m.* (very vulgar)
NOTE (1): This comes from the verb *enculer* meaning "to sodomize" or literally "to enter through the ass."
NOTE (2): **cul** *m.* ass.

enfifré *m.*
NOTE: This comes from the verb *enfifrer* meaning "to sodomize."

enfoiré *m.*
NOTE: This comes from the verb *enfoirer* meaning "to sodomize."

englandé *m.*
NOTE: This comes from the verb *englander* meaning "to sodomize."

enviandé *m.*
NOTE: This comes from the feminine noun *viande* meaning "meat."

filer du chouette *exp.* (very popular) • (lit); to give some ass.

fiotte *f.*

folle *f.* "queen."

gazier *m.* • (lit); gas man, gas fitter.

gerboise *f.* • (lit); Jerboa.

lopaille *f.*

lopart *m.*

lope *f.*

lopette *f.*

mettre sa chemise en véranda *exp.* • (lit); to put one's shirt out on the veranda.

minot *m.*

papaout *m.*
NOTE: This comes from the verb *empapouter* meaning "to sodomize."

pédé *m.* Abbreviation of: *pédéraste.*

pédéro *m.* Variation of: *pédé.*

pédoc *m.* Variation of: *pédé.*

pédoque *m.* Variation of: *pédé.*

plongeuse *f.* • (lit); diver.

pointeur *m.* one who likes a man's penis.
NOTE: **pointe** *f.* penis, dick • (lit); point.

poulette *f.* • (lit); young hen.

prendre du petit *exp.* (very popular) • (lit); to take some ass.

qui est de la famille tuyau de poêle *exp.* • (lit); who is in the family of homosexuals.
NOTE: **tuyau de poêle** *m.* homosexual world • (lit); stovepipe.

rivette *f.*
NOTE: This comes from the verb *riveter* meaning "to rivet."

sœur *f.* • (lit); sister.

tante *f.* (very popular) extremely effeminate man • (lit); aunt.

tantinette *f.* Variation of: *tante*.

tantouse *f.* Variation of: *tante*.

tantouze *f.* Variation of: *tante*.

tapette *f.* (very popular)
NOTE: **tapette** *f.* • **1.** gay, "fag" • **2.** tongue.

travelo *m.*

Lesbian

éplucheuse de lentilles *f.*
• (lit); lentil washer.
NOTE: **lentille** *f.* clitoris
• (lit); lentil.

gavousse *f.* This is a *javanais* transformation of *gousse*
SEE (1): ***Street French***, le javanais, p. 144.
SEE (2): *gousse*.

godo *f.*

gouchotte *f.*

goudou *f.*

gougne *f.*

gougnette *f.*

gougnotte *f.*
NOTE: **se gougnotter** *v.* to make love between two women.

gouine *f.* (very popular)
NOTE: **se gouiner** *v.* to make love between two women.

gousse *f.* (very popular)
NOTE: **se gousser** *v.* to make love between two women.

gousse d'ail *f.* • (lit); garlic clove.
NOTE: This is a popular pun on the feminine noun *gousse* meaning "lesbian, dyke" since the noun *gousse* literally means "clove (of garlic)."
SEE: *gousse*.

mangeuse de lentilles *f.*
• (lit); lentil eater.
NOTE: **lentille** *f.* clitoris
• (lit); lentil.

marchande d'ail *f.* • (lit); garlic merchant.
SEE: *gousse d'ail*.

qui tape l'ail *exp.* • (lit); who smells of garlic.
SEE: *gousse d'ail*.

qui est de la maison tire-bouchon *exp.* • (lit); who is of the lesbian world.
NOTE: **maison tire-bouchon** *f.* lesbianism • (lit); corkscrew house.

vrille *f.* • (lit); corkscrew.

To Sodomize

baiser à la riche *exp.* • (lit); to fuck in the style of the rich.

caser *v.* • (lit); to stow (something) away.

casser le pot *exp.* • (lit); to break the pot.
NOTE: **pot** *m.* buttocks • (lit); pot.

casser la rondelle *exp.* • (lit); to break the ring.
NOTE: **rondelle** *f.* anus • (lit); ring, small round disc.

défoncer la pastille *exp.* • (lit); to smash through the lozenge.
NOTE: **pastille** *f.* anus • (lit); lozenge.

emmancher *v.*

empaffer *v.*

empaler *v.* • (lit); to impale.

empapaouter *v.*

empétarder *v.* • (lit); to receive something through the back.
NOTE: This is an "antonym" of the verb *pétarader* meaning "to backfire."

emproser *v.*

encaldosser *v.*

enculer *v.*
NOTE: This comes from the masculine noun *cul* meaning "ass."

enfifrer *v.* • (lit); to insert the fife.
NOTE: This comes from the masculine noun *fifre* meaning "fife" or "small flute" but has taken the slang connotation of "penis, dick."

enfoirer *v.* • (lit); to "bring something in through one's annus."
NOTE: This is an "antonym" of the verb *foirer* meaning "to have diarrhea."

englander *v.* • (lit); to insert the mast.
NOTE: This comes from the masculine noun *gland* meaning "mast" but has taken the slang conotation of "penis, dick."

planter *v.* • (lit); to seed.

pointer *v.*
NOTE: This comes from the feminine noun *pointe* literally meaning "point" but has the slang connotation of "penis, dick."

prendre de l'oignon *exp.* • (lit); to get some onion.
NOTE: **oignon** *m.* annus • (lit); onion.
ALSO: **prendre du petit** *exp.* • NOTE: **petit** *m.* annus • (lit); small (area).

tourner la page *exp.* • (lit); to turn the page.

troncher *v.*
NOTE: This comes from the feminine noun *tronche* meaning "log."

To Be Bisexual

jazz-tango (être) *exp.* • (lit); to
be jazz-tango.

marcher à voile et à vapeur
exp. • (lit); to walk by sail
and by steam.

qui joue sur les deux tableaux
exp. • (lit); who plays in both
scenes (of theater).

INSIDE INFO (2): *BEING OBSCENE UNINTENTIONALLY*

When I first arrived in Paris as a fifteen-year-old American, I was enthusiastically welcomed by my relatives who were anxious to hear my reputedly flawless French. In a matter of only a few hours, I managed accidentally to call my uncle

A. **"bêtes"**   *not*   **"pets"**

Vous avez des bêtes?   *Vous avez des pets?*
Do you have any pets?   Do you have any farts?

B. **"bettrave"**   *not*   **"beet" (bite)**

Passez-moi les bettraves,   *Passez-moi les bites,*
s'il vous plaît.   *s'il vous plaît.*
Pass me the beets, please.   Pass me the dicks, please.

C. **"donner un baiser"**   *not*   **"baiser"**

Son mari, y lui a donné un baiser   *Son mari, y l'a baisée*
à la porte avant d'partir.   *à la porte avant d'partir.*
Her husband gave her a kiss   Her husband fucked her
at the door before leaving.   at the door before leaving.

D. **"j'ai chaud"**   *not*   **"je suis chaud"**

Maman, j'ai chaud!   *Maman, j'suis chaud!*
Mom, I'm hot!   Mom, I'm really in heat!

E. **"j'ai mal au cou"**   *not*   **"j'ai mal au cul"**

Quand j'regarde trop la télé,   *Quand j'regarde trop la télé,*
j'ai mal au cou.   *j'ai mal au cul.*
When I watch too much T.V.,   When I watch too much T.V.,
I get a pain in my neck.   I get a pain in my ass.

F. **"j'ai pu faim"**   *not*   **"j'suis plein(e)"**

Ça va. J' ai pu faim.   *Ça va. J' suis plein(e).*

No more, thanks. I'm satisfied.   No more, thanks. I'm pregnant.

G. **"j'me réjouis"**   *not*   **"je jouis"**

J' me réjouis de te r' voir.   *Je jouis de te r' voir.*

I'm so delighted to see   Seeing you again makes
you again.   me cum.

H. **"j'suis contre"**   *not*   **"j'suis con"**

La libération des femmes – vous   *La libération des femmes – vous*
êtes pour ou contre?   *êtes pour ou con?*

Women's rights... are you pro   Women's rights... are you pro or
or con?   totally stupid?

I. **"oie"**   *not*   **"gousse"**

On va manger d' l' oie   *On va manger d' la gousse*
pour Noël.   *pour Noël.*

We're going to eat goose   We're going to eat some dyke
for Christmas.   for Christmas.

J. **"répéter"**   *not*   **"repéter"**

Tu peux l' répéter, s' te plaît?   *Tu peux l' repéter, s' te plaît?*

Can you repeat that again,   Can you fart that again,
please?   please?

K. **"salut"**   *not*   **"salaud"**

M. DuBois! Salut!   *M. DuBois! Salaud!*

M. DuBois! Hello, there!   M. DuBois! You bastard!

L. **Rule: Never eat with one hand in your lap!**

In France, it is considered very rude and downright obscene to rest one hand in
your lap while eating at the table. They assume you must be doing something
"dirty" to yourself or to your neighbor!

ANSWERS TO LESSONS 11-15

LESSON ELEVEN - *Derrière le Volant*

Practice the Vocabulary

A. 1. b   5. a
    2. c   6. b
    3. b   7. c
    4. a   8. b

B. 1. branle   6. merde
    2. couilles   7. cul, bordel
    3. déconner   8. anglais
    4. renifler   9. saloperie
    5. pet   10. égout

C.

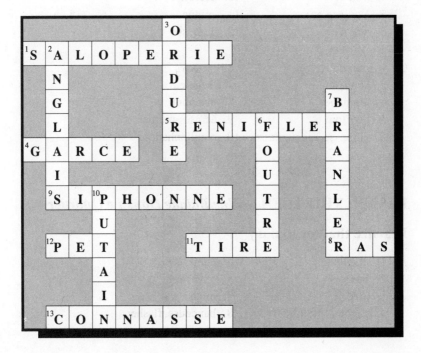

INSIDE INFO:

Practice Using Slang Driving Terms

A. 1. C   9. L
   2. H   10. A
   3. M   11. I
   4. G   12. E
   5. K   13. F
   6. N   14. B
   7. J   15. 0
   8. D

LESSON TWELVE - *Le Dîner Habillé*

Practice the Vocabulary

A. 1. asperge   7. tignasse   B. 1. b   6. c
   2. couillonnades   8. jacasser   2. b   7. b
   3. châsses   9. dents du fond   3. a   8. a
   4. trou   10. décrotter   4. b   9. b
   5. à quinze pas   11. cradoc   5. a   10. a
   6. ballot   12. gerbosse

C. 1. rougnotte, trou   6. jacasses
   2. dégueulé   7. lèche-cul
   3. pouliche   8. patapouf
   4. bouftou   9. écrases-merde
   5. gerbosse, ragoûgnasse   10. couillonnades

LESSON THIRTEEN - *Une Balade Dans Le Quartier*

Practice the Vocabulary

A. 1. michetonner   5. panier
   2. boxif   6. fenêtrière
   3. mac   7. miché
   4. capote, chtouille   8. bandeuse, flasher

B. 1. bandeuse
    2. draguer
    3. mac
    4. entre-jambe
    5. capote

    6. cuisses
    7. bagatelle
    8. pince
    9. pelle

LESSON FOURTEEN - *Au Métro*

Practice the Vocabulary

A. 1. a
    2. a
    3. b
    4. a
    5. b

    6. b
    7. a
    8. b
    9. b

B. MOTS CROISÉS:

¹M	O	L	A	R	D	²E	R	
						M		
					³M	O	R	B	A	⁴C
						E		O
			⁷T	O	R	C	H	E		L
		⁸C			D			O
⁹C	H	I	A	S	S	E		⁵P	I	S	S	E
		C			R			S
		A					⁶F	E	U

LESSON FIFTEEN - *À la Boîte de Nuit*

Practice the Vocabulary

A. 1. C   5. H   B. 1. chouquette   5. gousse
    2. E   6. D   2. honteuse   6. cuir
    3. G   7. A   3. outillé   7. pédé
    4. F   8. B   4. voile   8. gâteau

REVIEW EXAM
FOR LESSONS 11-15

[Answers to Review, p. 216]

A. Underline the appropriate word(s) that best complete(s) the sentence.

1. Y m'énerve, c'ui-là. Y raconte que des (**écrases-merdes, capotes, couillonnades**).

2. Elle a une (**pouliche, chiée, barbaque**) d'enfants.

3. Michelle, è vient d'avoir un bébé, et moi, j'savais même pas qu'elle était en (**cloque, boxif, morbac**).

4. J'peux pas la blairer. C't'une vraie (**honteuse, connasse, chiasse**).

5. J'ai trop mangé. J'ai les (**emmerdeurs, chiottes, dents du fond**) qui baignent.

6. E fréquente les lits, celle-là. Faut dire qu'elle a la (**cuisse, tignasse, bandeuse**) légère.

7. Arrête d'faire ça! Oh, quel (**torche-cul, mac, emmerdeur**)!

8. Elle est très belle, c'te fille. E fait (**débagouler, flasher, molarder**) les mecs, facile.

9. C'est (**cradoc, connasse, gerbosse**), c't'hamburger. J'peux pas l'bouffer!

10. Ces deux filles-là, è s'(**gouinent, décrottent, morfalent**).

B. Complete the sentences by using the appropriate word(s) from the list below. Make any necessary changes.

chiasse	anglais	bordel
entre-jambe	débagouler	décrotter
couillon	gousse	pédé
morfaler	pouliche	torche-cul

1. Elle est belle, c'te _____ -là.

2. Ma sœur, elle est pas contente aujourd'hui pasqu'elle a ses _____ .

3. Y est carrément stupide, c'ui-là. Mais quel _____ !

4. T'es tout sale! Va te _____ avant de v'nir à table.

5. J'avais la _____ quand j'ai découvert qu'y'avait un cambrioleur dans ma chambre!

6. Au restaurant, on a fait qu'se _____ .

7. Mais c'est l'_____ dans c'te maison!

8. Y fréquente que les mecs. J'crois qu'c't'un _____ .

9. Y est constipé d'l'_____ .

10. Sa sœur, elle est très masculine. J'me d'mande si c't'une _____ .

11. J'suis malade. J'ai envie de _____ .

12. Y'a pas de _____ dans c'W.C.

C. Choose the correct definition of the term(s) in boldface.

1. **cradoc:**
   a. propre   b. sale   c. content

2. **casser les couilles:**
   a. partir   b. énerver   c. arriver

3. **boudin:**
   a. voiture   b. grand nez   c. prostitué

4. **débagouler:**
   a. rire   b. pleurer   c. vomir

5. **dégueu:**
   a. dégoûtant   b. agréable   c. intéressant

6. **capote:**
   a. préservatif   b. verre   c. restaurant

7. **écrases-merde:**
   a. chaussures   b. pieds   c. enfants

8. **jacasser:**
   a. partir   b. faire l'amour   c. parler

9. **tignasse:**
   a. fille   b. cheveux   c. garçon

10. **molarder:**
    a. cracher   b. avoir peur   c. pleurer

D. Match the English with the French.

☐ 1. He's very effeminate.

☐ 2. I'm gonna try and pick up that girl.

☐ 3. I blew it!

☐ 4. I think he's a closet queen.

☐ 5. He's got the worst breath!

☐ 6. He tried to French kiss her.

☐ 7. I've gotta go take a leak.

☐ 8. I think he's A.C.-D.C.

☐ 9. She's really hung up on sex.

☐ 10. It stinks in here.

☐ 11. Get a load of her hair.

☐ 12. I bet that's her pimp.

A. **Elle est vraiment portée sur la bagatelle.**

B. **J'parie qu'c'est ça son mac.**

C. **Y fait très chouquette, lui.**

D. **Regarde un peu sa tignasse.**

E. **J'vais essayer de draguer c'te fille-là.**

F. **Y a essayé d'lui rouler une pelle.**

G. **Ça rougnotte ici.**

H. **Y tue les mouches à quinze pas!**

I. **J'l'ai foutu en l'air!**

J. **J'dois aller faire pleurer mon colosse.**

K. **J'crois qu'y marche à voile et à vapeur.**

L. **J'crois qu'c't'une honteuse.**

ANSWERS TO REVIEW FOR LESSONS 11-15

A.
1. couillonnades
2. chiée
3. cloque
4. connasse
5. dents du fond
6. cuisse
7. emmerdeur
8. flasher
9. gerbosse
10. gouinent

B.
1. pouliche
2. anglais
3. couillon
4. décrotter
5. chiasse
6. morfaler
7. bordel
8. pédé
9. entre-jambe
10. gousse
11. débagouler
12. torche-cul

C.
1. b
2. b
3. c
4. c
5. a
6. a
7. a
8. c
9. b
10. a

D.
1. C
2. E
3. I
4. L
5. H
6. F
7. J
8. K
9. A
10. G
11. D
12. B

UNIT THREE - *Popular Abbreviations*

-A-

accro *adj. accroché(e);* hooked. *Y est accro à la drogue;* He's hooked on drugs.

accu *m. accumulateur;* accumulator, storage cell or battery. *Recharger les accus;* To have another drink or eat.

aéro *m. aérogramme;* aerogram.

agreg & **agrég** *f. agrégation;* competitive state exam for teaching positions.

alcolo *m. alcoolique;* "wino."

amphés *f.pl. amphétamines;* amphetamines.

amphi *m. amphithéâtre;* amphitheater.

ampli *m. amplificateur;* amplifier.

ap' *m. appétit;* appetite. *Bon ap'!;* Have a good meal!

appart' *m. appartement;* appartment.

aprèm *m. après-midi;* afternoon.

archi *m. architecte;* architect.

aristo *m. aristocrate;* aristocrat.

arti *f. artillerie;* artillery.

astap(e) *exp. à s'taper le derrière (cul) par terre;* so funny as to touch one's butt (ass) on the ground (from laughing so hard). *C'est astap!;* That's a scream!

au p.p.p.d.c. *exp. (ô-pé-pé-pé-dé-cé) au plus petit poil du cul;* **1.** terrific • **2.** dead accurate.

auto *m. autographe;* autograph.

auxi *m. auxiliaire;* auxiliary.

-B-

bac *m. baccalauréat.*

b.c.b.g. *adj. (bé-cé-bé-gé)* **1.** *bon-chic-bon-genre;* well-bred. *Y est très b.c.b.g.;* He's very classy • **2. b.c.b.g.** *adj. beau-cul-belle-gueule;* nice-ass-pretty- face.

b.d. *f. (bé-dé) bande dessiné;* comic strip.

biblio *f. bibliothèque;* library.

bob *m. bobsleigh;* bobsled.

Boul' Mich' *m. Boulevard Saint-Michel.*

bus *m. autobus;* bus.

-C-

cafèt *m. cafétéria;* cafeteria.

calendo *m. camembert.*

calva *m. calvados.*

cambrio *m. cambrioleur;* burglar.

came *f. camelote;* junk.

cap *adj. capable;* capable.

cara *m. caractère;* disposition. *Elle a un mauvais cara;* She has a lousy disposition.

champe *m. champagne;* champagne.

choco *m. chocolat;* chocolate.

ciné *m. cinéma;* movie theater.

colo *m. & f. colonie de vacances;* camp.

comp *f. composition (école);* composition (school).

compal *f. composition (école);* composition (school).

compote *f. composition (école);* composition (school).

condisse *f. condition;* circumstance.

consomme *f. consommation;* drink.

converse *f. conversation;* conversation.

cop *m. copain;* friend.

corbi *m. corbillard;* hearse.

cré *adj. sacré;* blessed.

crebleu! *interj. Sacré bleu!;* Holy cow!

crédié! *interj.* or **crédieu!** *Sacré Dieu!;* Good God!

crème *m. café crème;* coffee with cream.

crénom! *interj. Sacré nom de Dieu!;* Good God!

cristi *interj. sacristi;* holy cow.

croco *m. crocodile;* crocodile. *un sac en crocro;* a purse made of crocodile skin.

crono *m. chronomètre;* stopwatch.

-D-

d'acc *interj. d'accord;* okay.

d'achar *adv. acharnement;* hard. *Y travaille d'achar;* He's working hard.

déca *m. café décaféiné;* decaffeinated coffee.

def *adj. défoncé;* high on drugs.

deg *adj. dégueulasse;* disgusting.

dégueu *adj. dégueulasse;* disgusting.

demi *m. demi-litre;* glass of beer.

démo *m. & f. démonstration;* demonstration (cassette).

der *m. le dernier;* the last one. *C'est l'der des ders;* It's the very last one.

deuche *f. deux chevaux;* two horsepower.

diame *m. diamant;* diamond.

diap *m. diapositif;* slide, transparency.

dico *m. dictionnaire;* dictionary.

disco *m. discothèque;* discotheque.

disserte *f. dissertation;* essay.

docu *m. document;* document.

dorto *m. dortoire;* dormitory.

-E-

écolo *m. écologiste;* ecologist.

estome *m. estomac;* stomach.

exhibo *m. exhibitionniste;* exhibitionist.

exo *m. exercice;* exercise.

expo *m.* **1.** *exposé (au lycée);* report (in school)
• **2.** *exposition;* exposition, show.

-F-

fantaise *f. fantaisie;* fantasy.

foot *m. football;* soccer.

formide *adj. formidable;* fantastic.

-G-

g.d.b. *f. (gé-dé-bé) gueule de bois;* hangover.

géo *f. géographie;* geography.

gol *m. mongolien;* idiot.

goldo *f. Gauloise;* Gauloise cigarette.

-H-

hebdo *m. hebdomadaire;* weekly paper or magazine.

hivio *m. hiver;* winter.

homo *m. homosexuel;* homosexual.

hosto *m. hôpital;* hospital.

-I-

illuse *f. illusion;* illusion.

impec *adj. impeccable;* impeccable.

imper *m. imperméable;* raincoat.

inco *adj. incorrigible;* incorrigible.

indic *m. indicateur;* police informer.

info *f. information;* information.

ino *adj. inoccupé;* unemployed.

inox *adj. inoxydable;* stainless.
acier inox; stainless steel.

instit(e) *n. instituteur, -rice;* teacher, "teach."

invite *f. invitation;* invitation, "invite."

i.v.g. *f. (i-vé-gé)interruption volontaire de grossesse;* abortion.

-J-

jars *m. jargon;* jargon.

j.v. *m. (gi-vé) jeune voyou;* young thug.

-L-

lab *m. laboratoire;* laboratory.

Latin *m. le Latin (le Quartier Latin);* the Latin Quarter (of Paris).

lavabe *m. lavabo;* bathroom.

le Sébasto *m. le boulevard de Sébastopol;* the Boulevard Sébastopol (in Paris).

lino *m.* **1.** *linoleum;* linoleum • **2.** *linotype;* linotype.

loco *f. locomotive;* locomotive. *faire la loco;* to smoke like a chimney.

-M-

M. *f. merde;* shit.

m'dame *Prn. madame;* ma'am, Mrs.

m'sieu *Prn. monsieur;* sir.

magase *m. magasin;* store.

magnéto *m. magnétophone;* tape recorder.

manif *f. manifestation;* demonstration.

maso *n. masochiste;* masochist.

mat' *m. matin;* morning.

maths *m.pl. mathématiques;* math.

max *m. maximum;* maximum.

maxi *m. maximum;* maximum.

mécano *m. mécanicien;* mechanic.

mélanco *adj. mélancolie;* melancholy.

mélo *m. mélodrame;* melodrama.

mer *adj. merveilleux;* marvelous.

météo *f. météorologie;* meteorology.

micro *m. microphone;* microphone.

mob *f. Mobylette;* motorbike.

Montparno *Prn. Montparnasse.*

moto *f. motocycle;* motorcycle.

Mouffe *Prn. la Mouffe (rue Mouffetard).*

-N-

nature *adv. naturellement;* naturally.

-O-

occase *f. occasion;* opportunity.

opé *f. opération;* operation.

-P-

p.b.i. *m. (pé-bé-i)* "*pas de bouches inutiles;*" "no unwelcomed guests."

p.d. *m. (pé-dé) pédéraste;* "fag."

parano *adj. paranoïde;* paranoid.

pardeusse *m. pardessus;* overcoat.

pédé *m. pédéraste;* "fag."

péno *m. penalty (football);* penalty (soccer).

périf *m. périphérique;* the freeway encircling Paris.

p.g. *m. (pé-gé) Prisonnier de Guerre;* P.O.W.

pharmace *m. pharmacien;* pharmacist.

philo *m. philosophie;* philosophy.

phono *m. phonographe;* record player.

p.h.s. *m. (pé-ash-ess) Réunion "pour hommes seulement";* stag party.

pitaine *m. capitaine;* captain.

poke *m. poker;* poker. *taper un poke jusqu'à l' aube;* to play poker till dawn.

popu *adj. populaire;* popular.

populo *adj. populaire;* popular.

porno 1. *f. pornographique;* pornographic • **2.** *adj. pornographie;* pornography.

postère *m. postérieur;* rear end.

prem *m. premier;* the first, the best. *J' suis prem en maths;* I'm an ace at math.

pro *m. professionnel;* professional.

prof *m. & f. professeur;* teacher.

projo *m. projecteur (cinéma);* projector (movies).

prolo *adj. prolétaire;* proletarian. *Tes fringues, è font prolos;* You look like a real pleb in those clothes.

promo *f.* **1.** *promotion;* marketing promo • **2.** class. *La promo de '89;* The class of '89.

proprio *m. propriétaire (m.) / propriote (f.)*; boss, owner.

psi; *psychiatre* • **1.** *m.* psychiatrist, "shrink" • **2.** *adj.* psycho.

psycho *f. psychologie;* psychology.

pub *f. publicité;* advertisement.

pull *m. pullover;* pull-over sweater.

-Q-

Quartier *m. le Quartier (le Quartier Latin).* SEE: *Latin.*

quèque *adj. & adv. quelque;* some. *quèque part, quèque chose, etc.;* somewhere, something, etc.

-R-

R.U. *m. restaurant universitaire;* university restaurant, commons.

réac *adj., m.& f. réactionnaire;* reactionary.

récré *f. récréation;* playtime, break time, etc.

resto *m. restaurant;* restaurant.

rétro *m. rétroviseur;* rearview mirror.

-S-

sado *adj. & m. sadique;* sadistic.

Saint-Ger *m. Saint-Germain-des-Prés.*

saxo *m. saxophone;* saxophone.

sensass *adj. sensationnel;* sensational.

smok *m. smoking;* tuxedo.

snack *m. snack-bar;* snack bar.

suite *adv. tout de suite;* right away.

sup *adj. supplémentaire;* extra *une heure sup';* an hour overtime.

super *m. supercarburant;* four-star
  gasoline.

sympa *adj. sympathique;* kind,
  nice.

système D. *m. système démerde;*
  "plan for getting out of trouble."

trav *m.pl. travaux forcés;* hard
  labor.

-U-

unif *f. uniforme;* uniform.

-T-

télé *f. télévision;* television.

télévise *f. télévision;* television.

tévé *f. télévision;* television.

transfo *m. transformateur;*
  transformer.

-V-

v'là *prep. voilà;* there.

vacs *f.pl. vacances;* vacation.

Versigo *Prn. Versailles.*

véto *m. vétérinaire;* veterinarian.

volo *adv. à volonté;* at will.

GLOSSARY

This glossary contains all the slang words and expressions used in the dialogues.

-A-

à-côtés *m.pl.* perks • (lit); that which is on the side.

à deux doigts (être) *exp.* to be on the verge • (lit); to be two fingers away (from doing something).

à deux on se distrait, à trois on s'ennuie *exp.* two's company, three's a crowd • (lit); with two it's fun, with three it's boring.

à l'envers (les avoir) *exp.* to be extremely lazy • (lit); to have them (hands) inside out.
SYNONYM: **les avoir à la retourne** *exp.* to have them (hands) turned inside out.
ANTONYM: **être d'attaque** *adj.* to be very energetic, "rarin' to go" • (lit); to be (full) of attack.

à la page (être) *exp.* to be in the know, caught up • (lit); to be (caught up) to the page.
NOTE: **mettre qqn. à la page** *exp.* to bring s.o. up-to-date.

SYNONYM: **être à la coule** *exp.*
• (lit); to be in the flow.

à lui/elle le pompon *exp.* he/she takes the cake • (lit); to him/her the pom-pom.

à tout casser *exp.* at the outside • (lit); to break everything.
NOTE: **à tout casser** *exp.* fantastic.

à toute barde *adv.* very quickly.
SYNONYM: **à toute pompe** *adv.*

abouler (s') *v.* to arrive, to show up, to come along • (lit); to hand oneself over.
NOTE: **abouler** *v.* to hand over.
SYNONYM: **se pointer** *v.* • (lit); to point oneself.

abrevoir *m.* bar, pub • (lit); drinking trough.

accrocher un mari *exp.* • (lit); to hook a husband.
NOTE: **avoir l'accroche de qqn.** or **être accroché(e) de qqn.** *exp.* to be hooked on s.o.
ANTONYM: **avoir qqn. dans le nez** *exp.* to dislike s.o. • (lit); to have s.o. in the nose.

affranchir qqn. *v.* to bring one up to date, to give one the lowdown • (lit); to emancipate; to stamp (a letter, etc).
SYNONYM: **mettre qqn. à la coule** *exp.*

anglais (avoir ses) *exp.* to menstruate, to have one's period, "to be on the rag" • (lit); to have one's English.
NOTE: **avoir ses angliches** *exp. angliches* is slang for *anglais,* "English."

antiffer *v.* to enter.
SYNONYM: **encarrer** *v.* • This verb comes from the feminine noun *carrée* meaning "a room."
ANTONYM: **décarrer** *v.* to exit, to leave a room *(carrée).*

arriver sur le clou *exp.* to arrive on the dot • (lit); to arrive on the nail.
NOTE: Other synonyms of the verb *arriver* may certainly be used in this expression, i.e., *s'abouler, s'amener, débarquer, radiner, rappliquer, se pointer,* etc.

asperge *f.* very thin and tall person • (lit); asparagus.
ANTONYM: **bouboule** *m. & f.* fatso.
SEE: *patapouf.*

assiette au beurre *f.* cushy job • (lit); plate of butter.
NOTE: **c'est du beurre** *exp.* it's a cinch, a snap • (lit); it's butter.
SYNONYM: **fromage** *m.* • (lit); cheese.

assommer *v.* to annoy greatly. • (lit); to knock unconscious.
NOTE: **assommeur, euse** *n.* a crashing bore, a "pain in the neck."
SYNONYM: **casser les pieds à qqn.** *exp.* • (lit); to break one's feet.

asticoter *v.* to annoy greatly.
NOTE: **s'asticoter** *v.* to fight.
SYNONYM: **assommer** *v.* • (lit); to knock (s.o.) out • NOTE: **assommeur, euse** *n.* annoying person, pain in the neck.

attaquer *v.* to telephone (s.o.) • (lit); to attack.
SYNONYM: **bigophoner** *v.* • NOTE: **bigophone** *m.* telephone.

au bout de sa corde (être) *exp.* • (lit); to be at the end of one's rope.
NOTE: **être au bout du rouleau** *exp.* to be at death's door • (lit); to be at the end of the roller.

au bout du rouleau (être) *exp.* to be at death's door • (lit); to be at the end of one's roller.
SYNONYM: **être à l'article de la mort** *exp.* • (lit); to be at the critical moment of death.

au châsse *adv.* free • (lit); at the eye.
NOTE: *châsse* is slang for *œil* meaning "eye." In slang, *au châsse* means "free" or "nothing" since the eye has the same shape as zero.
SYNONYM: **à l'œil** *adv.*

au prix où est le beurre *exp.* with the cost of living • (lit); with the price of butter where it is.

-B-

badaboum *m.* free-for-all fight.
SYNONYM: **torchée** *f.*

bâfrée *f.* a huge meal, a real blow out.
NOTE: **se bâfrer** *v.* to pig out
SYNONYM: **gueuleton** *m.* This comes from the feminine noun *gueule* which is an insluting term

for "face," "mouth," or "head" but is literally translated as "the mouth of an animal."

bagne *m.* un pleasant job, grind • (lit); penal servitude.

balai *m.* year • (lit); broom.
SYNONYM: **pige** *f.*

balaise (être) *adj.* to be big and strong.
SYNONYM: **être baraqué** *adj.* to be built like a "brick shithouse" •
NOTE: This comes from the feminine noun *baraque* meaning "house."

balanstiquer *v.* to throw, to toss • (lit); to balance, to swing.
NOTE: This is a slang variation of the verb *balancer*.

ballot *m.* idiot, jerk.
NOTE: This comes from the verb *ballotter* meaning "to shake up, to toss about." Therefore, *un ballot* might be loosely translated as "one who has had his brains shaken around."
SYNONYM: **cave** *m.*

bamboula (faire la) *exp.* to party it up, to go out on a bender.

bandeuse *f.* pricktease • (lit); a woman who makes a man get a hard-on.
NOTE: **bander** *v.* to get a hard on • (lit); to tighten.

baquer (se) *v.* to take a bath • (lit); to "tub" oneself.
NOTE: This comes from the masculine noun *baquet* meaning "tub" or "bucket."

barbaque *f.* poor quality meat, "leather."
NOTE: *barbaque* is also used to refer to human skin, i.e. **sac à barbaque** *m.* sleeping bag

• (lit); meat sack.
SYNONYM: **bidoche** *f.*

barber (se) *exp.* to be terribly bored.
NOTE: **barber** *v.* to annoy.
SYNONYM: **se barbifier** *v.*

bas de laine *m.* savings, money put aside for a rainy day • (lit); woolen sock (into which money is hidden away).
SYNONYM: **un magot** *m.*

basculer un godet *exp.* to drink • (lit); to rock back a glass.
NOTE: **godet** *m.* glass.
SYNONYM: **s'en jeter un derrière le bouton de col** *exp.* • (lit); to throw one behind the collar button.

battants *m.pl.* hours • (lit); beaters.
NOTE: **battante** *f.* watch.
SYNONYM: **plombes** *f.pl.*

béni-bouftou *m.* one who eats constantly, "a pig" • (lit); a blessed eater of everything.
NOTE: The masculine word *bouftou* is actually a contraction of the slang verb *bouffer* meaning "to eat" and the masculine noun *tout* meaning "everything." Also seen spelled *béni-bouffe-tout*.
SYNONYM: **bâfreur** *m.* This comes from the slang verb *bâfrer* meaning "to eat heavily."

berge *f.* year.
SYNONYM: **pigette** / **pige** *f.*

bien fait pour sa gueule *exp.* it serves him/her right • (lit); well done for his/her face.
NOTE: **gueule** *f.* insulting term for "face," "mouth" or "head" • (lit); mouth (of animal).
SYNONYM: **c'est pain bénit** *exp.* • (lit); it's blessed bread.

bien outillé (être) *adj.* to be well hung • (lit); to be well tooled.
NOTE: **outil** *m.* penis, dick • (lit); tool.

bien tassé(e)s *adj.* solid (said of hours) • (lit); well compressed, packed.

biler (se) *v.* to worry oneself, to get all worked up • (lit); to make oneself bile (from worrying too much).
NOTE: **se faire de la bile** *exp.* to worry oneself, to get all worked up.
SYNONYM: **se faire du mauvais sang** *exp.*

biseneusseuse *f.* prostitute, whore • (lit); businesswoman.

bistrot *m.* café-bar.
SYNONYM: **troquet** *m.*

blanche comme un cachet d'aspirine (être) *exp.* to be white as a ghost • (lit); to be white as an aspirin tablet.

bocal *m.* house, premises, place • (lit); jar.
SYNONYM: **baraque** *f.* house • (lit); barracks.

bof *interj.* • Used to denote indifference.

bomber *v.* to drive quickly; to move fast (like a bomb).

bordel *m. & expl.* • (lit); brothel, whorehouse • **1.** When followed by *de, bordel* is used to intensify the expletive that it precedes: *Merde!;* Shit! • *Bordel de merde!;* Holy shit! • **2.** *Bordel de* may also be used along with other intensifiers: *Bordel de putain de;* fucking mess.
NOTE: **foutre le bordel** *exp.* Pronounced: *fout' le bordel;* to make a fucking mess.
SEE: *foutre.*

borgnoter *v.* to look.
NOTE: This comes from the adjective *borgne* meaning "blind in one eye."

bouboule *m. & f.* fatso.
SYNONYM: **patapouf** *m.* (used only for men).

bouchon *m.* traffic jam • (lit); stopper of wine bottle which prohibits any liquid (or in this case, cars) from getting through.

bouchon (prendre du) *exp.* to get older • (lit); to take some from the stopper (or "to let some liquid" or "age" in this case, "to seep past the stopper of the bottle").
SYNONYM: **monter en graine** *exp.* Said of aging wine.

boucler son égout *exp.* to shut one's mouth • (lit); to shut one's sewer.
NOTE (1): **boucler** *v.* to shut • (lit); to buckle or fasten.
NOTE (2): **égout** *m.* mouth, trap, kisser • (lit); sewer.

boudin *m.* **1.** fat woman • **2.** prostitute, whore • **3.** tire (of a car) • **4.** penis • (lit); blood sausage.

boumer *v.* to be going very well • (lit); to be booming.
SYNONYM: **carburer** *v.* • (lit); to carburate.

bourré(e) (être) *adj.* to be dead drunk, ripped • (lit); to be stuffed or packed tight (with alcohol).
NOTE: **être bourré(e) à bloc , à zéro;** to be bombed out of one's mind • *à bloc, à zéro;* completely.

bouts de bois *m.pl.* • (lit); ends of wood • sticks of furniture.

boxif *m.* brothel, whorehouse.

braise *m*. money, "dough" • (lit); live charcoal.
SYNONYM: **fric** *m*.

branler *v*. **1**. *se branler;* to masturbate, to beat off • **2**. *s'en branler;* not to give a damn, "a rat's ass."

briquer *v*. to clean thoroughly, to scrub.
NOTE: **se briquer** *v*. to clean oneself, to freshen up.
SYNONYM: **astiquer** *v*.

brouillé(e) (être) *adj*. to be hopelessly bad at something • (lit); to be jumbled, mixed, confused.
NOTE: **être brouillé(e) avec qqn.** *adj*. to be on bad terms with s.o.

-C-

c'est le moins qu'on puisse dire *exp*. • (lit); that's the least you can say.
SYNONYM: **tu parles!** *exp*. you said it!

c'est moi qui te le dis *exp*. • (lit); I'm telling you.

c'est pain bénit *exp*. it serves him/her right • (lit); it's blessed bread.
SYNONYM: **c'est bien fait pour sa gueule** *exp*. (lit); it's well done for his/her face.

c'est pas de refus *exp*. don't mind if I do • (lit); it's not refused.

ça, c'est le bouquet *exp*. that's the last straw • (lit); that's the bouquet.
SYNONYM: **c'est la fin des haricots!** *exp*. • (lit); that's the end of the beans!

ça me connaît *exp*. that's right up my alley • (lit); it knows me.

SYNONYM: **être dans ses cordes** *exp*. to be right up one's alley.

ça passe comme une lettre à la poste *exp*. Said of anything that is easy to do • (lit); to go through like a letter to the post office.
SYNONYM: **ça va comme sur des roulettes** *exp*. • (lit); it's going (smoothly) as if it were on rollers.

ça s'arrose *exp*. that calls for a drink • (lit); that waters itself.
NOTE (1): **s'arroser la gorge** *exp*. to wet one's whistle.
NOTE (2): **arroser** *v*. to buy the drinks.

caca *m*. crap.

cafetière *f*. head • (lit); coffeepot.
SYNONYM: **caillou** *m*. • (lit); pebble.

cale dent *m*. snack • (lit); that which steadies "hunger."
NOTE: **avoir la dent** *exp*. to be hungry.
SYNONYM: **casse-croûte** *m*. snack • (lit); crust breaker (as in "to break bread").

caler le bide (se) *exp*. to take the edge off one's hunger • (lit); to steady one's stomach.
SYNONYM: **se caler les amygdales** *exp*. to eat well • (lit); to steady one's tonsils.

cambrousse *f*. country, sticks, "Hicksville."
NOTE: **cambroussard(e)** *n*. one who lives in the country, hick.

cancérette *f*. cigarette • (lit); cancer stick.
SYNONYM: **clope** *f*.

capote *f*. condom, rubber • (lit); bonnet.

NOTE: **capote anglaise** *f.*
• (lit); English bonnet.

carabiné(e) *adj.* extreme, violent.

caroubler *v.* to put something under lock and key.
NOTE: This comes from the feminine noun *carouble* meaning "duplicate" or "skeleton key."
NOTE: **caroubler** *v.* to break into a house.
SYNONYM: **mettre qqch. sous clé** *exp.* to put something under lock and key.

carrosserie *f.* build (of person) • (lit); body (of car).
SYNONYM: **châssis** *m.* • (lit); chassis (of car).

casque (en avoir dans le) *m.* to feel tipsy • (lit); to get some in one's head.
NOTE: **casque** *m.* head • (lit); helmet.
SYNONYM: **être ébréché(e)** *adj.* to be tipsy, buzzed • (lit); to be chipped.

casquer *v.* to pay, to cough up (money).
SYNONYM: **douiller** *v.*

casser (ne pas se) *v.* not to put oneself out • (lit); not to break oneself.
ANTONYM: **se plier en deux** *exp.* to bend over backwards (to do something) • (lit); to fold oneself in two.

casser les couilles *exp.* to annoy (s.o.) greatly • (lit); to break one's balls.
NOTE (1): **casse-couilles** *m.* an annoying person; one who bugs the crap out of others • (lit); ball breaker.
NOTE (2): **en avoir plein les couilles** *exp.* to be fed up • (lit); to have had it up to one's balls.

SEE (1): *ras le cul (en avoir)*.
SEE (2): *couillon*.

cataloguer *v.* to size up (s.o.) • (lit); to catalogue; to list.
SYNONYM: **situer qqn.** *v.* • (lit); to situate (s.o.).

cavaler (se) *v.* to run away, to make a run for it.
NOTE (1): **être en cavale** *adj.* to be on the run (from the police), to be on the lam.
NOTE (2): **cavaler qqn.** *v.* to annoy s.o. greatly.

cent pas (faire les) *exp.* to pace • (lit); to do the one hundred steps.

c'est le moins qu'on puisse dire *exp.*
• (lit); that's the least one can say.
SYNONYM: **tu parles!** *exp.* you said it!

chahut *m.* loud noise, racket.
NOTE: **chahuter** *v.* **1.** to make a lot of noise • **2.** to boo a performer.
SYNONYM: **chambard** *m.*

changer de disque *exp.* to change the subject; to give it a rest • (lit); to change the record.
SYNONYM: **basta!** *interj.* enough! (Italian).

chapeau *m.* big boss, he who wears the big hat • (lit); hat.
SYNONYM: **singe** *m.* • (lit); monkey.

châsser *v.* to look, to get a load at (something or s.o.) • (lit); to eye.
NOTE: This comes from the masculine noun *châsse*, which literally means "a frame or mounting (of a pair of glasses)." However, in French slang, *châsse* is commonly used to mean "eye."
SYNONYM: **zieuter** *v.* This comes from the plural masculine noun

yeux meaning "eyes" since *les yeux* is pronounced "les **z**'yeux," hence the verb, *zyeux-ter* or *zieuter*.

chatouiller une serrure *exp.* to pick a lock • (lit); to tickle a lock.
SYNONYM: **crocher** *v.* to pick a lock with a hook *(un crochet)*.

chaud de la pince (être) *exp.* to be hot for women • (lit); to be hot for a woman's vagina.
NOTE: **pince** *f.* vagina • (lit); the gripper.

chauffer du même bois (ne pas se) *exp.* not to have anything in common • (lit); not to heat oneself with the same wood.

chercher la petite bête *exp.* to nitpick • (lit); to look for the little animal.
SYNONYM: **chercher des poils sur l'œuf** *exp.* • (lit); to look for hairs on the egg.

chiasse (avoir la) *f.* to be scared to death • (lit); **1.** to be scared shitless • **2.** to have diarrhea.
SEE: *chier*.

chiée *f.* a lot • (lit); a shitload.
SEE: *chier*.

chier (faire) *v.* to annoy greatly, to bug the shit out of s.o. • (lit); to cause to shit.
NOTE: **chiant(e)** *adj.* "fuckin'" annoying.
SYNONYM: **emmerder** *v.* This comes from the feminine noun *merde* meaning "shit" • NOTE: The verb *emmerder* is not quite as strong as the verb *chier*.

chier (se faire) *v.* to be bored shitless • (lit); to cause oneself to shit.
SYNONYM: **s'emmerder** *v.* This comes from the feminine noun

merde meaning "shit" • NOTE: The verb *emmerder* is not quite as strong as the verb *chier*.

chiottes *f.pl.* bathroom • (lit); shithouse.
NOTE: This comes from the verb *chier* meaning "to shit."

chopin *m.* a catch (love).
NOTE: This comes from the slang verb *choper* meaning "to catch."

chouïa *adv.* a small amount, a little bit.

chouquette *f.* effeminate, queeny, swishy.

chouraver *v.* to steal, swipe.
NOTE: **chouraveur** *m.* thief.

ciné *m.* Abbreviation of: *cinéma*.
SYNONYM: **cinoche** *m.*

cirer toujours le même bouton *exp.* to harp on a subject • (lit); always to wax the same button.
SYNONYM: **c'est toujours la même rengaine** *exp.* it's always the same old (repetitive) story.

claquer un muscle (se) *exp.* to pull a muscle • (lit); to use up, to burn out (a light bulb, etc.).

cloque (être en) *adj.* to be knocked up • (lit); to have a lump or swelling (from an insect bite, etc.).

coffrer (se faire) *v.* to get arrested • (lit); to get oneself put into a safe.
NOTE: **coffre** *m.* prison • (lit); safe.
SYNONYM: **se faire épingler** *v.* • (lit); to get oneself pinned.

cogne *m.* • policeman, cop.
NOTE: This comes from the verb *cogner* meaning "to bump, to hit."
SYNONYM: **flic** *m.*

coller *v.* **1.** to put (with force) • (lit); to stick • **2.** to give.
SYNONYM: **fiche(r)** *v.*

coller un biscuit (se faire) *exp.* to get a citation • (lit); to get oneself stuck with a biscuit.
NOTE: **biscuit** *m.* citation.
SYNONYM: **prune** *f.* citation, ticket.

coltiner qqch. (se) *v.* to do; to get stuck doing something • (lit); **coltiner** *v.* to carry a heavy load on one's back.

combientième *adv. On est l'combientième, aujourd'hui?;* What's the date today?

comme on fait son lit on se couche *exp.* you've made your bed, now lie in it • (lit); since one makes one's bed, one lies down (in it).

comme tout *adj.* very, extremely • (lit); like everything.

comment faire pour *exp.* how to go about doing something • (lit); how to do for.
SYNONYM: **comment ça se fait que** *exp.* how is it that • (lit); how does it do that.

compas dans l'œil (avoir le) *exp.* to have a good eye for measurements • (lit); to have the compass in one's eye.

connasse *f.* **1.** bitch; "cunt" • **2.** stupid woman • (lit); female genitals, cunt.
NOTE (1): The difference between definition **1.** and **2.** simply depends on the context and manner in which the word is used: *J'veux pas l'inviter. C'est une vraie connasse!;* I don't want to invite her! She's a real cunt! • *Je l'aime bien mais c'est une vraie connasse;* I like her

but she's a real idiot.
NOTE (2): *connasse* comes from the masculine noun *con,* which literally means "cunt."
NOTE (3): Also spelled *conasse.*

constipé de l'entre-jambe (être) *exp.* to be unable to get an erection, to be unable to get it up • (lit); to have a constipated middle leg.

corder *v.* to hit it off (with s.o.) • (lit); to string (together).
SYNONYM: **copiner** *v.* This is from the noun *copin(e)* meaning "pal."
ANTONYM: **semer** *v.* to drop (s.o.), to leave behind • (lit); to sow (seed).

corser (se) *v. l'affaire se corse!;* the plot thickens! • (lit); to make stronger (sauce, drink, etc.), to intensify.
ANTONYM: **se tasser** *v.* to calm down • (lit); to settle, set (of foundations).

coton (c'est) *adv.* it's difficult • (lit); it's cotton.
SYNONYM: **c'est duraille** *adv.* • (lit); it's hard • NOTE: This is a slang transformation of the adverb and adjective *dure* meaning "hard."

coucher sur la dure *exp.* to sleep on the floor • (lit); to sleep on the hard.
NOTE: **dure** *f.* floor.
SYNONYM: **coucher à barbette** *exp.* to sleep (on a matress) on the floor.

couillon *m. & adj.* **1.** *m.* idiot, jerk, fool • **2.** *adj.* silly, foolish, dumb.
NOTE: *couillon* comes from the feminine noun *couille,* meaning "testicle." Perhaps it could be best compared to the American slang word "dickhead," which is used to refer to s.o. who is a real jerk.

couillonnades *f.pl.* nonsense, crap, bullshit.
NOTE: This comes from the plural feminine noun *couilles* meaning "testicles, balls."
SYNONYM: **merde** *f.* • (lit); shit.
NOTE: **couillonnerie** *f.*

coup de fil *m.* telephone call • (lit); wire call.
NOTE: In the above expression, *fil* may be replaced with any number of slang synonyms for the word "telephone," i.e., *bigophone, bigorneau, cornichon, escargot, phonard, ronfleur, télémuche,* etc.

coup de matraque *m.* overcharging, rip-off, fleecing • (lit); a blow or hit by a bludgeon.
SYNONYM: **coup de massue** *m.* • (lit); a blow or hit by a club or bludgeon.

coup de pompe (avoir le/un) *m.* to be suddenly exhausted.
NOTE: **être pompé(e)** *adj.* to be pooped.
SYNONYM: **avoir le coup de barre** *exp.* to be suddenly exhausted • (lit); to feel like you were just hit over the head with a bar.

courtille (être de la) *adj.* to be on the short side.
NOTE: This comes from the adjective *court(e)* meaning "short."

couru (être) *adj.* to be bound to happen • (lit); to be run.

cracher *v.* to cough up money • (lit); to spit.
NOTE: **cracher** *v.* to drop off s.o.

cradoc *adj.* dirty, filthy.
NOTE: There are several variations of the adjective *cradoc* which are:

cracra / crade / cradeau (also *crado*) / *cradingue / crados.*

craspèque *adj.* filthy dirty.
SYNONYM: **cradeau** *adj.*
ANTONYM: **nickel** *adj.* spotlessly clean.

crever les yeux *exp.* to be under one's nose • (lit); to be killing one's eyes.
SYNONYM: **sauter aux yeux** *exp.* • (lit); to jump to the eyes.

croulants *m.pl.* parents, "old folks."
NOTE: This comes from the verb *crouler* meaning "to collapse, to crumble."
SYNONYM: **vieux** *m.pl.* • (lit); old folks.

cueillir *v.* to pick up (s.o.) • (lit); to pick (flowers, etc.).
ANTONYM: **cracher** *v.* to drop off (s.o.) • (lit); to spit.

cueillir (se faire) *v.* to get arrested • (lit); to get oneself picked.
NOTE: **cueillir** *v.* to pick up s.o.
SYNONYM: **se faire agrafer** *exp.* • (lit); to get oneself stapled.

cuir *m.* (especially homosexual) man who is into the leather scene, who wears leather • (lit); leather.

cuisse légère (avoir la) *exp.* to be loose, easy • (lit); to have a light thigh (that lifts at the drop of a hat).

cuite *f.* state of drunkenness • (lit); a frying (of one's brain cells due to excessive drinking).
NOTE (1): **prendre une cuite** *exp.* to get drunk.
NOTE (2): **se cuiter** *v.* to get drunk.
SYNONYM: **poivrade** *f.* • (lit); peppering • NOTE: **se poivrer** *v.* to get drunk • (lit); to pepper oneself.

-D-

dabuche *m.* father.
NOTE: The slang suffix *-uche* was added to the already slang word *dab* meaning "father."
SYNONYM: **vieux** *m.* • (lit); old man.
ANTONYM: **vieille** *f.* mother • (lit); old lady.

dans la dèche (être) *exp.* • (lit); to be in poverty.
NOTE: **déchard(e)** n. one who is always broke; hard up for cash.
SYNONYM: **être dans la débine** *exp.*

débagouler *v.* to barf, to puke, to spew.

déboisé (être) *adj.* to be bald • (lit); to be "untimbered."
SYNONYM: **être chauve comme un genou** *exp.* • (lit); to be as bald as a knee.

décamper *v.* to leave quickly, to clear out • (lit); to decamp.
SYNONYM: **prendre la tangente** *exp.* • (lit); to take the tangent (and slip away quickly).

décatir (se) *exp.* to lose one's beauty, to age. • (lit); to take off the gloss (of furniture, etc.).

déconner *v.* **1.** to talk absolute nonsense • **2.** to act silly and goofy.
NOTE: *déconner* comes from the masculine noun *con* meaning "cunt."
NOTE: *sans déconner?;* no fooling? (extremely popular).

décrocher *v.* to crack up, to go crazy • (lit); to take (a telephone, a towel, etc.) off the hook, to unhook.
SYNONYM: **dérailler** *v.* • (lit); to derail.

décrocher un contract *exp.* to land a contract • (lit); to unhook a contract.
SYNONYM: **accrocher une affaire** *exp.* to sew up a deal • (lit); to hook a contract.

décrotter (se) *v.* to clean oneself • (lit); to "un-dung" oneself.
NOTE: This comes from the feminine noun *crotte* meaning "dung, droppings (from a rabbit, horse, etc.)."
SYNONYM: **se décrasser** *v.* This comes from the feminine noun *crasse* meaning "(body) dirt."

dégauchir *v.* to find, uncover • (lit); to "un-left" (something).
NOTE: The verb *dégauchir* comes from the expression *mettre qqch. à gauche* meaning "to put something away, to store" or literally "to put something to the left."
SYNONYM: **dégotter** *v.*

dégraisser *v.* to make cutbacks • (lit); to skim the fat off (soup, etc.).
SYNONYM: **balayer** *v.* • (lit); to sweep.

dégueu *adj.* disgusting, that which causes vomiting.
NOTE: This comes from the verb *dégueuler* meaning "to vomit, to barf."

dégueuler ses tripes *exp.* • (lit); to throw up one's guts.
NOTE: **dégueulasse** *adj.* disgusting, that which makes one want to throw up.
SEE: *gerbosse.*
SYNONYM: **dégobiller ses tripes** *exp.*

déhancher (se) *v.* to wiggle one's hips • (lit); to dislocate one's hips.

démanger *v.* to itch to do something • (lit); to itch.

NOTE: **démangeaison** *f.* an itching to do something.

déménager *v.* to ransack a house • (lit); to move, to "unhome."
NOTE: **déménager** *v.* to talk absolute nonsense.
SYNONYM: **nettoyer** *v.* • (lit); to clean (out a house during a burglary).

dents du fond qui baignent (avoir les) *exp.* to be stuffed to the gills • (lit); to have back teeth that are floating.

déphasé(e) (avoir l'air) *adj.* to be/to feel out of it • (lit); to be out of phase (of electrical current).
SYNONYM: **ne pas être dans son assiette** *exp.* • (lit); not to be in one's plate.

dépieuter (se) *v.* to get out of bed • (lit); to unstake oneself.
ANTONYM: **se pieuter** *v.* to go to bed.
NOTE: **pieu** *m.* bed • (lit); stake.

dernier cri (le) *m. & adj.* the latest fashion • (lit); the latest cry • **1.** *m.* *C'est l'dernier cri d'Paris;* It's the latest style from Paris • **2.** *adj. Ça, c't'une chemise dernier cri;* That shirt is the latest thing.

désargenté(e) (être) *adj.* • This comes from the masculine noun *argent* meaning "money" or literally "silver" • (lit); "desilvered."
ANTONYM: **argenté(e)** *adj.*

dessus (avoir le) *exp.* • (lit); to have the upper (hand).

dévaliser *v.* to clean out (a store, a refrigerator, etc.) of its stock.

dix minutes de bon (avec) *exp.* with ten minutes to spare • (lit); with ten minutes that are (still) good.

doublé (faire un) *m.* to have twins • (lit); to do a double.

draguer *v.* to cruise (s.o.) • (lit); to dredge (a river, etc.).
NOTE: **dragueur** *m.* skirt chaser.

du bois dont on fait les flutes (être) *exp.* Said of s.o. who can be wrapped around one's finger • (lit); to be the wood of which flutes are made (i.e., soft and pliable).

-E-

écrases-merde *m.pl.* big shoes, "shit kickers" • (lit); shit smashers.

écrouler dans un fauteuil (s') *exp.* to flop into an armchair • (lit); to crumble or collapse into a chair.
SYNONYM: **s'affaler dans un fauteuil** *exp.* • (lit); to fall or drop into a chair.

écumer les bars *exp.* to bar hop • (lit); to scour, rove bars.

embellemerder *v.* to be hounded by one's mother-in-law.

emmerdement *m.* annoyances, complications, problems, etc. • (lit); that which bugs the shit out of s.o.
NOTE: **emmerder** *v.* to bug the shit out of s.o. (since the root word is *merde* meaning "shit").

emmerdeur *m.* annoying person, pain in the ass • (lit); one who bugs the shit out of others.

NOTE: This comes from the feminine noun *merde* meaning "shit."

en boucher un coin *exp.* to surprise, to flabbergast • (lit); to stop up a corner of it.
SYNONYM: **en boucher une surface à qqn.** *exp.*

en bourgeois *m.* plainclothesmen • (lit); like a citizen, townsman.

en nage (être) *adj.* to be dripping in sweat • (lit); **nage** *f.* swimming; rowing.

encadrer qqn. (ne pas pouvoir) *v.* to be unable to stand s.o. • (lit); to be unable to put s.o. into a frame (as one would a painting).
SYNONYM: **ne pas pouvoir blairer qqn.** *exp.* • (lit); to be unable to smell s.o. • NOTE: **blair** *m.* nose.

enterrer sa vie de garçon *exp.* to have a bachelor party• (lit); to bury one's life as a boy.

envoyer sur les roses (se faire) *exp.* to get fired (from office) • (lit); to get oneself sent on the roses.
SYNONYM: **se faire saquer** *exp.* • (lit); to get oneself sacked.

éponger le retard *exp.* to make up for lost time • (lit); to sponge up a delay.

épouser le gros sac *exp.* to marry into money (said of a man who marries a rich woman) • (lit); to marry the big sack (of money).

esquinter *v.* to ruin, to hurt • (lit); to exhaust.
SYNONYM: **bousiller** *v.* • (lit); to break.

essorer qqn. *exp.* to squeeze s.o. dry of money • (lit); to wring or spin dry s.o. (of all his money).

éterniser (s') *v.* to overstay and wear out one's welcome • (lit); to last forever, to drag on and on.

étoffe (avoir l') *exp.* to have the makings (of something) • (lit); to have the fabric.

étouffer qqch. dans l'œuf *exp.* to nip something in the bud • (lit); to smother something in the egg (so that it can never become full grown).

étriller *v.* to ripoff (s.o.) • (lit); to currycomb (s.o. of all his money).
SYNONYM: **rouler** *v.* to ripoff, to cheat • (lit); to roll.

-F-

faire cadeau du reste *exp.* to spare s.o. the details, to cut to the chase • (lit); to make a gift of the rest.

faire dans la dentelle *exp.* to put on kid gloves, to handle carefully • (lit); to make lace.

faire la loi *exp.* to lay down the law • (lit); to make the law.

faire le pont *exp.* to take Monday off • (lit); to make the bridge (from Saturday to Monday).
SYNONYM: **faire le Saint-Lundi** *exp.* • (lit); to make Saint Monday (hence, a holiday).

faire peau neuve *exp.* to turn over a new leaf • (lit); to make new skin.

faire sa déclaration *exp.* to pop the question • (lit); to make one's declaration (of love).

faucheur *m.* thief.
NOTE: This comes from the verb *faucher* meaning "to steal."
SYNONYM: **barboteur** *m.* • This comes from the verb *barboter* meaning "to steal."

fenêtrière *f.* prostitute who hangs out the window, window hooker.
NOTE: This comes from the feminine noun *fenêtre* meaning "window."

festonner *v.* to stagger about drunkenly • (lit); to walk in the pattern of festoons.

fiche qqch. en l'air *exp.* to chuck something away • (lit); to throw something into the air.
NOTE: The verb *fiche* has replaced its old form *ficher*.
SYNONYM: **foutre en l'air** *exp.* • The verb *foutre* has a much stronger meaning than its euphemism *fiche* and is extremely popular.

fini *adj.* through and through, complete • (lit); finished.
SYNONYM: **sacré(e) / beau (belle)** *adj.* • (lit); blessed / handsome (pretty).

flasher (faire) *exp.* to turn (s.o.) on • (lit); to make one's lights turn on.

flécher *v.* to stick together, to team up.

flubard *m.* telephone.
NOTE: **flubards** *m.pl.* legs.
SYNONYM: **cornichon** *m.* telephone • (lit); pickle (since its shape resembles that of a telephone receiver).

fondre *v.* to lose weight • (lit); to melt.
ANTONYM: **prendre de la brioche** *exp.* to get a gut • (lit); to take on brioche (bread).

fondu (faire un) *m.* to drop out of the picture, to fade away • (lit); to do a dissolve (as in the movie industry).

fouetter *v.* to stink to high heaven • (lit); to whip.
SYNONYM: **taper** *v.* • (lit); to hit.

fouiner *v.* to snoop around • (lit); to do like a weasel *(une fouine)*.
NOTE: **fouine** *f.* a snoop • (lit); weasel.

foutre *v.* This is an extremely popular verb with many different meanings, all of which are harsh since its literal translation is "to fuck." • **1.** (lit); to fuck • **2.** to fuck something up • **3.** to do, to make • **4.** to put • **5.** to give • **6.** *s'en foutre;* not to give a damn.
NOTE (1): *foutre* is also commonly used as an expletive: *Foutre!*; Fuck! SEE: *bordel.*

foutre en l'air *exp.* **1.** to chuck or get rid of something. *C'te carrière d'malheur, j'l'ai foutue en l'air!;* You can take this career and shove it! • **2.** to kill, to do away with. *Y s'est foutu en l'air;* He killed himself.
NOTE: **fiche(r) en l'air** *exp.* A less strong variation of: *foutre en l'air.*

fraise *f.* face • (lit); strawberry.
SYNONYM: **citron** *m.* **1.** face • **2.** head • (lit); lemon.

frapper le biscuit (se) *exp.* to worry oneself sick • (lit); to hit oneself in the head.
NOTE: **biscuit** *m.* head • (lit); biscuit.
SYNONYM: **se faire du mauvais**

sang *exp.* • (lit); to make oneself bad blood.
ANTONYM: **être peinard(e)** *adj.* to be calm and relaxed.

fréquenter les lits *exp.* to sleep around, to bed hop • (lit); to frequent beds.

frimeur, euse *n.* show off.
SYNONYM: **crâneur, euse** *n.*

frippes *f.pl.* clothes, threads • (lit); wrinkles.
SYNONYM: **nippes** *f.pl.* clothes • NOTE: **nipper** *v.* to dress.

frotter à qqn. (se) *v.* to tangle with s.o. • (lit); to rub up against s.o.

fumeron *m.* heavy smoker, chain-smoker.
SYNONYM: **fumer comme un pompier** *exp.* • (lit); to smoke like a fireman.

-G-

gagner son bifteck *exp.* to earn a living • (lit); to earn one's beefsteak.
SYNONYM: **blot** *m.* job, line of work.
NOTE: **la lutte au bifteck** *exp.* rat race.

garce *f. & adj.* **1.** *f.* bitchy woman or girl; bitch • **2.** *adj.* bitchy.

gargoulette *f.* throat • (lit); the gargler.
SYNONYM: **avaloir** *m.* • (lit); the swallower.

gerbosse *adj.* disgusting, that which makes one want to throw up.
NOTE: **gerber** *v.* to throw up.
SYNONYM: **dégueulasse** *adj.*

gluant *m.* baby • (lit); sticky, gummy (since a baby is always stuck to a

mother's breast).
SYNONYM: **criard** *m.*
• (lit); screamer.

gosier blindé (avoir le) *exp.* to be able to handle strong liquor, to be able to pack it away • (lit); to have the armored throat.
ANTONYM: **avoir la cuite facile** *exp.* to get drunk easily.
NOTE: **gosier** *m.* throat • (lit); gullet.

gouiner (se) *v.* to practice lesbianism, to make love between two women.
NOTE: **gouine** *f.* lesbian, dyke.

gourbi *m.* house • (lit); shack, dirty house.
SYNONYM: **baraque** *f.* house • (lit); barracks.

gousse *f.* lesbian, dyke.
NOTE: **se gousser** *v.* to practice lesbianism, to make love between two women.

grelots (avoir les) *m.pl.* to be afraid, to have the jitters • (lit); to have bells, sleigh bells.
NOTE: This expression might be translated as "to have bells that are jingling (because the possessor is shaking from fear)."
NOTE: **grelotter** *v.* to shake with fear • (lit); to jingle.

gros sur la patate (en avoir) *exp.* to have a lot on one's mind • (lit); to have a large amount on the heart.
NOTE: **patate** *f.* **1.** heart • **2.** head • **3.** big nose • **4.** peasant • **5.** punch (to the face).

grosse à pleine ceinture (être) *exp.* to be in an advanced state of pregnancy • (lit); to be fat to the point of filling an entire belt (on its last notch).

-H-

histoire crousillante *exp.* a good juicy
story • (lit); crispy, crunchy.
ANTONYM: **une histoire à dormir
debout** *exp.* a long and boring story.

honteuse *f.* homosexual man who has
not yet come out of the closet,
"closet queen" • (lit); ashamed.

hosto *m.* Abbreviation of: *hôpital*
meaning "hospital".

hyper *adv.* extremely • (lit); hyper.
SYNONYM: **archi** *adv.*

-I-

il y a à boire et à manger là-dedans
exp. there are good points and bad
points to it; "there are parts that are
easy to swallow and others that are
not." • (lit); there are things to drink
as well as things to eat there.

-J-

jacasser *v.* to chatter, to talk a lot.
NOTE (1): **jacasserie** *f.* endless
chatter.
NOTE (2): **jacasseur, euse** *n.*
chatterbox.
SEE: *mitrailleuse.*
SYNONYM: **bavasser** *v.* This comes
from the verb *baver* meaning
"to drool."

jambes en parenthèses (avoir les)
exp. • (lit); to have legs shaped like
parentheses, to be bowlegged.
NOTE: Any number of slang

synonyms for "legs" could easily
replace *jambes* in this expression
such as: *(m.pl.) bâtons, bégonias,
bouts de bois, compas, flubards,
gigots, nougats, piliers, pivots, etc.*
• *(f.pl.) baguettes, béquilles cannes,
gambettes, gambilles, guibolles,
quilles, etc.*
SYNONYM: **avoir les jambes
Louis XV** *exp.* • (lit); to have legs
like Louis XV.
ANTONYM: **avoir les jambes en X**
exp. to be knock-kneed • (lit); to
have legs in the shape of an X.

jeter de la poudre aux yeux *exp.* to
pull the wool over one's eyes
• (lit); to throw powder in one's eyes.

jeter un coup d'œil *exp.* to have a
look • (lit); to throw a "quick" eye.
NOTE: **jeter un œil** *exp.*

jouer des badigoinces *exp.* to eat well
• (lit); to play the lips.
NOTE: **badigoinces** *m.pl.* lips.

jour chrômé *m.* nonworking day
(i.e., Sundays, holidays, etc.)
• (lit); chromed day.

Jules, jules *m.* man in general;
boyfriend; husband. • (lit); Julius.
ANTONYM: **Julie, julie** *f.* girlfriend,
wife.

-L-

la couler douce (se) *exp.* to have it
easy • (lit); to flow sweetly through
it (life).

laisser qqn. en carafe *exp.* to jilt s.o.,
to leave s.o. high and dry • (lit); to
leave s.o. like a carafe (after it's
been all used up).

SYNONYM: **laisser qqn. en plan**
exp. • (lit); to leave s.o. just
standing there like a plant.

lanterne *f.* eye • (lit); lantern.
SYNONYM: **mirette** *f.* This comes
from the verb *mirer* meaning
"to look."

lardu *m.* policeman • (lit); the "fat
one."
NOTE: This comes from the
masculine noun *lard* meaning
"fat" or "bacon."
SYNONYM: **flic** *m.* cop.

larme *f.* a drop • (lit); tear.
NOTE: **larmichette** *f.*

le dernier cri *m. & adj.* the latest
fashion • (lit); the latest cry.

lèche-cul *m.* kiss-ass • (lit); lick-ass.
NOTE: **faire du lèche-cul** *exp.* to
kiss ass.

lèche-vitrine (faire du) *exp.* to go
window-shopping • (lit); to go out
licking store windows.

lécher la pomme (se) *exp.* to make
out, to neck, to suck face • (lit); to
lick each other's face.
NOTE: **pomme** *f.* face • (lit); apple.
SYNONYM: **se sucer le citron** *exp.*
• (lit); to suck each other's face •
NOTE: **citron** *m.* face • (lit); lemon.

-M-

mac *m.* pimp.
NOTE: **macquereau** *m.*

Machin(e) *n.* What's-his-name;
What's-her-name.
NOTE: When in lowercase, the

meaning of *machin* becomes
"thing" or "thingamajig."

magase *m.* Abbreviation of: *magase*
meaning "store."

mains baladeuses (avoir les) *exp.*
• (lit); to have wandering hands.

malheureux *adj.* measly, mere
• (lit); wretched, poor.

marcher à voile et à vapeur *exp.* to
be bisexual, to be A.C.-D.C.
• (lit); to walk by sail and by steam.

mardoche *m.* Monday.

marida (se) *v.* Slang transformation of
se marier meaning "to get married."
SYNONYM: **se caser** *v.* to place, file
(something).

marne *m.* work.
NOTE: **marner** *v.* to work hard.
SYNONYM: **boulot** *m.*

maton *m.* policeman, cop • (lit); looker.
NOTE: This comes from the verb
mater meaning "to look at carefully."
SYNONYM: **flic** *m.*

mener une vie de paillasson *exp.* to
lead a fast life • (lit); to lead a life
of a doormat.
NOTE: This expression conjures
up an image of a person who
welcomes many different "house
guests" on a regular basis as does
a doormat.

menottes *f.pl.* child's little hands
• (lit); handcuffs.
NOTE: Other words used in
reference to a child are: **lolo** *m.*
milk, **peton** *m.* foot, **quenotte** *f.*
tooth.

merde *f. & expl.* • (lit); shit • **1.** *f.* shit
• **2.** *expl.* shit • **3.** good luck •
4. "No." • **5.** *Y s'prend pas pour*

d' la merde; He thinks he's hot shit. • **6.** *être dans la merde;* to be in hot water • **7.** *avoir un œil qui dit merde à l'autre;* to be cross-eyed. (lit); to have one eye that says shit to the other.
NOTE (1): **merder** *v.* to screw up.
NOTE (2): **un(e) petit(e) merdeux, euse** *m. & f.* little squirt • (lit); a little shit.
NOTE(3): **merdique** *adj.* shitty.

mettre à la coule *exp.* to bring (s.o.) up-to-date, to give (s.o.) the low-down • (lit); to put (s.o.) in the flow.
SYNONYM: **mettre à la page** *exp.* • (lit); to bring (s.o.) up to the page (of events).

mettre la louche au panier *exp.* to feel up a girl • (lit); to put the ladle in the basket.
NOTE (1): **louche** *f.* hand • (lit); (soup)ladle.
NOTE (2): **panier** *m.* vagina • (lit); basket.

mettre son véto sur qqch. *exp.* to draw the line, to put one's foot down • (lit); to put one's veto on something.

miché *m.* prostitute's client, john.

michetonner *v.* to pay for sex • (lit); to be a *miché;* john.

mitrailleuse *f.* chatterbox • (lit); machine gun.
SYNONYM: **tapette** *f.*
1. blabbermouth • **2.** gay man, "fag" • (lit); tongue.
SEE: *jacasser.*

molarder *v.* to spit, to hawk a loogie.
NOTE: **molard** *m.* gob of spit or phlegm, loogie.

mollo-mollo *adv.* carefully, cautiously.
SYNONYM: **tout doucement** *adv.* very carefully • (lit); all sweetly.

mon chou *exp.* sweetheart • (lit); my cabbage.

montrer (toute) sa boutique *exp.* to expose oneself, to flash • (lit); to show (all) of one's goods.

morbac *m.* annoying little child, brat • (lit); crab(louse), pubic louse.

mordre *v.* to understand, to get it • (lit); to bite.
SYNONYM: **piger** *v.* to understand.

morfaler (se) *v.* to stuff oneself with food.
NOTE: **morfale** *m.* / **marfalou** *m.* glutton, pig.
SYNONYM: **s'empiffrer** *v.* This comes from the slang masculine noun *pif* meaning "nose, schnoz-zola." Therefore, *s'empiffrer* might be loosely translated as "to eat until it's coming out of one's nose."

mouchodrome *m.* bald head • (lit); a launching pad for flies.
NOTE: **piste d'envol pour mouches** *f.* • (lit); launching pad for flies.
SYNONYM: **un genou** *m.* • (lit); a knee.

-N-

ne pas être aussi bête qu'on en a l'air *exp.* • (lit); not to be as dumb as one looks.
NOTE: Any slang synonym of *bête* could be used in this expression such as: *con, déplafonné, empaillé,*

empaqueté, emplâtré, enflé, fada, dingue, etc.

nicher *v.* to live • (lit); to build a nest, to nest.
SYNONYM: **crécher** *v.*

-O-

oiseau *m.* • (lit); bird.
SYNONYM: **un drôle de moineau** *m.* • (lit); a strange sparrow.

on apprend pas à un vieux singe à faire la grimace *exp.* you can't teach an old dog new tricks • (lit); you can't teach an old monkey to smile.

on sait jamais sur quel pied danser *exp.* you never know where you stand with him/her • (lit); you never know which foot to dance with.

ordure *f.* • (lit); dirt, filth, trash • This is commonly used as an expletive to refer to a thoroughly contemptible person. *Qu'est-c'que tu fous là, ordure?!;* What the hell are you doing there, you scum bag?!

-P-

papa gâteau *m.* man who takes care of a younger man (or woman) financially in exchange for sexual favors, sugar daddy • (lit); father cake.

paquet de bleues *m.* a packet of Gauloise cigarettes • (lit); a package of blues (since Gauloise

cigarettes come in a blue packet).
SYNONYM: **paquet de goldu** *m.*

parler boulot *exp.* to talk shop • (lit); to talk work.
NOTE: **boulot** *m.* work.

pas cher *exp.* cheap • (lit); not expensive.

pas croyable *adj.* unbelievable, terrific.
NOTE: This is a popular replacement for *incroyable.*
SYNONYM: **génial(e)** *adj.*

patapouf *m.* fatso.
ANTONYM: **planche à pain** *f.* very thin person • (lit); ironing board.
SYNONYM: **bouboule** *m. & f.*

pâtée maison *f.* a thrashing.

pavé dans la cour (n'avoir plus de) *exp.* to be toothless • (lit); to have no more pavement in the courtyard.

pédé *m.* (very popular) pederast, fag.
NOTE: This is an abbreviation of: *pédéraste* which is sometimes seen as simply *P.D.* or *pédé.* Although the noun *pédéraste* is not an insulting term, note that in its abbreviated form, it becomes extremely derogatory.

peigner (se) *v.* to fight, "to tear out each other's hair" (especially of women) • (lit); to comb one's hair.
NOTE: **se crêper le chignon** *exp.* • (lit); to frizz each other's bun (of hair).

pendre la crémaillère *exp.* to have a housewarming • (lit); to hang the pot hook.

perdre les pédales *exp.* to lose control of one's temper • (lit); to lose (control of) the pedals.

SYNONYM: **voir rouge** *exp.* • (lit); to see red.

pet de lapin (ne pas valoir un) *exp.* said of something worthless • (lit); not to be worth a rabbit's fart • *C'te télévision, ça vaut pas un pet d'lapin;* This television isn't worth a damn.

péter le feu *exp.* to be very energetic • (lit); to fart fire.
NOTE: **avoir la pétasse** *exp.* to be horribly frightened • (lit); to have the farts.

petits souliers (être dans ses) *exp.* to be very embarrassed or ill at ease • (lit); to be in one's little shoes.

peur bleue *f.* intense fear • (lit); blue fear.
SYNONYM: **trouille** *f. J'avais la trouille, moi;* I was scared shitless.

pigette *f.* year.
SYNONYM: **berge** *f.*

piper qqn. sur le tas *exp.* to catch s.o. red handed • (lit); to lure s.o. on the stack.
SYNONYM: **prendre qqn. sur le tas** *exp.* • (lit); to take s.o. on the stack.

piquer une ronflette *exp.* to take a nap • (lit); to take a little snore.
NOTE (1): **piquer** *v.* to take, to grab.
NOTE (2): *ronflette* comes from the verb *ronfler* meaning "to snore."

pisse *f.* urine • (lit); piss.

pistonner *v.* to recommend s.o. for a job, to pull strings (for s.o.).
SYNONYM: **chapeauter** *v.* to recommend s.o. for a job, to help s.o. become a boss *(un chapeau).*

pleurer mon colosse (faire) *exp.* to urinate, to take a leak • (lit); to make one's giant cry.

plombard *m.* • plumber.

plumes *f.pl.* hair • (lit); feathers.
SYNONYM: **tignasse** *f.*

plus on est de fous plus on rit *exp.* the more the merrier • (lit); the crazier we are, the more we'll laugh.

pompe-la-sueur *m.* slave driver • (lit); sweat pumper.

pompes (faire des) *f.pl.* to do push-ups • (lit); to do pumps.

popote (faire la) *exp.* kitchen, cooking • (lit); mess, canteen (military).
SYNONYM: **faire la tambouille** *exp.*
NOTE: **cuistot(e)** *n.* chef.

porté(e) sur la bagatelle (être) *exp.* to have sex on the brain • (lit); to be carried (away) on love making.

porté(e) sur la bouffe (être) *exp.* to be driven by food • (lit); to be carried by food.
NOTE: **bouffe** *f.* food / **bouffer** *v.* to eat.
SYNONYM: **raffoler de qqch.** *exp.* to be wild about something.

porter comme un charme (se) *exp.* to be fit as a fiddle • (lit); to carry oneself like a charm.
ANTONYM: **se sentir patraque** *adj.* to feel sick.

portrait tout craché (c'est le) *m.* the spittin' image • (lit); the complete spit.

poulaille *f.* audience, public.
SYNONYM: **galerie** *f.*

pouliche *f.* young girl, chick.
NOTE: **poulette** *f.*
SYNONYM: **nana** *f.* (very popular).

pour comble de malheur *exp.* to make matters worse • (lit); as an overflowing of misfortune.
ANTONYM: **mettre du beurre dans les épinards** *exp.* to make matters easier.

prendre les virages sur les chapeaux de roues *exp.* to screech around bends (in the road) • (lit); to take bends on the hats of the wheels.

prendre pour de la petite bière (ne pas se) *exp.* to think highly of oneself, to be conceited • (lit); not to take oneself for a little beer.
SYNONYM: **se croire sorti(e) de la cuisse de Jupiter** *exp.* to think of oneself as having come from Jupiter's thigh.

prendre un petit à-côté *exp.* to have extramarital sex • (lit); to take a little something on the side.

près de ses sous (être) *adj.* to be stingy, tight-fisted • (lit); to be close to one's money.
NOTE: **sous** *m.pl.* money; coins.
SYNONYM: **les lâcher avec un élastique** *exp.* • (lit); to release them (coins) with a rubber band.

presto *adv.* immediately (from Italian)
NOTE: illico-presto *adv.* Variation of: *presto.*
SYNONYM: **dare-dare** *adv.* quickly.

pris(e) au dépourvu (être) *exp.* to be taken off guard • (lit); to be taken short (as in destitute).

promenade *f.* something easy to do, a cinch, a snap, a piece of cake • (lit); a (cake)walk.

prononcer le conjugo *exp.* to tie the knot • (lit); to announce the taking of one's conjugal vows.

proprio *m.* (male) owner; landlord • (lit); Abbreviation of: *propriétaire.*
NOTE: **propriote** *f.* (female) owner.

putain *f., expl. & adj.* **1.** *f.* whore, prostitute • **2.** *expl.* Used to denote surprise. *Putain!;* Wow! • **3.** *expl.* Also, used to signify anger, frustration. *Putain! Damn!*
NOTE: putain de *adj.* damn, fucking. *C'te putain d'bagnole!;* This fucking car! *Putain de* is often used in conjunction with *bordel de* to further condemn the noun that it modifies: *Cette putain de bordel de voiture!;* This goddamn fucking car!

-Q-

quelle mouche le pique *exp.* what's bugging him? • (lit); what fly bit him.

quoi de neuf? *exp.* • (lit); what's new?
SYNONYM: **qu'est-ce qu'il y a de nouveau?** *exp.*

-R-

ragoûgnasse *f.* low quality food, grub.
SYNONYM: **graillon** *m.* • (lit); burnt fat.

ramasser la chtouille *exp.* to get the clap • (lit); to gather venereal disease.

ras le cul (en avoir) *exp.* to be fed up • (lit); to have had it up to the brim of one's ass • *J'en ai ras l'cul d'ces d'voirs!;* I've had it with this homework!
SYNONYM: **en avoir ras le bol** *exp.*

to have had it up to the rim of the bowl. *J'en ai ras l'bol de lui!;* I've had it with him!

ravigoter (se) *v.* to perk up oneself, to revive oneself.
SYNONYM: **se requinquer** *v.*
ANTONYM: **partir en brioche** *exp.* to go downhill.

rebecter (se) *v.* to start feeling better (after an illness), to pick oneself back up.
SYNONYM: **se refaire la cerise** *exp.* to redo one's face • NOTE: **cerise** *f.* • (lit); cherry • **1.** face • **2.** head.

rebiffer *v.* to snub s.o.
SYNONYM: **snober** *v.* • NOTE: **snobinard(e)** *n.* snob.

recharger les accus *exp.* to set 'em up (the glasses for another round of drinks) • (lit); to recharge the batteries.
SYNONYM: **recharger les wagonnets** *exp.* to recharge the tip carts.

réglo (être) *adj.* to be on the level, normal.
NOTE: This comes from the verb *régler* meaning "to regulate, to keep (something) in order."
SYNONYM: **être terre-à-terre** *adj.* to be down to earth.

rem *f.* • verlan for *mère;* mother.
NOTE: **rep** *m.* verlan for *père;* father.

rembrayer *v.* to get back to work, to get cracking • (lit); to put the clutch back in.
NOTE: **embrayer** *v.* to get to work • (lit); to put in the clutch.

renifler *v.* • (lit); to sniff • *J'peux pas la renifler!;* I can't stand (even smelling) her!

rester comme deux ronds de flan (en) *exp.* to be flabbergasted • (lit); to stay there like two slices of custard (hence "motionless").
SYNONYM: **en rester baba** *v.* to be speechless with astonishment.

rétamé(e) (être) *adj.* to be bombed • (lit); to be retinned (to be so drunk that one can barely move as if made of tin).
SYNONYM: **être bourré(e)** *adj.* • (lit); to be stuffed (of alcohol).

réussir *v.* to be good for one's health • (lit); to succeed (in digesting something).

réveil pénible *exp.* a rude awakening • (lit); an painful awakening.

rien à faire *exp.* no way • (lit); nothing doing.
SYNONYM: **rien à chiquer** *exp.* • (lit); nothing chewing (English equivalent: "I'm not swallowing that").

rien lui échappe *exp.* • (lit); nothing gets by him/her.

rincer l'œil (se) *exp.* to enjoy looking at something provocative.

roméo *m.* an alcoholic drink consisting of rum and water; *rhum et eau = roméo.*

roteuse *f.* bottle of champagne • (lit); the burper; that which causes burping.
NOTE: **roter** *v.* • (lit); to burp.
SYNONYM: **champe** *m.*

rougnotter *v.* to stink, to smell to high heaven.
SYNONYM: **schlinguer** *v.* / **schlingotter** *v.*

rouler les biscottos *exp.* to swagger, to strut (said of a bodybuilder)

• (lit); to roll one's biceps.
NOTE: **biscotto** *m.* bicep.

rouler une pelle à qqn. *exp.* to French kiss • (lit); to roll s.o. a scallop (since scallops are wet and slippery).

-S-

Sainte-Touche (la) *f.* • (lit); the blessed payday.
NOTE: **toucher** *v.* to receive one's salary.

saler la note *exp.* to pad the bill • (lit); to salt the bill.
NOTE: **être salé(e)** *adj.* to be expensive.

saloperie *f.* **1.** junk, trash. *C'est d'la vraie saloperie;* That's absolute junk • **2.** dirty language, smut. *Arrête de dire des saloperies comme ça!;* Stop talking such filth! • **3.** a dirty trick. *Y m'a fait une saloperie;* He did a real rotten thing to me. ALSO: **saloperie de** *adj.* filthy, junky, disgusting. *Quelle saloperie de temps!;* What lousy weather!

sans rigoler *exp.* no kidding • (lit); without laughing.
NOTE: **rigoler** *v.* to laugh.
SYNONYM: **sans blague** *exp.* • (lit); without a joke.

sapes *f.pl.* clothes, "threads".
NOTE: **se saper** *v.* to get dressed.
SYNONYM: **fringues** *f.pl.* • NOTE: **se fringuer** *v.* to get dressed.

sauver les côtelettes (se) *exp.* to save one's hide • (lit); to save one's cutlets or chops.
NOTE: **se sauver** *v.* to leave quickly.

serrer les fesses *exp.* to have courage, to hang in there • (lit); to squeeze the cheeks of one's buttocks.

simple comme bonjour (c'est) *exp.* it's easy as pie • (lit); it's easy as hello.
SYNONYM: **c'est bête comme chou** *exp.* • (lit); it's silly as cabbage.

siphonné(e) (être) *adj.* to be nuts, crazy • (lit); to be siphoned (of all sanity).
SYNONYM: **être cinglé(e)** *adj.*

soupé (en avoir) *exp.* to be fed up • (lit); to have eaten (all one can).
NOTE (1): **souper** *v.* to eat supper • NOTE (2): **souper** *m.* supper.
Commonly heard as: *A la soupe!;* Come and get it!
SYNONYM: **en avoir ras le bol** *exp.* • (lit); to have had it to the rim of the bowl.

sous le sceau du secret *exp.* on the qt • (lit); under the seal of secrecy.

-T-

tabasser *v.* • to beat up (s.o.).
NOTE: **passer qqn. à tabac** *exp.* to beat s.o. to a pulp.

taper *v.* • (lit); to strike, hit.
NOTE: **taper** *v.* • to stink.

taper sur le système *exp.* to annoy.
SYNONYM: **casser les pieds à qqn.** *exp.* • (lit); to break s.o.'s feet.

tapin (faire le) *m.* to work the streets (as a prostitute).
NOTE: **tapineuse** *f.* prostitute.

tarbouif *m.* nose, honker, "shnozzola."
SYNONYM: **tarin** *m.*

tête en compote (avoir la) *exp.* to have a terrible headache • (lit); to have a head that feels like compote.
SYNONYM: **avoir les pieds en compote** *exp.* to have aching feet.

tignasse *f.* insulting term for "hair."
SYNONYM: **tifs** *m.pl.* hair
• NOTE: *Tifs* is a non-insulting synonym for *tignasse*.

tiraillement *m.* tension, friction
• (lit); pulling, yanking.
NOTE: This comes from the verb *tirailler* meaning "to pull in different directions."

tire *f.* car • (lit); puller • *Félicitations! J'ai entendu dire qu't'as acheté une nouvelle tire!;* Congratulations! I heard you bought a new car!
NOTE: This comes from the verb *tirer* meaning, "to pull."
SYNONYM: **bagnole** *adj.* (very popular).

tire-au-flanc *m.* a lazy individual
• (lit); a "pull-by-his-side," one who has to be pulled while on his side because he's always lying down.
NOTE (1): **tirer au flanc** *v.* to be lazy.
SYNONYM: **cossard** *m.* lazy bum •
NOTE (2): **avoir la cosse** *exp.* to be lazy.
ANTONYM: **péter le feu** *exp.* to have a lot of energy • (lit); to fart fire.

tirer les ficelles *exp.* to run the show
• (lit); to pull the strings (of a theater curtain).

tissu de mensonges *exp.* pack of lies
• (lit); a tissue of lies.

tomber à pic *exp.* to arrive in the nick of time • (lit); to fall like a pickaxe.
SYNONYM: **tomber bien** *exp.*

tomber sur qqn. *exp.* to run into s.o. (somewhere) • (lit); to fall on s.o.

toquante *f.* watch.
NOTE: This refers to that which goes "tic toc."

torche-cul *m.* toilet paper
• (lit); ass-wipe.

tour du cadran (faire le) *exp.* to sleep round the clock • (lit); to take a tour of the face of the clock.
SYNONYM: **faire la grasse matinée** *exp.* to sleep in • (lit); to make the fat morning.

tout oreilles (être) *exp.* • (lit); to be all ears.

Trifouillis-les-Oies *prn.* boonies, boondocks, toolies, sticks, any imaginary far away place.
NOTE: **Tripatouille-les-Oies** *prn.*

trognon *n. & adj.* sweet, cute.

trotte *f.* a long distance • (lit); a trot.
NOTE: **se trotter** *v.* to leave.

trou *m.* place, dive • (lit); hole.
SYNONYM: **bled** *m.*

trouver porte de bois *exp.* to find no one at home • (lit); to find a wooden door.

tuer les mouches à quinze pas *exp.* to have bad breath • (lit); to kill flies fifteen paces away.
SYNONYM: **repousser du goulot** *exp.* • (lit); to repel from the mouth
• NOTE: **goulot** *m.* mouth, gullet.

-U-

un de ces quat' *exp.* one of these days
  • (lit); one of these four (mornings).
  NOTE (1): This is a shortened version
  of the expression *un de ces
  quat' matins* meaning "one of these
  four mornings."
  NOTE (2): *quat'* is an contraction of
  quatre.

-V-

vache (oh, la) *exclam.* wow!
  • (lit); oh, the cow (American
  equivalent: holy cow!).
  SYNONYM: **ça alors!** *exp.* • (lit); that
  then!

vanné(e) (être) *adj.* to be exhausted
  • (lit); to be winnowed.
  SYNONYM: **être lessivé(e)** *adj.*
  • (lit); to be washed out (of all
  energy).

viser *v.* to get a look at (something)
  • (lit); to take aim at (something).
  SYNONYM: **gaffer** *v.*

vite fait (s'en jeter un) *exp.* to have a
  quickie (with s.o.) • (lit); to throw
  oneself a "quickly done."

vivre à la colle *exp.* to be unmarried
  and living together • (lit); to live
  like glue.

voir de toutes les couleurs (en) *exp.*
  to be having a very hard time of it,
  to be going through the mill
  • (lit); to see it from every color.

Now you can listen to...

STREET FRENCH

and

MORE STREET FRENCH

...while you drive!

It's just virtually impossible to learn a language fully without hearing it spoken. Too often, students who have traveled abroad tell me that after years of French study, they are able to express themselves with a reasonable amount of ease, yet have enormous difficulty understanding *how* the natives speak!

The biggest complaint is that it always seems to be easier to recognize written words than those that are spoken so quickly and colloquially by the natives; this doesn't have to be the case!

Now, *Street French* and *More Street French* are available on cassette to help you understand any Parisian who is *câblé.** The cassettes encompass all the dialogues in each book and are organized in three fun, clear, easy-to-use steps:

- **EAR TRAINING**
  (Dialogue in French slang)

- **PRONUNCIATION TIPS**
  (How to sound like a native)

- **PRONUNCIATION PRACTICE**
  (Where you talk to the tape!)

To receive a current price list on the cassettes available, please send in a self-addressed stamped envelope to:

OPTIMA PrePress
11072 San Pablo Avenue, Suite 151
El Cerrito, CA 94530

*****câblé(e) (être)** *adj.* to be with it, in the know, "cool" • (lit); to be plugged in (to what is currently "in")